LONDON, NEW YORK,
MELBOURNE, MUNICH, AND DELHI

Editors Fran Baines, Kitty Blount, David Pickering, Bradley Round, Sadie Smith
Art editors Ann Cannings, Sheila Collins, Leah Germann, Catherine Goldsmith,
Joanne Little, Sharon Spencer, Claire Watson
Senior art editor Joanne Connor
Senior editors Shaila Awan, Carey Scott
Managing editors Gillian Denton, Linda Esposito, Andrew Macintyre
Managing art editors Julia Harris, Clare Shedden, Jane Thomas
Production controllers Kate Oliver, Erica Rosen, Rochelle Talary, Charlotte Trail
Special photography Andy Crawford, Geoff Dann, Ellen Howden, Ray Moller,
Gary Ombler, Steve Teague
Picture researchers Angela Anderson, Kathy Lockley, Alex Pepper,
Deborah Pownall, Sarah Pownall, Bridget Tily
Picture librarians Clare Bowers, Sue Hadley, Sarah Mills
DTP designer Siu Yin Ho
Jacket designer Neal Cobourne

For Bookwork Ltd:
Editor: Annabel Blackledge
Art editor: Kate Mullins

Consultants
Christianity: Annette Reynolds, AD Publishing Services Ltd.;
Jon Reynolds, Diocesan Director of Education
Islam: Batul Salazar
Judaism: Dr Jonathan Romain
Buddhism, Hinduism, Sikhism, and Introduction: Peggy Morgan, President,
British Association for the Study of Religions

See our complete
catalogue at
www.dk.com

Contents

Avalokiteshvara, the Bodhisattva of compassion

Illustration from a Lutheran Bible

The Hindu god, Ganesh

INTRODUCTION

Ancient religions

ALTHOUGH TODAY'S RELIGIONS have roots stretching far back into the past, religion existed long before they started. It is believed that all the world's ancient peoples had some form of religion and most worshipped a number of gods and goddesses. These religions have now died out, with reasons for this ranging from the collapse of empires to the introduction of new religions, but they have left behind a legacy for us to study.

Dragon symbol of Marduk, Mesopotamian creator-god

Mesopotamia

One of the world's first great civilizations developed in Mesopotamia (modern Iraq) around 5,000 years ago. The Mesopotamians believed that many of their gods lived in the sky and controlled the movements of the Sun, the Moon, and the stars. So their priests became skilled astronomers, observing the night sky and working out a calendar to help them time their rituals correctly.

Ishtar, goddess of love

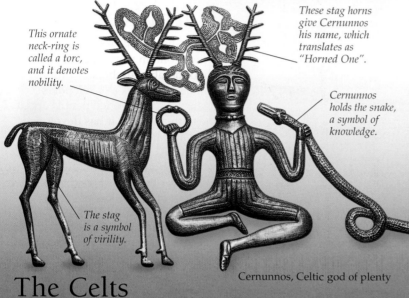

This ornate neck-ring is called a torc, and it denotes nobility.

These stag horns give Cernunnos his name, which translates as "Horned One".

Cernunnos holds the snake, a symbol of knowledge.

The stag is a symbol of virility.

Cernunnos, Celtic god of plenty

The Celts

The Celtic peoples lived in western Europe during the first millennium BCE. They had priests called druids who led worship, made sacrifices to their gods, and predicted the best times to sow and harvest crops. The Druids also organized seasonal festivals, such as the spring celebration known as Beltane.

NATURAL FORCES

Ancient peoples believed that there were a host of gods and goddesses, each of which controlled an aspect of the natural world, from thunder to the Sun. It was a harsh world that early people lived in, but they believed that if the gods were contented, then conditions on Earth would be favourable and they would avoid disasters. As such, the main aim of ancient religion was to keep these gods happy by worshipping them and making offerings and sacrifices.

Sun god
Ra-Atum

Egyptian painting from around 800 BCE

	CELTIC	MESOPOTAMIA	EGYPT	GREECE & ROME
GODS AND GODDESSES	**Sucellus** was king of the Celtic gods. He was a god of spring who woke up the plants by banging the ground.	**Tiamat**, goddess of the oceans, existed before the rest of the cosmos was created.	**Horus** was the falcon-headed sky god.	**Zeus** (Greek) /**Jupiter** (Roman), was king of the gods.
	Belanus was a god of fire and light.	**An**, the sky god, ruled over other Mesopotamian deities.	**Osiris** was king of the underworld, an underground region which people thought looked like Egypt.	**Hades** (Greek) /**Pluto** (Roman), was god of the underworld.
	Mother Goddess was often shown as three women carrying baskets of food.	**Nanna** was the moon god.	**Isis** was the wife of Osiris and mother of Horus.	**Aphrodite** (Greek) /**Venus** (Roman), was goddess of love and beauty.
		Ereshkigal was the goddess of the underworld. She was invisible to humans.	**Anubis** was the god of funerals. He took the form of a jackal.	**Poseidon** (Greek) /**Neptune** (Roman), was the ocean god, who could cause and quell storms at sea.
	Taranis was the thunder god.			

Egypt

The long-lasting ancient Egyptian civilization (3000–30 BCE) was based on the banks of the River Nile. In the baking climate of Egypt, the people relied upon the rain and river to water their crops, so many people prayed to the gods and goddesses that controlled the Nile, the weather, and the soil's fertility. The Egyptians established elaborate beliefs about life after death. They believed that there were eight separate elements of their soul that survived death to perform different roles.

Greece and Rome

The gods and goddesses of the ancient Greeks (c. 750–200 BCE) took human form and lived on a sacred mountain called Mount Olympus. They loved, fought, and behaved just like ordinary people, but they could have a powerful effect on everyday life. The Romans (c. 509 BCE–410 CE) adopted these Olympian gods after conquering Greece, but changed their names. Later, many Romans converted to Christianity.

Zeus

Zeus is usually portrayed as a strong, bearded man with curling hair.

EARLIEST RELIGIONS

The earliest peoples left no written records so what little we know about their religions comes from temples and other remains. Stonehenge, in southern Britain, was a religious site 5,000 years ago and was continuously rebuilt or added to over thousands of years. The ring of tall stones that remains today has been there for approximately 4,000 years.

Indigenous religions

IN MANY PARTS OF THE WORLD, people still lead a traditional or tribal lifestyle, living in small villages, hunting or growing their own food, and following a local, or indigenous, religion. Although many indigenous religions have died out with the spread of the major world faiths, some still survive. These diverse religions have one important common feature, a respect for a world of spirits – invisible, supernatural beings who are seen as gods, the souls of deceased ancestors, or as beings that inhabit every part of the natural world.

Ancestoral respect

Most indigenous religions believe that the dead live on as spirits. People honour their ancestors because they form a close link between the living and higher spirits who control life on Earth. Believers hope that their ancestors will encourage the higher spirits to look favourably on those who are still alive. Many peoples create poetry, music, pictures, or sculptures in honour of their ancestors.

Maori ancestor figure

ANCESTORS

Dreamtime: Australian aborigines believe that this was the period when ancient ancestors moved across the Earth creating all its physical features. Dreamtime is honoured in their art and ceremonies.

Totem poles: the indigenous peoples of northwestern North America carve totem poles to represent their ancestors and the tribe's relationship to the earliest spirits.

Stone statues: on Easter Island, in the Pacific, are huge stone heads that have stood for hundreds of years. They are thought to be images of ancestors of the people that used to inhabit the island.

The Days of the Dead: a combination of a Christian festival and an indigenous celebration, this Mexican festival includes offerings to ancestors' souls.

Sacred sites

Uluru

Striking features in the landscape, such as mountains, rocks, and rivers, are seen in many indigenous religions as the dwelling-places of powerful spirits. They are greatly revered, and ceremonies and rituals are performed at them to channel their power.

PLACES

Uluru: formerly known as Ayers Rock, this is a sacred place for Australian aborigines. Some tribes believe that their ancestors were born from Uluru.

Taishan: this Chinese mountain is home of the god Tung-yüeh Ta-ti, Emperor of the Eastern Peak. Devotees of traditional Chinese religion have climbed the mountain for thousands of years to pay respect to him.

Mount Fuji: for the followers of Japan's Shinto religion, this is the home of several gods and is the centre of the world. It is also a sacred place for Japanese Buddhists.

The Valley of the Chiefs: found in Montana, USA, this valley is sacred to many tribes of the Plains people, who still hold ceremonies there. The valley has a large number of indigenous rock drawings.

Natural world

Followers of most indigenous religions believe that spirits dwell throughout the natural world. While some spirits are mischievous or evil, many are friendly to people and are said to give humans the essentials for survival. Each kind of spirit performs a different role, such as helping crops to grow. A variety of different rituals in honour of these spirits are therefore used to help human life to thrive.

Trees are believed to contain spirits.

SPIRITS

Tree spirits: these provide fruit or offer protection. In places such as Borneo, shamans make sacrifices in front of trees to keep the tree spirits contented.

Rocks: spirits that have control over the surrounding landscape may live in rocks. The bushmen of the Kalahari in Africa draw pictures of the spirits on sacred rocks, to ensure that the spirits will remain there.

Water spirits: these control life-giving water. People in the uplands of Tibet throw offerings into lakes to appease the water spirits.

Bird and animal spirits: many native North American peoples traditionally offer prayers to animal spirits, in the hope that their hunters will be forgiven for taking animals for food.

Deities

African god

Most believers of indigenous religions worship a number of gods. These are supreme beings who have existed for all time, who have the ability to create, or who rule over entire parts of both the spirit and natural world. Sacrifice plays a major part in worship of the gods.

GODS

Creator gods: these made the world or brought the earliest human ancestors into being.

Sea gods: looking after the waters, these gods control the amount of fish to be caught and have power over storms and currents.

Mother goddesses: these may take part in the creation of the world, protect human mothers, and keep the soil fertile.

Sky gods: these may take the form of birds and are often said to cause thunder and lightning.

Tricksters: mischievous gods who play pranks on humans or cause accidents.

THE SHAMAN

Ceremonies in most indigenous religions are led by the shaman, a combination of priest, doctor, and fortune-teller. Shamans make sure that shrines and sacred places are looked after. They also organize festivals, treat the sick, and carry out rituals in which they claim to acquire some of the power of the spirits by travelling to the spirit world or becoming possessed by a spirit.

A shaman in Borneo performs a ceremonial dance.

DRUM POWER

Music and dance are used in most indigenous rituals that summon the spirits. The shaman takes the lead, beating his drum continuously to a powerful rhythm, which many of those present may take up by dancing and chanting. This can carry on for hours, and when the right moment arrives, it is believed that one of the inhabitants of the spirit world is summoned.

A Chukchi man plays a shaman's drum in Northern Siberia, Russia.

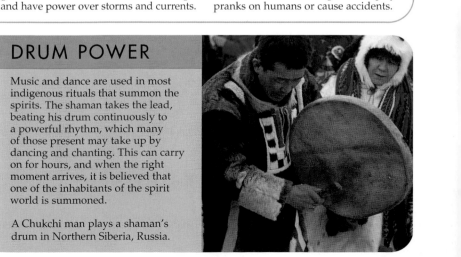

15

Sacred texts

ALL THE MAJOR WORLD religions have a book or collection of books that contain the main ideas and beliefs of the faith. Some texts are believed to contain the actual words of God. As people began to travel more, religions gradually spread from their places of origin. This led to a need for the beliefs to be written down, so that the teachings and ideas would remain constant. Sacred texts usually contain a variety of material, such as stories of the early teachers and prophets, hymns of praise, and instructions on how to live a good life.

Writing it down

Jewish scribe makes a copy of a *Torah* scroll

Many sacred texts began as spoken words that people memorized and passed on by word of mouth. But as religions spread, their leaders felt that it was vital to make sure that new believers were taught the scriptures accurately, so priests and scholars began to write down the sacred texts and make copies. In some faiths, especially Judaism and Islam, handwritten copies of the scriptures are still treated with special reverence.

Printed word

A copy of the Gutenberg Bible, the first printed Christian Bible, produced in 1455

Printing was invented in China by the 8th century CE, but European inventors did not work out how to print texts until the 15th century. In both places, religious books were among the first to be printed. These rapidly produced multiple copies made books cheaper and helped the spread of religious ideas. Many who could not afford hand-written texts could buy a printed book and study the scriptures for the first time.

PICTURE POWER

Before the modern era, few people could read, so religious leaders often tried to find different ways of teaching people. Christian priests used pictures, such as this stained-glass window, to show episodes from the Bible. Carvings on Buddhist and Hindu temples played a similar role. Islam and Judaism, by contrast, placed a greater stress on the written word.

Stained-glass window showing Jesus teaching in the synagogue

Decorated page from a 14th-century copy of the Qur'an

Past and future

Sacred texts often look back to the past. In explaining the early history of a faith and its followers, they can give identity to an entire religious community. But they can also look ahead to the future, with predictions about what will happen to us when we die and prophecies about future events in the life of the faith. This stone statue (right) is a visualization of the future Buddha, Maitreya, as predicted in Buddhist holy scriptures.

Stone carving of Maitreya, Kathmandu, Nepal

Arabic text written in Rayhani *script*

Richly decorated border

GOD'S WORD

Some scriptures have a special status because they are believed to contain the words of God, words that have always existed, just like God himself. These sacred words are preserved in their original language, such as Arabic for the Muslim Qur'an, and are copied by hand in beautiful calligraphy.

Book as sacred object

Copies of any sacred book are treated with a great respect and are often kept in a special place, such as the Ark in a synagogue or the special throne in a Sikh *gurdwara*. They are carried and read with care, and an effort is made not to mark or smudge the text itself.

Reading the *Guru Granth Sahib*, the Sikh sacred book

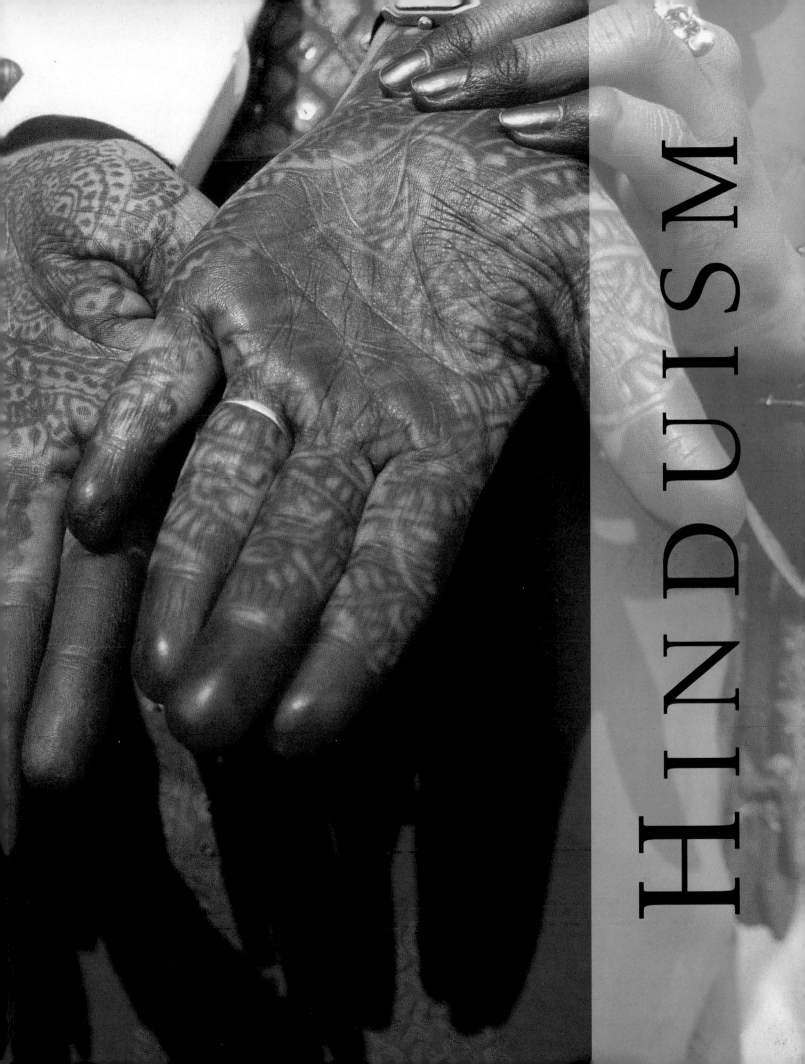

HINDUISM

The Hindu faith

Hinduism began in India, where it has been evolving for over 5,000 years. There are also many Hindus elsewhere in Asia, in Africa, the Caribbean, and Europe. Their faith is as varied as this wide geographical spread. Some Hindus believe in one god, others honour many gods, or believe that the faith's many deities are all aspects of one supreme being. Many of their other beliefs vary, for there is no standard creed and no standard rituals. But all Hindus share the idea of rebirth, believing that all living things are part of an ongoing process of life, death, and rebirth. Hindus seek to break out of this cycle by means of *moksha*, or release. The concept of *dharma* is also important in Hinduism. *Dharma* means law, duty, justice, and virtuousness, emphasizing that correct behaviour is central to the faith.

INDUS VALLEY
In Pakistan's Indus valley, archaeologists have found the remains of a civilization dating back to 2,500 BCE. At the Indus cities of Harappa and Mohenjo-daro they found statues of deities that may be the ancestors of the Hindu gods, such as this statue of a priest king.

HOLY LIFE
Sadhus are respected holy people who devote their lives to religion. They study holy texts, practice yoga, and eat only simple food. *Sadhus* usually live alone as hermits or in monastic communities, and give religious guidance to those who need it. Both the *Vedas* and the *Upanishads* (Hindu holy texts) stress the importance of such spiritual teachers.

Pilgrims prepare to bathe ritually in the purifying waters of the Ganges.

Vessel in which passers-by can leave money and food for the sadhu

Prayer beads

A *sadhu* prays on the street in Sarnath, India.

SACRED RIVER
The River Ganges flows from the Himalayas of north central India, southeast through Bangladesh, and into the Bay of Bengal. For Hindus, the Ganges is a sacred river, worshipped as the goddess Ganga. Many people make the pilgrimage to the Ganges, especially to the city of Varanasi (Benares), where the river is said to be most purifying. At religious festivals thousands of people gather on the banks here.

Krishna, visualised as a cowherd

The flute is the traditional symbol of the cowherd.

SACRED COW
In Hinduism, cows are associated with Krishna (left), the eighth avatar (manifestation) of the god Vishnu. As a child, Krishna spent some time as a cowherd. So, to feed a cow is a way of worshipping Krishna. In ancient times, the cow was considered to be a mother goddess and today cows are still sacred – a Hindu would never kill a cow. Many Hindus also refuse to kill any other living animal and are vegetarian.

It is said that the cows became still when they heard Krishna's flute.

SACRED SYLLABLE
Hindus believe that the sacred sound *om* or *aum* existed at the beginning of time and that the vibrations caused by its sounding brought about the creation of the world. This special syllable is therefore uttered at the start of all rituals and before meditation. The three letters of one of its spellings, A, U, and M, represent the three parts of the *Trimurti* (pp. 30–31). A represents Brahma, U stands for Vishnu, and M is Shiva.

A Hindu family

"Hinduism is more a culture than a creed."

RADHAKRISHNAN, FORMER PRESIDENT OF INDIA

INFLUENTIAL HINDU
One of the most influential Hindus of the 20th century was Mohandas K. Gandhi (1869–1948), who spent his life working for India's independence from British rule. A devout Hindu, Gandhi was inspired by several doctrines of the faith, especially the concept of *ahimsa*, or non-violence. He was convinced he could win political victory without harming others, and his success inspired millions – Hindus and non-Hindus alike.

Gandhi making the traditional namaste gesture, which means "I bow to the divine in you"

STAGES OF LIFE
Hindu scriptures stress the importance of family life. The role of *grihastha* (householder) marks an important stage of life for all Hindus. In terms of spiritual enlightenment, there are various stages through which an individual hopes to pass. Passing these stages means that the individual is eventually able to escape *samsara*, the endless cycle of rebirth and reach *moksha* – liberation – and hence be at one with Brahman (God).

Three great gods

SACRED SOUND
OM or AUM is the eternal syllable. It is said or sung before and after all prayers.

ONE OF OLDEST OF THE major world religions, Hinduism developed in one of the most populous and diverse places on earth, India. As a result, Hinduism takes many forms and has hundreds of different gods, some of which have many different titles and names. Yet Hinduism is still one religion. Many Hindus explain this by saying that all the gods are part of one overall absolute reality, known as Brahman, which is revealed in various ways. One way in which Brahman is revealed to Hindus is as the *Trimurti*, a trio of the great gods Brahma, the creator, Vishnu, the preserver, and Shiva, the destroyer and re-creator. Of the three, Vishnu and Shiva are among the most widely worshipped of all Hindu deities. Vishnu is referred to in scriptures as the luckiest of the gods and stands for compassion, law, and order. Shiva takes a variety of different forms, summed up in his 1,008 names. Many of these names refer to Shiva's rule over the natural world, so he is called Kedarnath (Mountain Lord) and Gangadhara (Bearer of the Ganges).

Brahma has four heads; this sculpture shows three of them

BRAHMA THE CREATOR
Brahma's exclusive purpose is creation. Unlike Vishnu and Shiva, he does not contain opposites within himself, and so he never destroys what he has created. According to one tradition he arose out of the "egg of the universe". Originally he only had one head. He acquired three more when he created woman. After cutting her from his own body he fell in love with her, but she hid herself from him. So that he could always see her from every side, he grew heads to the right, left, and behind.

HINDUISM

GODS?
Brahma, Vishnu, Shiva, Sarasvati, Kali, Lakshmi, and many others

THE AFTERLIFE?
Reincarnation

SCRIPTURES?
Vedas, Upanishads, and others

MAJOR FESTIVALS?
Divali – New year Festival of Lights
Holi – Spring festival
Janmashtami – Birthday of Krishna
Shivaratri – Main festival of Shiva

SACRED ANIMAL?
Cow is the symbol of Earth

Smaller figures represent two of the four Vedas *(earliest holy scriptures)*

VISHNU THE PRESERVER
Vishnu contains and balances good and evil, and all other opposites, within himself. His main task, as preserver, is to maintain the divine order of the universe, keeping the balance between good and evil powers. When evil gets the upper hand Vishnu comes down to Earth to restore the balance, taking the form of one of ten manifestations called avatars – beings in whom he lives throughout their lives (p. 32). Vishnu is often called "the infinite ocean of the universe".

"More are the names of God and infinite are the forms through which He may be approached."

HINDU SAINT RAMAKRISHNA (1836–1886)

The flaming halo around Shiva symbolizes the cosmos.

Shiva's whirling hair holds flowers, snakes, a skull, and a small figure of the goddess Ganga (the sacred river Ganges).

As Shiva beats the drum, he summons up a new creation.

Shiva's vertical third eye gives light to the world.

The flame is a symbol of the fire with which Shiva destroys the universe.

This hand points to the left foot, beneath which the worshipper can find safe refuge.

Left foot is a symbol of liberation

SHIVA AS "LORD OF THE DANCE"
Shiva is both destroyer and re-creator. He is depicted in many forms. As Nataraja, Lord of the Dance (the form shown here), he brings the dance or cycle of life to an end in order that a new cycle of life may begin. This statue illustrates a legend in which he subdued 10,000 heretics (non-believers) by dancing on the demon of ignorance.

Apasmarapurusa, the black dwarf, demon of ignorance

Shiva dances in a ring of flames.

Shiva is adored by two sages (wise men); the one on his right has the lower body of a snake, the one on his left has tiger legs.

This sage has the legs of a tiger.

Flowers, symbols of purity, and rebirth, are used to decorate temples and statues.

Hindu gods

The flute is a symbol of the cowherds who raised Krishna.

ALTHOUGH THERE ARE MANY MANIFESTATIONS OF GOD, most Hindus devote a majority of prayer to one god or goddess – often the one that has been worshipped by previous generations of their family. At special times of their lives, though, Hindus may worship other gods, taking a new-born child to a local mother goddess' shrine for a special blessing, for example. In addition, Hindus will also pray to gods and goddesses who control specific aspects of life, such as Sitala, who controls the spread of smallpox, or Manasa, who protects against poisonous snakes. So Hindu temples usually have shrines to a number of the manifestations to whom people may offer worship.

KRISHNA
Krishna, the eighth avatar of Vishnu (p. 30), is considered a god in his own right. Usually portrayed as a child or youth, he often carries a flute, an instrument played by the cowherds who raised him. Krishna had a happy childhood and devotees explain that he brings them happiness in turn. Many colourful stories are are told about Krishna in the Mahabharata (p. 40) and the Puranas.

Krishna's skin is blue, the colour of the oceans and the sky.

Rama seated on a throne with Sita, his consort

RAMA
The lord Rama, the seventh avatar of Vishnu, is worshipped as a god in his own right. He is seen as an honest and virtuous figure, as well as being the perfect son, husband, and ruler. These exceptional qualities are described in the Ramayana (p. 38), the epic that recounts his heroic deeds. They make him one of the most popular of all Hindu deities.

Varaha dives into the ocean to rescue Earth.

THE BOAR-HEADED AVATAR
The boar-headed Varaha is Vishnu's third avatar. When a demon named Hiranyaksa dragged the Earth to the bottom of the sea, Varaha plunged in after it. After thousands of years of fighting, Varaha killed the demon. He then bore the weight of Earth on his tusks, and lifted it out of the sea.

Figurine of the god Ganesh

GANESH
Ganesh is the god of wisdom. He has the power to help humans and is known as the "remover of obstacles". Before beginning any new undertaking – from sitting an exam to getting married – it is customary to pray and make offerings to Ganesh. Ganesh did not originally have an elephant's head – his father, the great god Shiva, mistakenly beheaded him. To restore life to his son, Shiva cut off the head of a passing elephant and placed it on Ganesh's shoulders.

YAMA, GOD OF DEATH
The first man to die, Yama became the ruler of the dead. He judges people when they die and guides them to the dwelling-place of the ancestors. He makes a fearsome figure, riding on his buffalo and sometimes accompanied by two fierce-looking, four-eyed dogs. When a person dies, their soul has to hurry past these creatures to get into Yama's kingdom.

Ganesh is shown sat on a lotus flower, a symbol of purity.

THE MOON GOD
The Hindu Moon god, Chandra, is usually portrayed as a young man. He is said to have special influence over people's health. Chandra is also considered a fertility god, since the dew that falls on the plants overnight and gives them life was once believed to have come from the Moon.

Chandra, the Moon god.

KARTTIKEYA, GOD OF WAR
Shiva's son Karttikeya is the god of war, and a popular deity in southern India. According to one story he was born in order to rid the world of the destructive demon Taraka. He rode into battle on his peacock, which is a symbol of his immortality, and killed Taraka and a number of other demons.

The Great Goddess

THE COUNTLESS GODDESSES in Hinduism differ widely in their character and powers. However, many of them are seen as separate aspects of one being – the mother goddess Mahadevi, also known as the Great Goddess. Mahadevi can take a variety of forms, most of whom appear as consort (companion) to the three principal Hindu gods – Brahma, Shiva, and Vishnu. In their different forms, these goddesses can be gentle and benevolent, or fierce warriorlike beings. Thousands of lesser goddesses are also worshipped. These are often nature deities, worshipped in specific parts of India.

The goddess Sarasvati

Sarasvati is usually portrayed as a beautiful woman with four arms

Lotus blossom is a symbol of the soul

FAIR OF SPEECH
Consort of the god Brahma, Sarasvati is the goddess of learning and the arts. She was thought to be able to create anything that came into her husband's mind and was said to have invented the Sanskrit language in which the Hindu scriptures are written. Worshipped in places such as schools and libraries, she is also known as Vagishvari – the goddess of speech.

BRINGER OF GOOD FORTUNE
One of the most popular Hindu deities, Lakshmi is the goddess of wealth, beauty, and good luck. The consort of Vishnu, she is seen by his side in each of his different avatars (p. 32). So, when Vishnu appears as Rama, Lakshmi becomes his faithful wife Sita. Because she is a bringer of luck and happiness, Lakshmi's image is often carved above house doors, so that she may bring good fortune to all those who live inside.

The goddess showers wealth on her followers.

Lakshmi is usually shown sitting on a lotus.

The goddess is shown on water because she is said to have emerged from the sea at the time of the creation.

Painting of Lakshmi of the type displayed in many Hindu homes

FEARSOME FORCE
The fierce goddess Kali is known as a slayer of demons and usually appears with a weapon and occasionally with the skulls of her victims. She is the consort of Shiva and is sometimes shown dancing on cremation-grounds or holding a severed head. However, there is a positive side to her destruction in that she fights evil and all that is bad in the world.

Shiva   Parvati

LOVING CONSORT
Parvati is the more benign version of Shiva's consort. Her name means "daughter of the mountain" and she is said to have been born out of the rocks of the Himalayas. Gentle and caring, she makes a good counterpart to Shiva the destroyer, and is worshipped widely. Parvati is normally portrayed sitting at Shiva's side.

Weapon represents Kali's destructive power

This statue shows Kali encircled by flames.

A statue of the goddess Kali

Durga is traditionally shown riding on the back of a lion.

WOMAN WARRIOR
Durga, like Kali, is an often warlike embodiment of Shiva's partner. She is known for her battles with the demons, notably the buffalo-demon, Mahishasura, who were always waging war against the gods. But Durga also has a creative side, being famous for her skill in growing plants, especially herbs. Her festival, celebrated at harvest-time, makes clear her link with the fertility of the soil.

THE GODDESS AS CONSORT
Hindu gods and their consorts are often shown sitting close together in paintings or statues, like a human married couple. But sometimes the closeness of god and goddess is explained in a different, more spiritual way. As well as a male character, each god also has a female side, known as a *shakti*, and this is represented by the goddess.

Krishna and his consort Radha

Sacred teachings

THERE ARE TWO MAIN groups of Hindu sacred texts. The first are known as *shruti* ("things heard"), because they are believed to be words that have always existed and were heard by scholars directly from God. Because they are God's words, these scriptures, known as the Vedic writings, have the highest authority. The other texts are the *smriti* (things remembered) writings. These were composed by scholars and poets long ago and include texts on subjects such as ritual, law, and mythology, the two epics (pp. 38-41), and writings connected with the worship of deities such as Vishnu, Shiva, and the Great Goddess.

READING AND WRITING
The Hindu scriptures were originally transmitted by word of mouth from one priest to another. Eventually, they were written down in the ancient Sanskrit language (above) of India, and later they were printed. But even today, Hindus place a great stress on listening to the sacred texts, and priests often prefer to recite the scriptures from memory rather than to read from a printed copy.

The three white lines on this Brahmin boy's forehead means he is a devotee of Shiva.

THE VEDAS
In the past, it was normally only boys of the Brahmin, or priestly class, who studied the *shruti* texts. The central Vedic writings (which are *shruti*) are the *Vedas* themselves, a collection of hymns, melodies, and chants in praise of the various deities. Additional Vedic writings are made up of the *Brahmanas*, prose texts which concern ritual, the *Aranyakas*, which discuss worship and meditation, and the *Upanishads*, which deal with the philosophy of Hinduism.

Agni's three heads are topped by flames.

Varuna, god of the sky and water

Agni, god of fire

Indra, god of war

Indra rides a white elephant named Airavata.

Copy of a Veda mounted on a stand

THE VEDIC GODS
Many of the earliest Hindu gods are praised in the hymns of the *Vedas*, which were probably collected over 3,000 years ago. These deities may appear in many different forms. The fire god, Agni, for example, may take the form of lightning, the Sun, or the fire in the hearth. Indra is considered to be the most powerful of the Vedic gods, and the scriptures describe him as lord of the heavens and a destroyer of demons.

"From delusion lead me to truth. From darkness lead me to Light. From death lead me to immortality."

BRIHAD-ARANYAKA UPANISHAD 1, 3, 28

THE *PURANAS*

Among the most important *smriti* texts are the *Puranas*. These include stories of the gods and goddesses, accounts of the creation, destruction, and recreation of the world, and tales of the *manus* (human ancestors). The *Puranas* also contain information on a range of subjects, from theology and ritual to science and astrology. The most famous of the *Puranas* is the *Bhagavata-Purana*, which recounts the life of Krishna. *Bhagavata-Purana* means "stories of the Lord" in Sanskrit.

Part of the *Bhagavata-Purana* (left)

A group meets to read and discuss Hindu texts.

THE *UPANISHADS*

These sacred texts are based on the teachings of gurus whose pupils sat close by them to listen to their words – the word *Upanishad* means "near-sitting" in Sanskrit. The *Upanishads* deal with a number of key doctrines, including the belief that the soul passes through a cycle of deaths and rebirths, and that it is possible to attain release from this process.

Stories from the life of Krishna are illustrated on the scroll.

Text and illustrations reproduced on silk paper

Sanskrit text written in Devanagri script

Balinese Hindus praying

THE CORRECT RITUALS

Hindus, like these women praying in a temple in Bali, have certain guidelines to follow whilst praying or performing religious rituals. The *Brahmanas* are texts used by Brahmins, or priests, to pass on these teachings. As well as containing instruction on matters of prayer and ritual, the *Brahmanas* discuss ancient rites of sacrifice as well as rituals that are still performed today.

The *Ramayana*

ONE OF THE TWO great epics of Hindu literature, the *Ramayana* is a dramatic poem of some 96,000 verses, telling the story of Rama, one of the avatars (manifestations) of the god Vishnu. Although it is traditionally believed to be the work of a legendary sage called Valmiki, the poem was actually written by several authors at different times, in the ancient Sanskrit language. It is full of gripping stories and adventures and deals with many interesting themes – love and deception, war and peace, and good and evil. The *Ramayana* covers the whole lifespan of Rama from his childhood and youth, through his exile and struggles against the demon Ravana, to his return to his homeland and peaceful rule as rightful king. So, although much of the poem describes struggles and battles, its final message is one of peace and reconciliation and the victory of good over evil.

Rama reclining on a five-headed snake

A maiden, possibly Sita

RAMA
The seventh avatar of Vishnu (p. 32), Rama was the eldest son of Dasharatha, King of Ayodhya in northeastern India. Dasharatha had three wives, and Rama was the eldest of four brothers. One of the wives, Kaikeyi, persuaded the King to make her son Bharata heir to the throne, instead of Rama, who was the oldest. Rama eventually married Sita, a beautiful and virtuous young woman who was the daughter of another king, Janaka.

The 10-headed Ravana watches the battle from his palace.

Soldiers from Rama's army fight alongside an army of monkeys.

A figurine of Hanuman

HANUMAN
The monkey-god Hanuman, one of the most popular Hindu deities, plays an important role in the *Ramayana*. The poem celebrates his cunning, bravery, magical powers, and devotion to Rama. In one episode, Rama's enemies wrap Hanuman's long tail in an oily cloth and set it alight. Hanuman turns this to his advantage by flying over the enemy city of Lanka and setting it on fire. He then flies over the sea and dips his tail into the water to put out the blaze.

Rama listens to the monks as they describe Ravana and his demons.

2 THE ABDUCTION OF SITA

Hearing of Sita's beauty, Ravana decided to kidnap her, take her to his kingdom in Lanka, and make her his queen. He tricked Rama into chasing a beautiful deer deep into the forest and then imitated Rama's voice to call Lakshmana to his aid. This left Sita on her own and Ravana was able to carry her off to his palace. When Sita would not give in to his wishes, Ravana had her imprisoned in his palace gardens, guarded by 100 demons.

Ravana, disguised as a holy man, kidnaps Sita.

Sugriva, the monkey king

1 EXILE IN THE FOREST

When Bharata became heir to the throne, Rama was sent into exile, to live in the forest for 14 years. His wife Sita and devoted brother Lakshmana joined him there. Monks, living as hermits in the forest, told them how demons, ruled by their king the 10-headed Ravana, murdered anyone they met. Rama and Lakshmana vowed to kill the demons and defeat Ravana. They soon had an encounter with Ravana's sister, Shurpanaka, which resulted in a battle in which they killed many of the demons.

3 SUGRIVA THE MONKEY KING

Searching for Sita, Rama and his brother met a band of monkeys led by their king, Sugriva. One of the monkeys, Hanuman, told Rama that he had seen Ravana abducting Sita. Sugriva told Rama how he himself had been dethroned by his own brother. If Rama would help Sugriva get back his throne, Sugriva and his army would help Rama win back Sita. So Rama and Lakshmana helped defeat Sugriva's brother and soon Hanuman was on his way to Lanka to search for Sita.

Demons are represented as having boars' heads.

4 THE BATTLE AT LANKA

With the help of the monkey army, a great causeway was built so that Rama and his allies could cross to Lanka. Then a huge battle began, in which many of the monkeys were killed or wounded. To heal them, Hanuman flew to Kailasa Mountain and brought back the entire hill, with healing herbs growing on it. Soon the army was revived, and Ravana and his demons were killed.

Rama's followers provide a feast to celebrate his coronation.

5 RAMA IS CROWNED

After the defeat of Ravana, Rama and Sita returned to Ayodhya, where Rama was crowned king. For a while, Sita was banished because Rama suspected her of being unfaithful, but eventually the couple were reconciled, and Rama ruled in peace. The story shows how Vishnu sends his avatars to Earth to put things right when evil becomes powerful. Hindus celebrate Rama's triumphant return every year at the festival of Divali (p. 46).

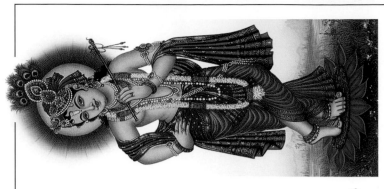

The Mahabharata

LIKE THE *RAMAYANA*, THE *MAHABHARATA* is a much-loved epic poem, written in the Sanskrit language and added to over many generations. It includes a rich mix of myth, folk tale, and philosophy. Its main story concerns the rivalry between two families, culminating in a great battle that is eventually won by the "good" family, the Pandavas. Meanwhile, dozens of different subplots incorporate hundreds of characters that include demons and gods as well as human beings. The poem stresses the horrors of war by showing the sadness of the Pandava leader, Yudhishtira, at the devastation wrought on the two families. The *Mahabharata* also emphasizes the teachings central to Hindu faith, and its best-loved section, the *Bhagavad Gita* (meaning "Song of the Lord"), teaches the importance of duty and devotion to the supreme god.

KRISHNA

The god Krishna is one of the most important characters in the *Mahabharata*. On the eve of the battle between the Pandavas and their cousins, Krishna gave the two sides a choice – one could have Krishna's huge army, the other could have Krishna himself. The Pandavas chose Krishna.

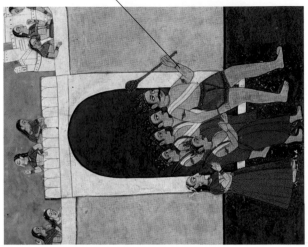

The Pandavas and Yudhishttira's wife Draupadi set off into exile.

3 THE DICE GAME

The Dhartarashtras cheated Yudhishtira in a game of dice, winning his kingdom and his riches. They then forced the Pandavas into a long exile. But when the Pandavas were eventually able to return, the Dhartarashtras still refused to give them back their kingdom.

1 THE FIVE PANDAVAS

At the heart of the *Mahabharata* is the story of the five Pandavas, the sons of the deceased king Pandu. The eldest Pandava, Yudhishtira, became king in his father's place when he died, but the family still had to face the rivalry of their 100 cousins, the Dhartarashtras, who also laid claim to the throne.

2 THE DHARTARASHTRAS

The 100 Dhartarashtras were the sons of the blind king Dhritarashtra and his wife Gandhari. But they were also incarnations of demons, sworn mischief-makers, and enemies of the gods who supported the Pandavas. They continously abused and attacked their rivals, planning to trick Yudhishtira out of his kingdom.

Gandhari wore a blindfold in sympathy with her blind husband.

Arjuna has thrown his enemies into the air.

5 FINAL JOURNEY TO MOUNT MERU

Towards the end of the epic, many of the characters reach the end of their lives. Years after the great battle, the Pandavas decide to retire from the world to the home of the gods (heaven), Mount Meru. The journey is a long and hard one, and some die on the way.

BHAGAVAD GITA

The *Bhagavad Gita* contains a conversation held between the Pandava brother Arjuna and Krishna just before the battle. In it, Krishna reveals how through work, devotion, and duty a person can achieve liberation, or *moksha* – release from the cycle of rebirth. Only when *moksha* is reached can a Hindu be at one with Brahman (God).

Krishna acts as Arjuna's charioteer.

The Pandava prince Arjuna

A scene from the *Bhagavad Gita*

"To those who are constantly devoted and worship Me with love, I give understanding by which they can come to Me."

KRISHNA IN *BHAGAVAD GITA* 10:10

4 BLOODY BATTLE

The Pandavas won back their kingdom in a fierce 18-day battle with their cousins, the Dhartarashtras. Afterwards, Dhritarashtra and a number of his followers retreated to the forest. But it was a sad victory for the Pandavas – many members of their family were killed in the fighting.

Arjuna is shown as an archer in battle.

Temples and worship

HINDUS BUILD ELABORATE temples where they can worship their gods, but worship, or *puja*, also takes place at a small shrine in the home. The centrepiece of both temples and shrines is an image of one of the Hindu gods or goddesses. Hindus regard these images as the dwelling places of the deity they represent, and a key part of *puja* is *darshan* – viewing the image and being in the god's presence. In addition, *puja* involves making offerings of food, money, or incense to the god and worshippers may also sing hymns and recite prayers.

PORTABLE SHRINE
For daily worship, many Hindu families set up small shrines in their homes dedicated to a personally favoured god. This example is a shrine to Vishnu. Offerings of food can be made at the shrine and prayers are said, either by individuals or by the household as a whole.

Rose-water sprinkler

Incense burner

PURIFICATION
Ritual cleanliness is important in Hinduism. Hindus often bathe before *puja* and worshippers sprinkle water on the face and feet of the image, so that they are symbolically clean. Incense may also be burned to purify the air.

Kum Kum

Milk and water

PUJA TRAY
The items on this tray are used by the priest during the preparation for temple worship. He uses the red dye, or *Kum Kum*, to make a red mark on the worshippers' foreheads, to which he adds a grain of rice. A mixture of milk and water is used to cleanse the image of the god.

Temple entrance, where worshippers remove their shoes

Central tower

Main shrine, or garbhagriha, houses the statue of Vishnu

Sacred pool provides pleasing setting for the gods

Tanks provide water for worshippers to wash

Entrance to the shrine is guarded by deities such as Lakshmi

VISHNU TEMPLE
Hindu temples can be large and complex, and this plan shows an early 19th-century temple to Vishnu in southern India. The temple has shrines to many gods that worshippers visit before arriving at the large central shrine. This space houses an image of Vishnu beneath the central tower.

A priest preparing offerings by a lake

Sarasvati, goddess of the arts

Elephant-headed god Lord Ganesh

TEMPLE CARVINGS
Hindu temples may be richly decorated on the outside with carvings showing the gods and goddesses. These brightly painted temple carvings adorn the Sri Murugan Temple near Hampi, India. The interiors of temples are usually plainer, so that worshippers can concentrate on the main image of the god.

BRAHMIN PRIESTS
A member of the Brahmin (priestly class) normally leads worship at a Hindu temple. It is his job to act as a link between the other worshippers and the god. He begins worship by chanting to summon the deity to the temple. He then makes offerings on behalf of the other worshippers.

Roof is decorated with ornate carvings

MOUNTAIN-SHAPED TEMPLE
Hindu temples often have tapering towers that stand out clearly amongst the lower buildings around it. These tall towers remind worshippers of Mount Meru, where the gods are said to live. The towers have another symbolic purpose – they create a visible link between heaven and Earth. The largest tower normally roofs the temple's main shrine and there may be smaller towers over other parts of the temple.

Hindu temple, Bali, Indonesia

A festive calendar

FESTIVALS ARE HUGELY important in the Hindu faith because they are seen as celebrations of God's creation – life itself. Many festivals are local events, and hundreds of different ones take place in India's towns and villages. Most are joyous, colourful occasions when music rings out from the temples and processions fill the streets. The Hindu year follows the lunar calendar and festivals are often held at certain phases of the Moon or coincide with other events in the heavens such as solstices or eclipses. The actual celebrations vary from the flamboyant, outdoor festivals of the hot, dry months to the quieter, indoor rituals of the rainy season. At this time, dangerous creatures such as snakes and scorpions come out from their hiding places. People hold festivals in order to alert the gods to the dangers they face and to ask for protection.

DAY OF GOOD FORTUNE

Makar sankranti is celebrated in mid-January, when the sun enters the constellation of *Makar* (Capricorn). It is considered to be a lucky time of the year and is observed in many parts of India as a harvest festival when people celebrate the fertility of the soil. In the Punjab, where January is the coldest month of the year, people light huge bonfires to celebrate this festival, which they call *Pongol*. Kite-flying is a traditional children's activity at this festival and some people take part in kite-flying competitions.

Colourful kites are flown as part of the Makar sankranti *celebrations.*

Children celebrating *Holi* in Varanasi, India

Brightly coloured powders (*gulal*) and spices used in the *Holi* celebrations

Coloured water for throwing at passers-by

COLOUR AND MOVEMENT

Holi takes place in March or April and is a festival that welcomes in the spring and celebrates the Hindu new year. It also commemorates the god Krishna's defeat of the winter demon, Holika. At *Holi*, many of the usual social restrictions are ignored and vegetarians may even eat meat. People light bonfires and throw dyed powder or squirt coloured water at one another, one of the practical jokes said to have been played by the young god Krishna. With all the fun and games, it is a festival particularly enjoyed by children.

The swastika is an ancient Indian symbol of the Sun and of good fortune.

A *rakhi*

The rakhi *is always tied on the right wrist.*

MARK OF PROTECTION

The festival of *Raksa Bandhan*, held in July or August, reminds Hindu men of their duty to protect their womenfolk. Young women tie bracelets of string or tinsel onto the wrists of their brothers or other men, who return the favour with a present and the promise of protection. The bracelets, known as *rakhis*, often bear the image of Santoshi Ma, daughter of the god Ganesh and a goddess especially revered by women in India.

Some festival sweets are decorated with pure silver leaf.

FESTIVAL FOOD

Many festivals are celebrated with lavish feasts, and in India they are particularly well-known for their sweets, known as *mithis*. Some are made of special ingredients, such as *tilgul*, a sweet made with sesame seeds that is eaten at the festival of *Makar sankranti*.

A tray of traditional Indian sweets

OFFERING TO THE GANGES

The River Ganges plays a central role in the *Kumbh Mela* celebrations. Hindus believe that the river can cleanse the spirit as well as the body. Bathing in the river during the festival is believed to wash away the taint of all the pilgrim's sins – and those of countless previous generations. People also give offerings to the Ganges, in the form of fruit, money, candles, or flowers, as a tribute to the life-giving power of the river's waters.

GATHERING OF MILLIONS

The festival of *Kumbh Mela* is held every 12 years at Allahabad in India. The festival takes its name from the word *kumbha*, meaning "pot", and probably began when people brought pots of grain to the River Ganges and dipped the seeds in the water to ensure their fertility. Today, millions make the *Kumbh Mela* pilgrimage, meeting on the banks of the Ganges to bathe, pray, and make offerings to the holy men. Stalls, side shows, and other entertainments create a vibrant atmosphere of celebration.

A pilgrim's offerings of candles float on the waters of the Ganges.

Honouring the gods

As WELL AS HAVING festivals which focus around the Hindu calendar, many important festivals are also held to honour a specific deity. These usually celebrate the birthday or marriage of a god, or an important event in the life of a deity. For example, there are festivals which commemorate the achievements of Rama, as told in the Hindu epic the *Ramayana* (pp. 38–39). Festivals can be localized celebrations focusing on a temple's favoured god, or on a much larger scale, huge events celebrated in Hindu communities throughout the world, honouring great gods such as Shiva. In addition, many Hindu families observe a weekly festival day, with longer rituals and special foods, for the god they personally worship. For example, devotees of Shiva celebrate on Mondays while followers of Ganesh observe his festival on Wednesdays.

DIVALI, THE FESTIVAL OF LIGHTS
Divali is a five-day festival held in October or November. Its main focus celebrates the return of Rama from exile, as told in the *Ramayana* (pp. 38–39). People decorate their homes, temples, and streets with oil lamps, candles, and coloured electric lights.

CELEBRATING PARVATI
The festival of *Gangaur* honours the goddess Parvati. Images of the goddess are cleaned and dressed in beautiful clothes made especially for the occasion. These women are dressing a statue of Parvati at Mandawa, near Delhi.

Shiva's three eyes symbolize the Sun, the Moon, and the fire of wisdom.

Statue of Shiva, India

Shiva usually carries a trident.

BIRTHDAY OF GANESH
Worshippers celebrate the birth of the god Ganesh at the festival of *Ganesh Chaturthi* in August or September. At home they set up small clay statues of the god, whilst larger images are paraded through the streets. At the end of the festival, the statues are taken to a river or lake, where they are dropped into the water – taking with them the next year's worth of misfortune.

Ganesh Chaturthi in Bombay, India

Statue is adorned with garlands

SACRED TO SHIVA
The eve of each new full moon is a special night sacred to Shiva. However, on the new full moon of January/February, or in February/March in other parts of India, Shiva's festival of *Mahasivatri* is celebrated to commemorate the god's marriage to Parvati. On the day of *Mahasivatri* devotees spend the whole night singing praises of Shiva, and sometimes reading from the *Shiva Purana* (a Hindu holy scripture). Everyone enjoys a lavish feast on the following day.

Ganesh is adorned with a royal headdress.

TRIBUTE TO DURGA

Navaratri, the festival of "nine nights", takes place in September or October in honour of the goddess Durga. Durga's victory over the buffalo-headed demon *Mahishasura* (p. 35) is the special event that is celebrated. People decorate statues of the goddess and may dance around her shrines. On the fourth day of the celebrations, statues of the goddess are immersed in rivers. But this is also a solemn time. Many people fast, and all offer worship to the goddess, giving the festival its popular name of *Durga puja*.

THE TENTH DAY

Dussehra, or the "tenth day" occurs immediately after *Navaratri* and is a celebration of Rama's victory over the demon Ravana (pp. 38–39). Episodes from the *Ramayana* are re-enacted and images of Ravana are burned. Traditionally, husbands worship with their wives, as Rama did with Sita.

Dancers dress as characters from the Ramayana.

Dussehra celebrations in Karnataka, India

BUDDHISM

Introducing Buddhism

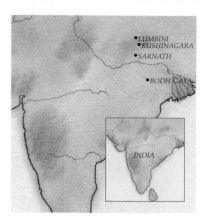

BIRTHPLACE OF BUDDHISM
Many people believe that Buddhism was born when the Buddha preached his first sermon (p. 64) at Sarnath, near Benares (now called Varanasi) in northern India. Buddha's birth at Lumbini (p. 56), his enlightenment at Bodh Gaya, and his death at Kushinagara (p. 58) are also central to the story of Buddhism.

BUDDHISM BEGAN in India in the 5th century BCE (before the common era, the term used by non-Christians for BC). It spread across Asia and is now practised by people all over the world. Buddhism is not based on belief in a god or gods. It is instead founded on the teachings of its leader, the Buddha, "the enlightened one". The Buddha taught his followers how to conquer suffering and distress and advised them on how to lead their lives. By following his example, Buddhists move closer to the heightened state of awareness, or enlightenment (p. 58), experienced by the Buddha himself.

Yogis meditating in different positions

TRAINING THE MIND
Early Buddhists learnt the skill of meditation from ancient Indian traditions, such as yoga. Meditation is a way of training, calming, and purifying the mind. Buddhists often begin meditation by concentrating on their breathing. They hope to go on to reach a deep understanding of the nature of life.

The Buddha is seen in Hinduism as an incarnation of the god Vishnu.

Mahavira statue from Adishwarji Jain temple, Bombay, India

FOLLOW THE LEADERS
When the Buddha was alive, another great religious leader, Mahavira, was attracting many followers. He was the leader of the Jains, who believe that their faith has always existed, but was rediscovered at this time. The popularity of both the Buddha and Mahavira shows that, at this time, India was a melting-pot of religious ideas.

Indra pays homage to the Buddha.

The Buddha sits on a throne decorated with lotus flowers.

Stone fragment showing the Buddha with Indra and Brahma

ADVICE FROM THE GODS
Many people in India at the time of the Buddha were Hindus, and he is often depicted alongside Hindu gods. Brahma, "the Creator", and Indra, "God of Rain and Warfare", are two of the most important Hindu gods. It is said that when the Buddha achieved enlightenment, Brahma and Indra persuaded him to teach others the truths that he had learnt. The Buddha knew this would not be easy.

PORTRAYING THE BUDDHA
Depictions of the Buddha vary greatly depending on where they come from and when they were made. But they all succeed in putting across a sense of the high esteem in which he is held. Statues of the Buddha are often golden and large. This stresses the fact that he was an important figure and worthy of reverence.

The Buddha wears a robe with a decorative border.

Modern statue of the Buddha made of gilded plaster

The Buddha's right hand is turned towards the ground in the Earth-witnessing gesture (p. 15).

Modern book containing Buddhist scriptures in Pali

LANGUAGES OF BUDDHISM
The early scriptures were written down in Pali, an Indian language. The sacred language of India in the Buddha's time was Sanskrit, but he encouraged his followers to use local languages and dialects. Buddhist words have two main forms. Pali is the form used in Theravada Buddhism (pp. 68–69) and in this book. Sanskrit, along with Tibetan and Chinese, is used in Mahayana Buddhism (pp. 72–73).

Thai Buddhist novice monk in the meditation position

THE BUDDHA'S FOLLOWING
Today, there are Buddhists all over the world. They come from many different places and traditions. The Buddha was a great teacher. He spent most of his time travelling and preaching with a group of followers. These followers grew in number and became the first Buddhist monks, who continued to spread the faith.

The Buddha's left hand is in his lap in the meditation gesture.

The Buddha's feet are crossed in the lotus position, a posture often used during meditation.

> *"Completely have I understood what must be understood, though others failed to understand it. That is the reason why I am a buddha."*
>
> **BUDDHACARITA**
> The meeting with the mendicant

It is said that the Buddha had webbed toes, rounded ankles, and projecting heels – these are some of the 32 marks of a great man (pp. 62–63).

The life of the Buddha

Burmese statue of the Buddha as a child

BABY BUDDHA
Many statues of the young Siddhatta show him pointing one hand to the Earth and the other to Heaven. After his birth, Siddhatta is said to have taken seven steps each to the north, south, east, and west. He then declared that he alone, on the Earth and in Heaven, was worthy to be revered.

THE MAN WHO WAS to become the Buddha was born Siddhatta Gotama during the 5th century BCE, in an area of India that is now part of Nepal. His family were from the upper class and, according to some accounts of his life, Siddhatta's father was the ruler of a tribe called the Shakya. Siddhatta was therefore a prince. He left his privileged background to seek for the truth of human existence and to reach the state of enlightenment. He finally became the leader of what is today one of the oldest and most widespread of all world faiths.

SIGNS OF GREATNESS
Accounts of Siddhatta's birth are full of signs predicting he would lead an exceptional life. He was born in a grove among woods near Lumbini when his mother was on her way to visit her family. In some accounts of the birth, the young prince emerged from his mother's side. He was said to be spotlessly clean when he was born and able to walk straight away.

"When born, he was so lustrous and steadfast that it appeared as if the young Sun had come down to Earth."

BUDDHACARITA
The birth of the bodhisattva

18th-century Tibetan painting showing the Buddha taking his first steps

A SHELTERED LIFE

Soon after Siddhatta was born, a holy man called Asita visited him at his father's palace. Asita predicted that Siddhatta would become either a great prince or a great religious teacher. Siddhatta's father wanted his son to follow in his own footsteps, so he made sure that Siddhatta lived a sheltered life, staying mostly within the royal palace.

The artist has given the palace a Chinese appearance.

18th-century Tibetan picture of Siddhatta in his father's palace

READY TO RULE

The young prince Siddhatta lived a life of luxury. This 10th-century Chinese painting shows him riding with one of his servants. Siddhatta's father protected him from life's hardships because he didn't want his thoughts to turn towards religion. Siddhatta married a beautiful young woman called Yashodhara, and it seemed that he would become a ruler of his people as his father wished.

Relatives mourn a dead man.

SEEING SUFFERING

When Siddhatta did leave the palace, his father ordered all signs of human suffering to be hidden. But one day Siddhatta caught sight of an old man bent double over his walking stick. The next day, he saw a sick man, and the day after that a funeral procession. On the following day, Siddhatta saw a holy man who had reached a state of calm by leaving behind all worldly comforts.

Siddhatta witnesses death for the first time.

18th-century Tibetan depiction of Siddhatta watching a funeral procession

Siddhatta's faithful servant says farewell.

Gods support the hooves of Siddhatta's horse, so that they make no noise as he leaves the palace in secret.

Siddhatta leaves the palace on his horse Kanthaka.

Section of frieze from the Amaravati stupa in southern India

Prince Siddhatta gives up his horse.

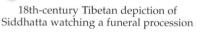

GIVING IT ALL AWAY

Siddhatta decided to give up the comforts of the palace, his fine horses and chariots, and his loving wife and newborn son, Rahula. He believed that this was the only way in which he would find out the truth about human suffering and achieve the peace of mind of the holy man he had seen.

Continued on next page

Continued from previous page

Great going forth

Siddhatta "went forth" into the world to achieve enlightenment. If he succeeded, he would escape the cycle of suffering, death, and rebirth (pp. 64–65) and develop a new understanding of life and the Universe. Siddhatta's quest was not quick or easy – he had to try several different routes before he finally succeeded.

18th-century Tibetan depiction of the Buddha cutting his hair

WORLDLINESS AND VANITY
Siddhatta prepared for his spiritual search by giving up everything to do with his worldly past. He shaved off his long hair, because in India at that time hair was thought to be symbolic of vanity.

Animal-faced demons surround Mara.

Mara carries a mace, ready to attack Siddhatta.

17th-century Japanese statue of the emaciated Siddhatta

Stone relief showing a group of demons in Mara's army

SIDDHATTA'S SEARCH
After studying with different spiritual teachers, Siddhatta continued his quest alone. He became an ascetic – someone who gives up all comforts – sleeping outdoors and eating only a little food. But this did not give him the answers he was searching for.

MARA'S ARMY
Mara is an embodiment of death and desire. He attacked Siddhatta with the help of his beautiful but deceitful daughters and his army of demons. Siddhatta called on the Earth Goddess to bear witness to his merit (p. 63), and Mara and his army ran away in fear.

THE ENLIGHTENED ONE
Siddhatta meditated under a tree (now known as the Bodhi Tree) at Bodh Gaya in northeast India. After three days and nights, he finally reached enlightenment. He was free from the fear of suffering and from the cycle of death and rebirth. He could truly be called the Buddha, "the enlightened one".

Leaves from a descendant of the first Bodhi Tree

Chinese depiction of the Buddha beneath the Bodhi Tree

Triptych showing the Buddha with two of his followers

FIRST FOLLOWERS
After achieving enlightenment, the Buddha meditated alone for several weeks. He then began to teach others, and soon followers such as Sariputta and Moggallana were learning how the Buddha had attained enlightenment. The Buddha had succeeded through neither extreme luxury nor through asceticism, but through following a Middle Way (pp. 66–67).

> *"His body gave him no trouble, his eyes never closed, and he looked into his own mind. He thought: 'Here I have found freedom.'"*

BUDDHACARITA
The enlightenment

The Buddha told his followers to be calm because he was passing on to his final death.

PASSING AWAY
About 45 years after reaching enlightenment, the time came for the Buddha to achieve parinibbana, or pass on to his final death. Scriptures record that he ate some poisoned food. Knowing that it would cause death, he stopped others from eating it. He then lay on his side and meditated until he passed away.

In depictions of his death, the Buddha always rests his head on his right arm.

Animals and demons mourn the death of the Buddha.

Living for buddhahood

Ancient Chinese wine pot in the shape of a monkey

HUNDREDS OF STORIES are told to help people understand the Buddha's teachings (pp. 64–65). Many of the tales concern the previous lives of the Buddha, before he was born as Siddhatta Gotama. They are called Jataka stories and form part of the scriptures in the Pali language (pp. 68–69). The stories show the Buddha-to-be reborn (pp. 64–65) in many different forms. In most cases, he carries out a virtuous deed or an act of self-sacrifice, showing his unique character and ensuring that each of his rebirths is a step on the way to buddhahood.

BODHISATTVA BIRD
The Tibetan story "The Buddha's Law Among the Birds" is similar in form to the Jatakas. Bodhisattva Avalokiteshvara (p. 75) turned himself into a cuckoo. After meditating for a year, he taught all the other birds that they should not be satisfied with the endless round of death and rebirth, but should study the teachings of the Buddha.

Serpents are often portrayed with many heads.

18th-century Burmese elephant chesspiece

BUILDING BRIDGES
"The Monkey King" is a tale about the King of Benares, who went out hunting monkeys. He saw a monkey king stretch his body across a river to make a bridge so his tribe could escape. In the process, the monkey king injured his back and could not escape himself. The King of Benares was so amazed by the monkey's self-sacrifice that he bathed the animal's wounds.

A MOVING TALE
"The White Elephant" is a tale about a fine white elephant who worked for a king. The king noticed that the elephant was sad and asked what was wrong. The elephant explained that he wanted to go back to the forest to care for his old, blind mother. The king was so moved that he let him return to the forest.

SERPENT'S SPIRIT
"The Serpent King" is about a serpent who often left his watery kingdom to fast, or go without food. One day, the serpent was caught by a human king. The serpent showed the king his beautiful underwater home. "Why do you want to leave this place?" asked the king. "Because I want to be reborn as a man and purify my spirit," replied the serpent.

Stone head of a Naga serpent

GREAT SACRIFICE
"The Hungry Tigress" is a tale about the Buddha-to-be in human form. He and one of his followers came across a starving tigress who was about to eat her own cubs. The Buddha-to-be sent away his follower, then offered his own body to the starving animal. Both the tigress and her cubs feasted on his flesh.

Shakra, "King of the Gods", is sitting in the posture of royal ease.

Limestone depiction of the Mandhata Jataka

Emperor Mandhata is surrounded by dancing women.

LETHAL LONGING
Emperor Mandhata, the subject of the "Mandhata Jataka", was a great emperor who lived in Heaven. But he was bored and longed for the pleasures of life on the Earth. Mandhata returned to the Earth, but he quickly aged and died, showing that all longing leads to suffering.

TEACHING TALES
Carved reliefs of the Jatakas, like these from Amaravati in India, appear on many stupas (pp. 92–93). The stories illustrate acts of selflessness and virtue, so they have always been used to teach people how to live their lives. In the days before most people could read, monks used the carvings in their lessons.

SELFLESS STAG
"The King and the Deer" is about a king who went hunting. He was going to kill a doe who had a fawn, but a stag stepped forwards to offer himself in place of the doe. The king was moved by the stag's bravery and vowed never to kill an animal again.

18th-century wooden statue of a deer from Thailand

Features, poses, and gestures

LONG BEFORE THE BUDDHA'S time on the Earth, Indian wise men said that there were 32 marks, or features, to be found on a great man. The Buddha had all of these, from the wisdom bump on his head to the wheels on the soles of his feet (p. 91), although not all are shown on every image of him. Each of the 32 features has a special meaning, as do the Buddha's various poses and hand gestures. They represent aspects of his character, and events and activities from his lives.

Copy of an early depiction of the Buddha from Burma

Copy of the Kamakura Buddha from Japan

FINGERS AND THUMBS
In this gesture, used during meditation, the palms of the hands face upwards and the fingers and thumbs touch at the tips. This forms a flattened triangle shape that symbolizes the Three Jewels of Buddhism (p. 66).

The wisdom bump on top of the Buddha's head resembles the turban that was worn by royalty and gods.

The urna between the Buddha's eyes is sometimes called a beauty spot or a wisdom eye.

Burmese Buddha with Mucalinda

SHELTER FROM THE STORM
This statue symbolizes an event in the Buddha's life. The Buddha was meditating during a rainstorm. A cobra called Mucalinda coiled himself around the Buddha and arched his hood over the Buddha's head to form a protective umbrella.

THE FACE OF THE BUDDHA
As depicted here, the Buddha is usually shown with a calm or withdrawn expression and with half-closed eyes, as if he is meditating. This statue also features some of the 32 marks. The Buddha has an urna, or spot, between his eyes and a wisdom bump. He also has elongated ear lobes, which symbolize wisdom and spiritual understanding.

The flame-like headdress represents the light of supreme knowledge.

Thai wooden Buddha in the meditating posture

Chinese painted wooden reclining Buddha

Thai bronze Buddha making the Earth-witnessing gesture

DEATH POSTURE
The Buddha is said to have died lying on his side in the reclining posture. The reclining Buddha is often shown wearing monk's robes (pp. 96–97) and resting his head on his right hand, while his left hand is on his hip. His expression is usually serene.

CROSS-LEGGED
When meditating, the Buddha is often shown with his legs crossed in the half-lotus position shown here. This posture had been used for meditation in yoga for many hundreds of years.

WITHOUT WEAPONS
This gesture, with the right hand raised to shoulder height, is common in images of the standing Buddha. It represents fearlessness and also blessing and friendship. It makes clear that the person making the gesture holds no weapon.

CALLING THE EARTH GODDESS
The Earth-witnessing gesture shown here symbolizes the moment in the Buddha's life when he touched the ground during his struggle with Mara. This gesture summoned the Earth Goddess. The Buddha called her to bear witness to the merit, or virtue, he had acquired in his previous lives and the steadfastness with which he withstood Mara's attack.

CALMING THE ELEPHANT
The Buddha is sometimes shown with both hands raised in a gesture of strength and fearlessness. According to one story, the Buddha was once attacked by an angry elephant. The Buddha channelled his great power into this simple gesture and calmed the beast.

"The soles of his feet were marked with wheels ... his fingers and toes were joined by webs ... a circle of soft down grew between his eyebrows ..."

BUDDHACARITA
Asita's visit

Standing Buddha making the gesture of fearlessness and friendship

Buddhist teachings

THE BUDDHA'S MOST important teachings concerned basic truths about existence and advice about how his followers should live. He told people that their lives were part of a repeating cycle of birth, death, and rebirth. The Buddha summed up the problems that most humans have to endure in Four Noble Truths about suffering (pp. 66–67). He then offered a way to overcome suffering through the Noble Eightfold Path. This path allows some people to break free from the cycle of rebirth and achieve the state of enlightenment.

The six realms of rebirth from the Wheel of Life

BORN AGAIN
The endless cycle through the realms of rebirth is known as samsara. Buddhists believe that, when a person dies, he or she is reborn and a new being is created. This new being could be an animal or even one of the gods. Buddhists do not believe in an essential soul or self, so each reborn being is distinct from the previous life.

Heaven, or the realm of the gods, is the highest of the six realms, but it is still only a step on the route to enlightenment.

The realm of the asuras is a place of envy and continuous war.

Yama, "Lord of Death", grips the wheel with his teeth.

The scenes around the edge of the wheel illustrate the law of kamma, in which every action depends on other actions.

THE FIRST SERMON
After his enlightenment, the Buddha went to a deer park at Sarnath, near the city of Benares in northern India. He explained to others the truths that had come to him under the Bodhi Tree and told them how they too might reach the state of enlightenment known as nibbana (p. 88).

WHEEL OF LAW
The Buddha's sermon at Sarnath became known as "the first turning of the Wheel of Law". The Buddha's teachings are also referred to as the dhamma, which means doctrine, truth, or law. The dhamma sums up the essence of the Buddha's ideas about human suffering and the way to end it.

Hand of the Buddha making the dhamma, or teaching, gesture

WHEEL OF LIFE
Tibetan Buddhists illustrate the cycle of rebirth with the Wheel of Life. The main body of the wheel shows the six realms into which one can be reborn. These are the realms of gods, humans, animals, asuras (warlike demons), hungry spirits, and Hell. Around the edge of the wheel, 12 scenes show how kamma works in human life (p. 88).

Wheel of Life from a Tibetan wall hanging

Copy of a decoration from the roof of the Potala Palace, Lhasa, Tibet

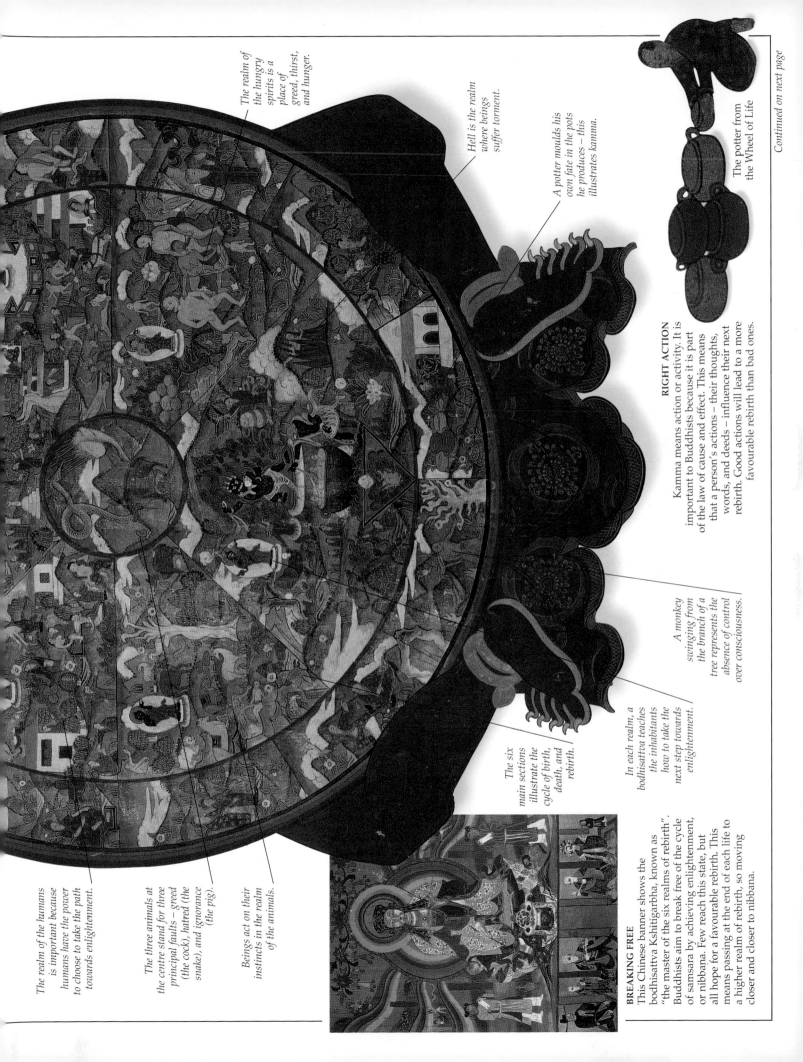

The realm of the humans is important because humans have the power to choose to take the path towards enlightenment.

The three animals at the centre stand for three principal faults – greed (the cock), hatred (the snake), and ignorance (the pig).

Beings act on their instincts in the realm of the animals.

The realm of the hungry spirits is a place of greed, thirst, and hunger.

Hell is the realm where beings suffer torment.

A potter moulds his own fate in the pots he produces – this illustrates kamma.

The six main sections illustrate the cycle of birth, death, and rebirth.

In each realm, a bodhisattva teaches the inhabitants how to take the next step towards enlightenment.

A monkey swinging from the branch of a tree represents the absence of control over consciousness.

The potter from the Wheel of Life

Continued on next page

RIGHT ACTION
Kamma means action or activity. It is important to Buddhists because it is part of the law of cause and effect. This means that a person's actions – their thoughts, words, and deeds – influence their next rebirth. Good actions will lead to a more favourable rebirth than bad ones.

BREAKING FREE
This Chinese banner shows the bodhisattva Kshitigarbha, known as "the master of the six realms of rebirth". Buddhists aim to break free of the cycle of samsara by achieving enlightenment, or nibbana. Few reach this state, but all hope for a favourable rebirth. This means passing at the end of each life to a higher realm of rebirth, so moving closer and closer to nibbana.

Continued from previous page

SUFFERING SICKNESS
This painting shows the Buddha helping a monk who is suffering through illness. The Four Noble Truths at the centre of the Buddha's teachings are closely linked to human suffering. The Buddha saw that people suffer when they crave for things they cannot have. For example, people may crave eternal life, even though everyone has to die.

The Middle Way

There are Four Noble Truths at the centre of the Buddha's teachings: all life is suffering, the cause of suffering is craving, the end of suffering comes with release from craving, and the release from suffering comes from following the Noble Eightfold Path. In order to follow the moral guidance of the Noble Eightfold Path, Buddhists must find the balance between luxury and hardship known as the Middle Way. They do not usually wear fancy clothes or rags, instead they dress practically. They do not normally feast or fast, instead they share simple meals.

The snake symbolizes hatred.

The cock symbolizes greed.

The pig symbolizes ignorance.

CONSTANT CRAVINGS
The animals in the centre of the Wheel of Life symbolize three faults that the Buddha believed people must overcome. These faults are hatred, ignorance, and greed – all of which involve craving. Hatred involves the craving to destroy. Ignorance and greed bring about craving for unnecessary things. The three animals chase each other in an endless circle, symbolizing the strong link between the three faults.

INSPIRING TEACHER
This Tibetan mural shows the Buddha teaching the Noble Eightfold Path. The eight parts of this path are right understanding, right intention, right speech, right action, right livelihood, right effort, right mindfulness, and right concentration. The path teaches Buddhists how to overcome greed, hatred, and ignorance, which lead to suffering.

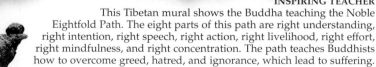

Carved figures embracing, from Borobudur stupa in Java

CONSEQUENCES OF CRAVING
These figures are wrapped up in the world of desire and craving and are ignoring the Noble Eightfold Path. Buddhists believe that it is important to find release from craving because craving leads to moral faults. These faults can, in turn, bring about a poor rebirth.

The eye is drawn upwards to the eight discs that decorate the spire.

Thai novice monk caring for a kitten

THE RIGHT JOB
Doi Suthep-Doi forest in Thailand is protected and cared for by Buddhist monks. Buddhists try to observe the Noble Eightfold Path in their livelihood, or work, just as they do in the rest of their lives. They avoid jobs that involve causing suffering to others, such as working as a butcher or trading in arms, and try to do work that benefits other living things. This is known as right livelihood.

This model stupa may once have contained relics of the Buddha.

Teardrop-shaped gems representing the Precious Jewels

PEACE AND HARMONY
The Buddha said that people should behave in a caring way towards other living things to encourage harmony in the world. This is known as right action. He taught people not to harm or kill other beings and not to steal. Early Buddhists reinforced this advice with Five Moral Precepts. These are to avoid harming others, stealing, sexual misconduct, lying, and taking drugs and alcohol.

LITTLE GEMS
The Buddha described three things, or Three Precious Jewels, for Buddhists to turn to when trying to follow the Noble Eightfold Path. They are the Buddha himself, his dhamma, or teaching, and the monastic community known as the sangha (pp. 96–99). Buddhists remember the Three Precious Jewels, which are often represented by three gems, every time they take the Triple Refuge (pp. 102–103).

Images of the Buddha decorate the model.

EIGHTS EVERYWHERE
The qualities of the Noble Eightfold Path are often represented on stupa spires by a series of eight discs. The Wheel of Law has eight spokes and the stupa at Borobudur is made up of eight levels. This repeated use of the number eight reminds Buddhists of the importance of the Noble Eightfold Path. The eight parts are of equal importance. Buddhists aim to practise them all together, because they reinforce each other.

The Buddha is in a meditational position.

The Buddha is touching the Earth with his right hand.

9th-century bronze model of a stupa

Detail from an Ashoka pillar, 3rd century BCE, Sarnath, India

Theravada Buddhism

Guardian spirits detail from the Tipitaka wall hanging

THERAVADA BUDDHISM IS practised mainly in Sri Lanka, Thailand, Laos, Cambodia, and Burma (also known as Myanmar). Theravada Buddhists traditionally place the greatest importance on the Buddha himself and on his teachings, written in Pali in the ancient scriptures. The sangha, or community of monks, are also central to this strand of the faith. In the past, the practice of meditation was restricted to monks, who could reach enlightenment. Ordinary people could only live a life of merit in the hope of a favourable rebirth. Today, however, many Theravada Buddhists practise meditation and hope to move quickly along the path to enlightenment.

The Tipitaka is being paraded on the back of an elephant.

SPREADING THE WORD
This lion-topped column is a trade mark of the great Buddhist emperor Ashoka, who ruled much of India during the 3rd century BCE. He built a number of stupas (pp. 92–93) and sent his followers across India to teach others the dhamma. Ashoka also constructed many huge columns inscribed with Buddhist scriptures and symbols (pp. 90–91).

TREASURED TIPITAKA
This wall hanging shows a procession in which the Pali scriptures are carried on the back of an elephant. The scriptures are known as the Tipitaka, or triple basket, because the manuscripts were originally carried in three baskets. Each basket held one of the three main parts of the scriptures – the Vinaya Pitaka, the Sutta Pitaka, and the Abhidhamma Pitaka.

200-year-old palm Pali scriptures in Burmese script bound with cord

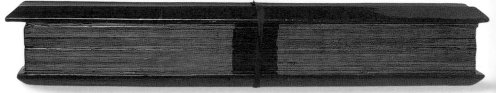

PALI ON PALMS
In South and Southeast Asia, Pali scriptures are traditionally written on pressed palm leaves. Narrow strips of leaves are bound with cords or ribbons and protected with a wooden cover. Pali is said by some to be the language used by the Buddha. It is a spoken language with no script of its own, so can be written in the script of any language.

20th-century palm scriptures in a wooden case bound with ribbons

WHAT'S INSIDE?

The first of the three parts of the Tipitaka scriptures, the Vinaya Pitaka, includes 227 rules by which Theravada monks must live (pp. 96–99). The second part, the Sutta Pitaka, contains the Buddha's teachings and other writings, such as the Jataka tales. The third and final part, the Abhidhamma Pitaka, is made up of philosophical writings about the Buddhist outlook on life.

FIRST EDITIONS

The scribes who made early copies of the Pali texts used a bronze stylus like this to write on palm leaves. They first prepared the leaves by cutting them to size, boiling them in milk or water, and rubbing them down to produce a smooth, pale finish. They then used the stylus to write out the texts in black ink. Some palm scriptures were highly decorated and coated with gold leaf.

Lacquered palm Tipitaka scriptures in Pali with Burmese script

Ananda's statue stands 7 m (23 ft) tall.

Giant statue of Ananda, Polonnaruwa, Sri Lanka

Modern Pali scriptures containing the Dhammapada

PALI IN PRINT

Modern scriptures like these are often printed on strips of card to mimic earlier palm versions. One of the most popular parts of the Tipitaka today is the Dhammapada. This collection of the Buddha's sayings is part of the Sutta Pitaka. It is full of advice about living well, doing good, and purifying the mind. Many Buddhists learn it by heart.

FAVOURITE FOLLOWER

The Buddha's cousin and favourite follower, Ananda, was one of the first arahats, or Buddhist saints. He had not reached enlightenment when the Buddha died, but he did so soon afterwards as a result of his deep devotion to the great teacher. All Theravada Buddhists hope to reach enlightenment and become arahats.

Buddhism moves south

TYPICALLY THAI
In Thailand, the Buddha is often shown making the Earth-witnessing gesture. The tightly curled hair style, pointed headdress, and fine features are also typical of statues of the Buddha from this part of the world.

Hundreds of golden ornaments adorn the elephant's red velvet costume.

DURING THE 3RD century BCE Buddhism spread southwards from India to the island of Sri Lanka. From here, news of the Buddha's life and teachings was carried along the trade routes across the Indian Ocean. It then reached Burma, Thailand, Cambodia, and Laos. Fine temples were built in cities such as Pagan, in Burma, and Angkor, in Cambodia, as the Buddha's teaching was spread all over the region. Theravada Buddhism is popular in these countries to this day. For example, more than 90 per cent of the population of Thailand follow this branch of Buddhism.

Buddhists at a religious procession in Kyaukpadoung, Burma

BUDDHIST BURMA
Processions are a notable part of Buddhism in Burma. The tradition began when local rulers became Buddhists as a result of strong links with India and Sri Lanka. They built large temples and took part in lavish ceremonies. Burma is now ruled by the military, but most of the people are still Buddhists.

Burmese-style peace pagoda, Birmingham, UK

BUILDING FOR MERIT
Theravada Buddhism has spread widely. There are now many Burmese-style buildings in the Western world. Burmese temples often have golden roofs, and Shwedagon pagoda in Burma is the world's largest gold-covered building. Buddhists build these monuments in the hope of gaining merit.

TEMPLE OF THE TOOTH
Sri Lanka's most precious relic is the tooth of the Buddha, kept at the Temple of the Tooth in Kandy. The Portuguese invaded Sri Lanka in the early 16th century and claimed to have destroyed the tooth. But locals claimed it was miraculously saved and built the temple to house it.

FANTASTIC FESTIVAL
This elephant and boy are taking part in Esala Perahera. This is a festival held every year in Kandy, Sri Lanka, in honour of the tooth of the Buddha. The festivities last for several nights. The highlight is a procession in which dancers, musicians, and elephants dressed in beautiful embroidered clothes parade through the streets. One of the elephants carries a case containing the sacred tooth.

The elephant's decorated covering is called a caparison.

Ornate Burmese alms bowl

GENEROUS GIFTS
This ornate alms bowl (p. 99) has a pointed lid that resembles the roof of a Burmese temple. It is typical of the lavish gifts given to Buddhist monks by Buddhist members of the public. Monks live simple lives, but people hope that these rich gifts will earn them merit.

Those taking part in the procession wear white clothing.

"These jars now hold the relics great in virtue, as mountains hold their jewelled ore."

BUDDHACARITA
The relics

Mahayana Buddhism

The text is a Chinese translation of the Diamond Sutra.

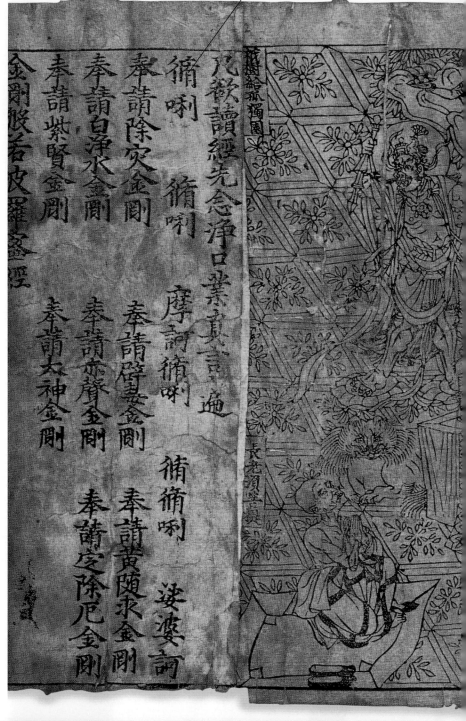

THE BRANCH of the faith called Mahayana, or northern, Buddhism developed in the 1st century CE (common era, the term used by non-Christians for AD). It spread across China, Mongolia, and Tibet, before reaching Vietnam, Korea, and Japan. Some Mahayana practices and beliefs differ from those of Theravada Buddhists. Mahayana Buddhists hope to become bodhisattvas (pp. 74–75). They have a more devotional approach both to the Buddha and to the bodhisattvas. They also have some scriptures, known as sutras, not used in Theravada Buddhism.

Spirit from the Diamond Sutra

CUTTING WORDS
This Chinese copy of the Diamond Sutra dates from 868. It is the oldest printed book in the world. As with other Mahayana scriptures, the Diamond Sutra was originally written in Sanskrit. Its title suggests that it is able to cut through ignorance like a diamond. The text is a sermon by the Buddha describing a bodhisattva's journey towards wisdom.

7th-century Korean wooden printing block

MIRROR IMAGE
Printing was developed in Korea in order to produce copies of the Mahayana scriptures. The printer had to carve a mirror image of the words of each section into a flat block of wood. This could then be coated with ink and pressed on to a scroll to make a copy of the text.

SHORT BUT SWEET
The Heart Sutra is a short, very popular scripture. It is recited regularly in numerous Mahayana monasteries, especially the Zen monasteries of Japan (pp. 86–87). The text is known as the "doctrine of emptiness". It says that, in order to become a bodhisattva, a person has first to achieve selflessness through wisdom and compassion.

Painting showing the Heart Sutra being written

The Buddha is making the teaching gesture with his right hand.

The bodhisattvas, with their haloes and crowns, listen to the Buddha's teaching.

Painting of Nagarjuna from the Ki monastery, Spiti, India

LOST AND FOUND

The scholar Nagarjuna was born in India, probably in the 2nd century. According to legend, he discovered and taught sutras that had previously been lost. He founded a school of Buddhism called Madhyamaka, which sought to find a middle way between extremes of thought, belief, and action. It had a huge influence on Mahayana Buddhism.

GUARDIAN AND GUIDE

The Lotus Sutra, shown here in Chinese script, describes the Buddha as a being dwelling in a paradise with thousands of faithful followers. He watches over people on the Earth with great compassion. The Lotus Sutra is an example of how skillfully the Buddha's teachings are adapted for people worldwide.

The Buddha wears a symbol of good fortune on his chest.

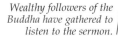

Many monks listen as the Buddha first speaks the words of the Diamond Sutra.

Wealthy followers of the Buddha have gathered to listen to the sermon.

Fan with text from the Sutra of the Lotus of Good Law

Detail from the Diamond Sutra showing musical spirits called Gandharvas

SIGNIFICANT SUTRAS

The sutras are so important to Mahayana Buddhists that words from them are often written on everyday objects such as fans. Sutra is a Sanskrit word used in Mahayana Buddhism for texts that are written as if spoken by the Buddha himself. These texts include the Pali suttas as well as works written originally in Sanskrit but surviving only in translations.

Other buddhas and bodhisattvas

SIDDHATTA GOTAMA is said to be just one of many buddhas. He was preceded by other people who had, like him, achieved supreme enlightenment and escaped the cycle of life, death, and rebirth. Buddhists believe that there are also people who reach the point of enlightenment but who remain in the realm of ordinary existence. They die and are reborn in order to help others reach enlightenment. These people are known as bodhisattvas. Like the buddhas, they are widely revered, especially in the Mahayana tradition.

AVOIDING ANGER
Akshobya, "the imperturbable" (calm and not excitable), avoided emotions such as anger so that he could achieve any task he set himself. He is said to dwell in a paradise in the east where there is no evil or suffering. He is one of the Jinas, or Cosmic Buddhas (p. 78).

Akshobya's right hand touches the Earth, indicating his enlightenment.

Dipankara's right hand is making the gesture of dhamma, or teaching.

Amoghasiddhi's right hand is in the position that represents fearlessness or blessing.

Vairocana's hands form the dhyana mudra, or meditational gesture.

Amoghasiddhi's left hand rests in his lap in a gesture of meditation.

CREATOR OF LIGHT
The first of the earlier buddhas was called Dipankara, which means "creator of light". A Jataka story tells how the Buddha himself, in an earlier life, met Dipankara and was greatly inspired by his wisdom and compassion.

SPIRITUAL SUCCESS
Amoghasiddhi is one of the Cosmic Buddhas and is most commonly depicted along with the others. This buddha's name means "he who does not work in vain" or "he who is always successful".

UNIVERSAL BUDDHA
Another of the Cosmic Buddhas, Vairocana is seen differently in various branches of Buddhism. For some, he embodies the Historical Buddha; for others, he is a supreme being who embodies the entire Universe.

BUDDHA OF THE FUTURE

Maitreya, whose name means benevolence or friendship, is known as "the Buddha of the future". It is said that, in thousands of years' time, he will leave the Tushita Heaven, the place where future buddhas dwell. He will then come to the Earth to be the next human buddha.

Maitreya stands, ready to step into the world.

FULL OF MERCY

Renowned for his mercy, Avalokiteshvara is also known as "the protector of the world". He is prepared to be reborn in any form to save living beings from suffering. Although he is widely revered as a male bodhisattva, in eastern Asia Avalokiteshvara is seen as a female figure. She is known in China as "the goddess of mercy", Kuan Yin (p. 83).

Tara wears the jewels and crown typical of a bodhisattva.

MOTHER OF BUDDHAS

Tara, meaning star, is also known as "she who saves". She is greatly revered in Tibet and is referred to as "the mother of all buddhas". Tibetans see her as the ancestor of their people. Tara can take many forms. The best known are the peaceful White Tara and the fierce Green Tara.

Manjushri holds a sword to cut through ignorance.

THE GENTLE HOLY ONE

The bodhisattva Manjushri, "the gentle holy one", is renowned for his wisdom. In Tibet, great teachers are sometimes said to be incarnations of Manjushri. He is often seen as "the master of all bodhisattvas" and is said to live in a paradise on top of a five-peaked mountain.

Tibetan Buddhism

A DISTINCTIVE type of Mahayana Buddhism developed in Tibet. As in other strands of the Mahayana, Tibetan Buddhists revere the bodhisattvas, in particular Avalokiteshvara and "the mother of all buddhas", Tara. But, like Theravada Buddhists, they place great importance on the role of monks as scholars and teachers. Tibetan Buddhism also has some unique elements, such as the mystical collection of writings and practices known as Tantric Buddhism. When communist China invaded Tibet in 1950, many Buddhist leaders had to leave the country. But this has made the faith stronger, because Tibetan Buddhism has spread all over the world.

FAMILY VALUES
These wooden figures from Tibet show a Buddhist monk and two members of his family. While the monk meditates, the members of his family turn prayer wheels. These figures show the importance of monks and lay people in Tibetan Buddhism – both can achieve buddhahood.

ANCIENT PRACTICES
This 17th-century French illustration shows an ascetic practising yoga. In the Tibetan strand of Buddhism, meditation is particularly important. The Tibetan word for meditation is "gom". It means to familiarize your mind with something of spiritual significance. Tibetan teachers pass on spiritual knowledge and the teachings of the Buddha through the practice of meditation.

PURE MINDFULNESS
This Tibetan lama (pp. 78–79) is chanting a mantra. A mantra is a word or series of words repeated over and over to help focus the mind during meditation. As the lama concentrates on the rise and fall of his voice and the meaning of the words he is chanting, all other thoughts fall away. He reaches a state of calm and "pure mindfulness".

The lama counts the beads as he chants.

A Tibetan lama's robes are similar in style to those of other monks and nuns (pp. 96–97).

RED HAT, YELLOW HAT

These monks belong to a school of Tibetan monks called the Gelugpas, or "Yellow Hats". Monasticism is very important in Tibetan Buddhism, and there are four main schools of monks. The other three schools are the Nyingmapa, Kargyupa, and Sakya. These monks all wear red hats.

BUDDHIST BEADS

Many Tibetan Buddhists carry prayer beads to help them count the number of times they repeat a mantra or the Triple Refuge (pp. 103–103). Most strings are made up of 108 beads, which is the number of desires that must be overcome before reaching enlightenment. Some prayer beads are made from the bones of dead holy men or lamas.

Prayer beads made of ivory, jade, and sandalwood

The weighted chain helps the wheel to turn.

Protective cover

Milarepa holds a hand to his ear, listening to the songs he wrote down.

18th-century Tibetan bronze statue of Milarepa

Milarepa wore thin, cotton robes because the type of meditation he practised generated heat.

The scroll contains a printed mantra.

Complete prayer wheel (above left) and prayer wheel opened out to show how it works

The metal spindle holds the scroll.

The handle is usually grasped in the right hand to spin the wheel.

SINGING SAINT

Milarepa was a sinner in early life, but he began to regret his actions and became a Buddhist. Milarepa joined up with a Buddhist wise man called Marpa. The pair founded the Kargyupa school of Buddhism, and Milarepa became Tibet's greatest saint. He wrote down thousands of Buddhist songs and became a teacher of other holy men.

"If you have deserved it ... a white light will guide you into one of the heavens ... you will have some happiness among the gods."

TIBETAN BOOK OF THE DEAD
The dawning of the lights of the six places of rebirth

ROUND AND ROUND

Tibetan prayer wheels contain a roll of paper on which the sacred mantra "Om mani padme hum" ("Hail to the jewel in the lotus") is written many times. When the wheel turns, the mantra spins, in effect being repeated continuously. This spreads blessings and well-being and calls up Avalokiteshvara.

Continued on next page

Tibetan lamas

The most senior monks (pp. 96–99) in Tibetan Buddhism are known as lamas. They are usually people who have achieved mastery of Tibetan-style meditation and the related rituals. Most exalted of all lamas are those known as tulkus. These lamas are believed to be reincarnations of saints or bodhisattvas. They are reborn to teach and to help people to follow the Noble Eightfold Path. Some of the most inspiring of all Buddhist teachers have been lamas and tulkus.

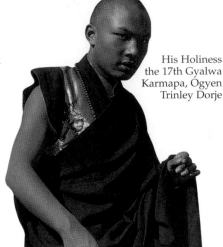

His Holiness the 17th Gyalwa Karmapa, Ögyen Trinley Dorje

ADORED ASHES

These medallions are made from the ashes of lamas who have been cremated after death. The ashes are mixed with clay, formed into discs, and then stamped with an image of the lama. Lamas are widely revered because they devote their lives to spiritual matters.

THE CHOSEN ONES

Towards the end of his life on the Earth, a lama or tulku usually gives clues to help his followers find the site of his next rebirth. After his death, monks follow these hints until they find a child who fits the description. The chosen child, like this young lama, is taken to a monastery to begin a life of study and spirituality.

"I now transmit to you the profound teachings which I have myself received from my Teacher and, through him, from the long line of initiated gurus."

TIBETAN BOOK OF THE DEAD
Preamble

Clay medallions preserving the ashes of venerated Tibetan lamas

Vairocana transforms delusion into wisdom.

Ratnasmbhava transforms pride and greed into wisdom.

Vajrasattva transforms hate into wisdom.

Amitabha transforms lust into wisdom.

Lama's ornate ritual headdress

THE BUDDHAS OF WISDOM

Ritual headdresses worn by lamas are usually decorated with depictions of the Cosmic Buddhas of Mahayana Buddhism. They are also known as "the buddhas of wisdom". These figures are very important because they are said to transform negative emotions into wisdom. This is a quality which, together with compassion, is one of the two most important aspects of enlightenment.

Potala Palace,
Lhasa, Tibet

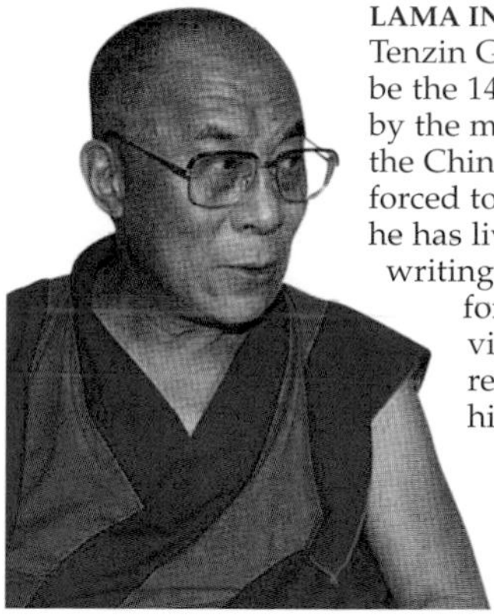

POTALA PALACE

This huge palace was built for the Dalai Lama at Lhasa in southern Tibet. The Dalai Lama is the head of the school of Tibetan monks called the Gelugpas. During the 17th century, the Gelugpas became the political, as well as the spiritual, leaders of Tibet. In 1950, Communist China invaded Tibet and brought this unique period of rule to an end.

LAMA IN EXILE

Tenzin Gyatso was declared to be the 14th Dalai Lama in 1937 by the monks of Lhasa. After the Chinese takeover, he was forced to leave Tibet. Since then he has lived in exile, teaching, writing, and campaigning for freedom without violence. He is widely revered, especially in his homeland of Tibet.

Ngawang Losang
Gyatso from Samye
monastery, Tibet

MUSIC FOR MEDITATION

This lama is holding a bell and a type of small drum called a damaru. Tibetan Buddhists use these instruments during rituals. The sounds they produce call on "the bodhisattvas of wisdom", provide musical offerings, and are a focus for meditation.

Tibetan lama
meditating with
a bell and drum

*The bell's handle
is shaped like a
vajra (p. 91).*

THE GREAT FIFTH

Ngawang Losang Gyatso (1617–82), the fifth Dalai Lama, was the first lama to rule Tibet. He built the Potala Palace and formed an alliance with the Manchus, the dynasty who ruled neighbouring China. He was a powerful but compassionate ruler and is known to Tibetans as the Great Fifth.

*The drum is carved
from wood and has
a brocade tassel.*

*Amoghasiddhi
transforms envy
into wisdom.*

*The bell's
beautiful
sound is said
to awaken the
listener from
ignorance.*

79

Continued on next page

Tantric Buddhism

This form of Buddhism is based on Tibetan texts called the tantras. It teaches that all thoughts and emotions, even negative ones, are part of the essential buddha-nature – the potential of all beings to reach enlightenment. Under the guidance of a guru, or spiritual teacher, Tantric Buddhists learn to identify with one of the Cosmic Buddhas, hoping to come to a deep understanding of buddha-nature. By using meditation and special rituals Tantric Buddhists aim to reach nibbana much more quickly than other Mahayana Buddhists, who follow the less direct path of the bodhisattvas.

PERFECT WORLD
Tantric Buddhists use complex representations of the Buddhist Cosmos, called mandalas, to help them meditate and reach harmony with buddha-nature. The Buddha Kalachakra sits in the centre of this 16th-century mandala with his partner, Vishvamata. They are surrounded by a series of enclosures containing gods and goddesses, making up a perfect world. Tantric Buddhists look at a mandala until they become absorbed in its ideal world and move towards harmony with Kalachakra.

RESISTING EVIL
Hevajra is a form of the Cosmic Buddha Akshobya. He is often shown embracing his partner, Nairatmya, and trampling figures underfoot. Hevajra has five heads, and his sixteen hands hold cups containing gods, ritual objects, and animals. He is an angry deity who uses his terrifying form to fight evil.

Hevajra's left hands hold cups containing gods of the elements, such as water and air.

The central area contains Kalachakra and Vishvamata.

Hevajra's right hands hold cups containing animals.

The second area contains 64 goddesses of speech, "the mothers of all mantras".

18th-century bronze statue of Hevajra and Nairatmya

The third area contains 360 deities in 12 lotus flowers.

"Masters of tantra" appear along the outer edges of the mandala.

80

He holds a magical staff in his right hand.

Tibetan gilt bronze statue of Padmasambhava

He holds a symbolic weapon in his left hand.

FLOWER CHILD

According to legend, the Indian monk Padmasambhava was born from a lotus blossom and was a form of the Buddha Amitabha. He helped to convert the Tibetans to Buddhism and taught them Tantric rituals. It is said that he used supernatural powers to repel demons who were preventing the spread of Buddhism in Tibet.

CLEARING THE WAY

Tantric Buddhists like these in Nara, Japan, put items such as grains into a fire at their temple. The objects placed in the fire stand for ignorance and for the emotions and thoughts that stand in the way of their enlightenment. The fire destroys the symbolic objects, helping clear the way to nibbana.

TANTRIC TEACHER

Tantric masters guide their followers in meditation, choosing the right methods and practices for each individual. They teach skills such as breath control, the memorizing of mantras, the use of ritual hand gestures called mudras, and the use of mandalas for meditation. All this brings their pupils closer to buddha-nature.

Chinese and Korean Buddhism

BUDDHISM CAME TO China from Central Asia and spread gradually eastwards across the country until it reached Korea. At first there were tensions between Buddhism and established Chinese philosophies such as Confucianism, but the different belief systems learnt to live together. They were even combined into a popular religion that saw the bodhisattvas as gods and goddesses who could help people in their everyday lives. China also produced its own schools of Buddhism, some based on intense study, and others based on a simpler path.

Hsüan Tsang mural, Mogao cave temple, Dunhuang, China

Lao Tsu, founder of Taoism, taught people to live a simple, self-sufficient life.

THREE FAITHS
This 18th-century Chinese painting is an artist's impression of what might have happened if the Buddha had gone to China. Two of the most famous Chinese thinkers, Lao Tsu and Confucius, are shown caring for the infant Buddha. The philosophers had different belief systems, but they respected others, and the three faiths usually got on well in China.

TRAVELLING TEACHER
Hsüan Tsang was born in Honan in China. He became a Buddhist monk in 620 and made a lengthy pilgrimage across China to India. The journey lasted 16 years and covered more than 64,000 km (40,000 miles). Hsüan Tsang's travels took him through Afghanistan and all around India, where he learnt Sanskrit. He translated many scriptures and brought them back to China.

Confucius, founder of Confucianism, taught people to respect others.

The infant Buddha

SUTRA STORAGE
This 13th-century lacquered Korean box was made to hold sutras. By the 7th century, Buddhism was flourishing in China, and some emperors were keen to spread the Buddha's teaching around their vast empire. Monks copied the sutras and distributed them across China and into neighbouring Korea. These precious manuscripts were often kept in beautiful boxes.

THE COMFORTER
Kuan Yin, the Chinese form of the bodhisattva Avalokiteshvara, inspires love all over China. She is the compassionate "Goddess of Mercy", who listens to the cries of those in distress. Many people keep an image of her in their homes and look upon her as a comforter of those who are sick, lost, or frightened.

LEARNED LOHAN
Chinese Buddhists recognize 18 immortal lohans, or saints. The lohans were followers of the Buddha to whom he entrusted his teachings before his final nibbana. All 18 lohans studied Buddhist law in great depth and eventually achieved enlightenment.

Statue of a lohan from Hebei Province, China

Kuan Yin is usually depicted wearing a crown – a symbol of royalty.

Stucco head of Bodhisattva Kuan Yin dating from the 8th or 9th century

RITUAL CLEANSING
These 12th-century water jars come from Korea, and similar ones are often seen in Korean paintings of the bodhisattva Avalokiteshvara. Monks often sprinkle water during ceremonies to cleanse ritually the statues and people present in the temple. Water containers like this are kept near the altar, or shrine. They are used with a sprinkler made from a willow branch.

Japanese Buddhism

From about the 7th century, travellers began to bring Buddhist ideas to Japan from China and Korea. By this time there were many different schools of Buddhism in China, all of which were part of the Mahayana strand of the faith. Most Japanese schools of Buddhism, such as Tendai, Shingon, and Jodo Buddhism, are based on forms that began in China. However, one new school, Nichiren Shu, was founded in Japan by a monk who began as a follower of the Tendai school.

Wooden head of Amida Buddha

TAKING IT EASY
Many different sects of Mahayana Buddhism are popular in Japan, so temples and statues of the Buddha are common and varied. This statue shows the Buddha in the royal ease posture. It is also known as the relaxation posture. It suggests harmony and indicates the Buddha's state of enlightenment.

PURE LAND PARADISE
Amida Buddha is extremely important in the Jodo, or Pure Land, school. Jodo Buddhists believe that Amida, "the Buddha of infinite light", dwells in a Pure Land, or paradise, in the west. Amida has displayed supreme goodness over a vast number of years, and it is said that all who turn to him will be reborn in the Pure Land.

PURIFYING FIRE

Rituals practised by members of the Tendai school include fire ceremonies. Tendai monks pray for 1000 days – taking only a little sleep and food each day – and tend fires as acts of purification. Some walk across hot ashes to demonstrate that their spiritual purification protects them from injury.

Firewalking ceremony in Hiroshima, Japan

PROTECTIVE POWERS

In Japan, the bodhisattva Avalokiteshvara is called Kannon and is revered by the Tendai, Shingon, Jodo, and other Japanese schools of Buddhism. Kannon can take male or female form. The bodhisattva is often portrayed standing in water, on a fish, or with other sea creatures. This serves as a reminder that Kannon is said to protect sailors and fishermen.

Gilded statue of Kannon

Kannon holds a golden lotus flower in her left hand.

SHARED SHRINE

There is a beautiful Tendai shrine at Nikko in central Japan, decorated with painted animals and gods. It has been a place of pilgrimage for hundreds of years. The shrine at Nikko is sacred to Buddhists and to followers of Japan's native religion, Shinto. It is popular because many Japanese people follow both faiths.

Peacock detail from the shrine at Nikko

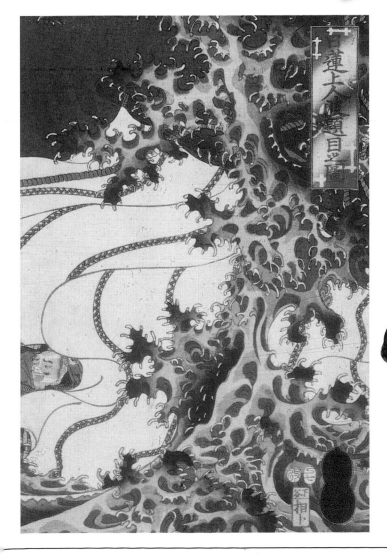

TAKING REFUGE

The Japanese monk Nichiren, seen in this trio of pictures using his faith to calm a storm at sea, was devoted to the Lotus Sutra. He developed a school of Buddhism based on study of the sutra, acceptance of its teachings, and the reciting of the phrase, "I take refuge in the wondrous Sutra of the Lotus."

Zen Buddhism

A FORM OF Buddhism called Ch'an began in China in the 6th century. The school was brought to Japan by a travelling monk called Eisai. The Chinese term Ch'an (which means meditation) became Zen in Japanese. The main feature of Zen is the use of meditation in order to discover the essential buddha-nature that is present in everything and everyone. Zen also has a distinctive style of teaching, often using riddles and stories to help people understand buddha-nature more clearly.

MARATHON MEDITATION
The Indian monk Bodhidharma (right) is said to be the founder of Ch'an Buddhism. He travelled to China to spread the Buddha's teachings and show people how to meditate. According to legend, Bodhidharma meditated in the lotus position for nine years and lost the use of his legs.

SURROUNDED BY BEAUTY
Zen monks, like the one in this Japanese painting on silk, are aware of the beauty and buddha-nature in everything around them. They spend long periods of time meditating in order to encourage natural clarity of mind and move closer to this ever-present buddha-nature.

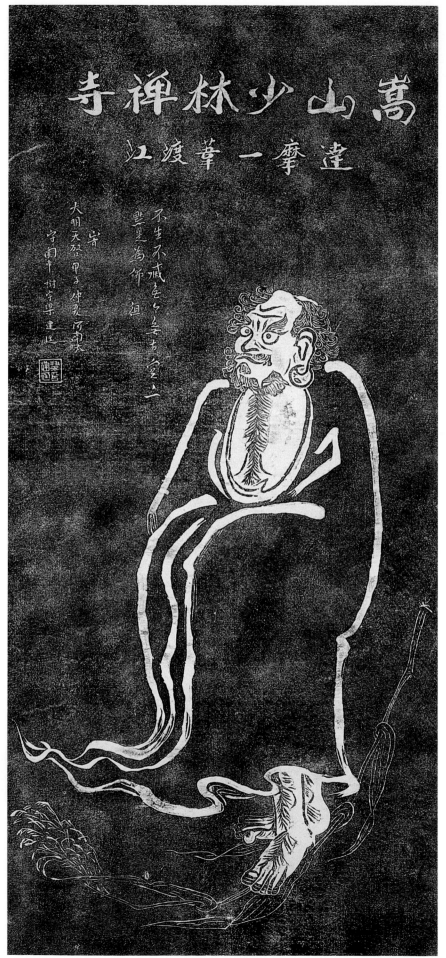

86

ABSTRACT ATMOSPHERE
Zen Buddhist temples, and sometimes the homes of Zen Buddhists, have gardens in which arrangements of stones and sand raked into abstract patterns produce a simple, calming effect. The atmosphere created by these Zen gardens is perfect for meditation. In the words of Bodhidharma, it allows Zen Buddhists to "see into their own nature" and perhaps achieve buddhahood.

"Those who perform meditation for even one session destroy innumerable accumulated sins; how should there be wrong paths for them?"

HAKUNI'S SONG OF MEDITATION
Zen meditation

Daitoku-ji temple garden, Kyoto City, Japan

THE ART OF WRITING
For the Chinese, calligraphy, or beautiful writing, is an art form that people practise for many years. Zen scholars in both China and Japan take calligraphy extremely seriously. They concentrate on the beauty of each character as they write it, in the hope that it will be true to the nature of the object or action it portrays.

This character reads "kokoro", which means "heart".

Fukusai-ji Zen temple in Nagasaki, Japan

INTERIOR DESIGN
The interior of this temple at Kyoto in Japan is in typical Zen style. It is simple and spacious, and decorated with paintings showing natural scenes. There are cushions for the monks to sit on when listening to teachings, and musical instruments such as large gongs for use during ceremonies.

TURTLE-TOPPED
One popular form of Kannon shows the bodhisattva standing on the back of a turtle. At this Zen temple, built in 1979, the whole roof has been built in the form of the turtle's back, with its head outstretched above the door. The statue of Kannon towers above. This is a modern version of traditional Zen buildings, whose large, curving roofs are often the dominant feature.

Demons and gods

BUDDHISM BEGAN IN India among people who believed in many different demons and gods. The Buddha taught that these were beings caught up in the cycle of birth, death, and rebirth, just like humans. These supernatural beings range from gods living in Heaven to demons in the realm of Hell at the very bottom of the Wheel of Life. Some Buddhists believe that all these beings have the power to influence the world. These Buddhists worship the gods in the hope that they will help them in their everyday lives.

SAND GODS
These Tibetan monks are making a mandala from sand of different colours. Each sand mandala is made for a specific ritual and is destroyed afterwards. Like other mandalas, sand mandalas are complex images of the Buddhist Universe. They feature hundreds of gods and goddesses, each intricately depicted in coloured sand.

The protective figure resembles Yama, who holds the Wheel of Life.

INNER DEMONS
In the Buddhist tradition, demons, known as asuras, are fearsome, weapon-wielding creatures who fight the gods. Buddhists in some places see these demons as forces to be feared, and they carry objects like this amulet to protect themselves. Other Buddhists regard the demons as portrayals of the negative feelings we all have, and which we must try to avoid.

Jewelled Tibetan amulet

A bodhisattva holds the light of hope.

Realm of desire and possession

LIFE ON THE EARTH
The 12 scenes around the edge of a Wheel of Life depict aspects of life on the Earth. They show figures who stand for different qualities. For example, a blind man represents ignorance, and a man picking fruit represents desire and possession. Many Buddhists look to the gods for help in handling the challenges of life on the Earth.

HOPE IN HELL
This section from a Wheel of Life shows Hell – the lowest of the six realms of rebirth. It is a place of torment where beings are tortured in both icy cold and scorching heat. Amongst the fear and anger in this realm of demons stands a bodhisattva. He preaches a message of hope, which is symbolized by the light of the fire he brings with him.

18th-century engraving of Yama

LORD OF DEATH

Some images of the ancient Indian god Yama show him riding a bull. In others he has a bull's head. Yama was absorbed into Buddhist culture as "Lord of Death", "King of Hell", and "protector of the Buddhist law". According to some traditions, he judges the dead and takes them to the correct realm to be reborn.

HAPPY IN HEAVEN

This section from a Wheel of Life shows the realm of the gods, or Heaven, where everyone is happy. Trees and flowers flourish, and there are fine palaces and stupas (pp. 92–93). A bodhisattva holding a lute stands at the centre. He reminds the gods that when their good kamma runs out they will have to be reborn in a lower realm.

NATURE SPIRITS

This 100-year-old Burmese folding book shows the variety of different forms taken by the demonic beings known as nats. These supernatural beings are nature spirits with a long history in Burma. Like the gods and goddesses of India, nats have been absorbed into local Buddhist belief.

Healing mantras in Burmese script surround the nats.

Indra travels on the back of a white elephant – a form of transport fit for a king.

11th-century Indian depiction of Indra, "King of the Gods"

KING OF THE GODS

In Hinduism, Indra is "King of the Gods". He holds a similar position among the gods and goddesses of the Buddhist realm of Heaven. Indra is also known as Shakra, "the mighty one", and in some of the sutras he is referred to as Vajrapani. He is a faithful guardian of the Buddha.

Buddhist symbols

IN THE EARLY DAYS of the Buddhist faith, symbols were often used in place of more complex images. An empty throne, for example, could be used to stand for the Buddha's presence, and a simplified Bodhi Tree could represent the moment of his enlightenment. Symbols have continued to appear in art, on objects, and in buildings. Some symbols are drawn from the natural world. Others may be ritual objects, items associated with the Buddha's life, or symbols that have been adapted from other faiths and traditions.

Chinese enamelled vase in the shape of two fish

FERTILE FISH
Fish have thousands of offspring, so in Buddhism these creatures are symbols of fertility. They are usually golden and are often portrayed in pairs, placed head to head. The fish, umbrella, treasure vase, lotus, conch shell, knot, banner, and wheel are the Eight Auspicious (lucky) Symbols of Buddhism.

Ceremonial conch with silk tassel

The knot symbolizes the infinite wisdom of the Buddha.

MAJESTIC ELEPHANT
The elephant is just one of the animals that often appears in Buddhist art. It is a quiet, strong creature that sums up the calm majesty aspired to by Buddhists. A rare white elephant even appears in the story of the Buddha's conception. Other animals appear at the centre of the Wheel of Life and as guardians of temples.

PRECIOUS PRINTS
Before his death, the Buddha stood on a rock at Kushinagara in Nepal facing towards the south. When he moved, he is said to have left his footprints in the stone. Ever since, images of these prints have been used as symbols of his presence on the Earth. They appear at many temple sites, where they are treated with special reverence. Pictures and carvings of the footprints are often covered with other Buddhist symbols.

Long, straight toes of even length are said to be one of the 32 marks of a great man.

The swastika is an ancient Indian symbol of good fortune.

Stone footprints from the Amaravati stupa in southern India

The footprints are framed by a border of intertwined lotus flowers.

The Wheel of Authority, which can have up to 1000 spokes, represents the Buddha as "King of the Dhamma".

This three-pointed symbol represents the Triple Jewel.

Lion guardian at a temple entrance, Birmingham, UK

REACH FOR THE SKY

The lotus is a symbol of spiritual growth. It grows in muddy water, but its stems and flowers reach upwards to the Sun, as if towards nibbana. The Buddha is often depicted on a throne made of lotus petals, and people bring lotus flowers as offerings to Buddhist shrines (pp. 100–101).

GUARDIAN LION

As Buddhism spread around the world, it adopted traditional symbols from the places where it took root. The use of lion statues to guard temples was originally a Chinese tradition. Many Buddhist temples now have lion guardians at their entrances.

PROTECTION AND POWER

In the Buddha's time, members of royalty were protected from the rain and sun by umbrellas held by servants. The umbrella became a symbol of protection and the Buddha's spiritual power. Stupas are often topped with umbrella-shaped carvings called finials (pp. 92–93).

Modern Buddhist parade umbrella

The umbrella is made of golden paper decorated with coloured thread.

SPIRITUAL WEAPON

Translated as either "diamond" or "thunderbolt", the vajra is a symbolic weapon. It is said to be able to cut through any substance. It is used, especially in Tibet, as a symbol of the spiritual power that can cut through ignorance. Some Buddhists hold the vajra in one hand and a bell in the other while chanting.

Vajra-shaped handle

Tibetan bell

Tibetan vajra

Stupas and pagodas

AFTER THE BUDDHA died, his body was cremated. His ashes were divided and buried in a number of different places in India. A large, dome-shaped mound called a stupa was built over the relics, or remains, at each burial place. Later, many other stupas were built all over the Buddhist world. Some were constructed over the remains of Buddhist saints, and others were built over copies of the scriptures. Many existing stupas were clad with decorative carved stone and given elaborate gateways. They soon became popular places of pilgrimage (p. 102). In China, Japan, and parts of Southeast Asia, tall structures called pagodas developed from the stupa form.

LITTLE AND LARGE
Model stupas like this are used for personal devotion at home. When visiting a full-size stupa, Buddhists walk around it as an act of respect to the relic kept there.

IN RUINS
This structure was built in the 5th century at Sarnath near Benares. It marks the site where the Buddha gave his first sermon. The stupa is now in ruins. The large, dome-shaped covering on the top has not survived, but the carved lower walls are still intact. The first stupa at this important site was built by the great Indian emperor Ashoka in the 3rd century BCE.

The stone cladding and gateway were added after Ashoka's time.

MAKING AMENDS
This stupa, on the site of an early monastery at Sanchi in India, was built by the emperor Ashoka. He became a Buddhist after leading his army into a battle in which thousands were killed. Ashoka regretted the violence and devoted himself to spreading Buddhism and erecting thousands of stupas and shrines.

A row of pillars, called ayaka, top the gateway through which pilgrims would enter the stupa.

The gateway is guarded by lions.

A rich young man has come to the stupa to make an offering.

CARVED IN STONE
This carved stone slab once decorated a stupa at Nagarjunakonda in southern India. It shows the great, curving shape of a stupa decorated with symbols and scenes from the Buddhist tales. In front of the gateway stands a young man, perhaps a prince, with several followers. The young man holds up his hand to make an offering to the Buddha, gaining merit as he does so.

19th-century illustration of Borobudur

SUPER STUPA

Borobudur is an enormous stupa in Java. The lower levels are richly decorated with relief carvings showing scenes from the Buddha's life. The upper levels are plainer, and contain a series of smaller stupas. Each of the small stupas on the upper levels contains a statue of the Buddha.

The umbrella-shaped finial is a symbol of kingship standing for the Buddha's spiritual rule.

Spirits offer garlands of flowers to the Buddha.

> *"There, with the appropriate ceremonies, they erected in their capital cities stupas for the relics of the Seer."*
>
> **BUDDHACARITA**
> The relics

A carving of the Buddha marks the centre of the stupa.

Engraving of a Chinese pagoda

TALL AND BEAUTIFUL

In China, Japan, and Korea, Buddhist relics are housed in pagodas. Chinese and Korean pagodas are usually built of stone or brick. Those in Japan are wooden. A long pole inside connects the relics buried at the base to the top of the structure. Pagodas are stunning buildings. They are often very tall and have ornate roofs with delicate, up-turned corners.

Temples and complexes

THE WALLS HAVE EYES
Above one of the entrances to the Baiju temple at Gyantse in Tibet, there is a mural of the Buddha's eyes, with the urna between them. The half-open eyes seem to watch over those who enter the temple. At the same time they bring to mind a state of deep meditation.

Mahabodhi temple, Bodh Gaya, India

The main tower is covered with detailed carvings.

ALL BUDDHIST TEMPLES contain statues of the Buddha. They are places in which Buddhists can gather and make offerings, and they also provide a focus for devotion and pilgrimage. Buddhist temples vary greatly in shape and size. Some are quite small, comprising just an entrance area and a simple inner shrine. Others are huge complexes, which may consist of many small stupas containing relics. Some temples are plain and unadorned. Others, such as the Mahabodhi temple at Bodh Gaya and the temples on the Silk Road in Central Asia, are decorated with stunning carvings and paintings.

TEMPLE BY THE TREE
The Mahabodhi temple at Bodh Gaya is one of the most important destinations of Buddhist pilgrimage. It marks the site where the Buddha became enlightened. Building work started in the 6th century next to a tree that is believed to be a descendant of the one under which the Buddha meditated. The large temple complex fell into disrepair between the 13th and 19th centuries, but was eventually restored and extended by monks and pilgrims.

The small stupas match the shape of the main tower.

Some of the miniature stupas contain the ashes of pilgrims who died at Bodh Gaya.

FACE TOWERS
The Bayon at Angkor in Cambodia is a beautiful temple built by the Khmer king Jayavarman VII (1181–1219). The enormous faces carved in the walls of the Bayon are said to represent the bodhisattva Avalokiteshvara, but they may be based on the features of Jayavarman himself.

CARVED IN CLIFFS
At Ellora, in the northwest of India's central Deccan region, more than 30 temples have been carved into the local cliffs. People cut their way through tonnes of solid rock to hollow out large halls and shrines. Pillars, statues, and vaulted ceilings have also been carved from the rock inside the cave temples.

Vajravira holds a staff above his head.

Vajravira's body is protected by golden armour.

Vajravira at the Taiyuin-byo shrine in northern Honshu

GREEN GUARDIAN
This figure, Vajravira, is one of the Four Guardian Kings. Found guarding entrances or shrines, especially in Japanese temples, the Guardian Kings are said to protect the four points of the compass. They are usually shown as warriors, wearing armour, brandishing weapons, and trampling on demons. Vajravira protects the west and can be identified by his green skin.

CROSSING THE STREAM
The walls and roof of this small temple at Ayuthaya in Thailand are reflected in the nearby water. As well as enhancing the beauty of the temple's surroundings, the water is an important symbol. Buddhists sometimes use the phrase "crossing the stream" to describe the process of passing through the world of suffering on the way to enlightenment.

This detail is called a cho fa, or "tassel of air".

The bargeboards are ornately carved.

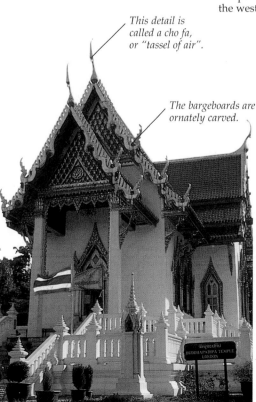

"When you have performed the acts of worship, help will come from the guardian angels."

BYA CHOS
The Buddha's law among the birds

WESTERN TEMPLE EASTERN STYLE
This British Buddhist temple, like many in the West, is built in a style influenced by the architecture of Southeast Asia. The pitched roofs, pointed windows, and carved details give the building an Eastern appearance. The "tassels of air" are said to be based on simplified statues of the bird Garuda, a Hindu god who protected people from evil.

Buddhist monks and nuns

Needle and thread

Razor

Water strainer

SOME BUDDHISTS JOIN the community of monks and nuns called the sangha. They devote their lives to understanding the Buddha's teachings and explaining them to others. In order to join the sangha, Buddhists take part in a ceremony called ordination. They promise to observe a set of rules that affect everything they do. Buddhist monks and nuns live simple lives. They wear plain robes, shave their heads, study, and meditate.

Alms bowl

WOMEN'S RIGHTS
In most branches of Buddhism, women like this Tibetan nun may be ordained and become members of the sangha. Some of these nuns have become important spiritual leaders. Women can become nuns in all traditions of Buddhism, but in Theravada Buddhism nuns have a lower status than monks.

Lid from alms bowl, used as a plate

FEW THINGS
Buddhist monks are allowed to have very few possessions. The basics are robes, a place to live, an alms bowl, and medicine. They may also own a razor, a needle and thread for mending their robes, a belt, and a strainer to ensure that insects are not swallowed along with drinking water.

Lower robe, worn around the hips

Upper robe, worn over the shoulder

Outer robe, worn for travel and sleeping

Belt or girdle

COMMON COLOUR
Monks' robes are traditionally dyed a saffron, or orangey-yellow, colour, as seen in this Thai mural. This is said to date back to the time when the Buddha founded the sangha. He and his followers made their robes by sewing together scraps of cloth and dyeing them a common colour.

ROBE RULES
A Buddhist monk is allowed three robes made of plain, dyed material. The colour of the robes varies according to the branch of Buddhism. In the Theravada tradition, the robes are yellow or orange. Tibetan monks wear maroon robes, and Zen members of the sangha wear black.

Both monks and novices shave their heads.

The upper robe is worn covering only the left shoulder within the monastery.

Thai novice monk in his simple hut

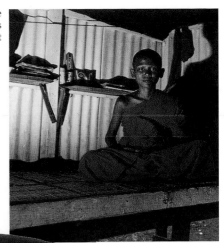

LET US BE HAPPY
In the early days of Buddhism, many monks lived in caves or other simple shelters. They spent much of their lives travelling from place to place. Monks and nuns today usually live in permanent monasteries, but they still live simple lives. A monk's life should be one of fulfilment. As one scripture says, "Let us be happy, then, we who possess nothing."

The upper robe is tied firmly around the novice's body.

These robes are made from cotton, but the scriptures also allow other plant-based fabrics to be used.

Traditionally, the robes are coloured using dyes derived from clay, plants such as the saffron flower, and other natural materials.

IN IT FOR LIFE
Boys as young as seven or eight may enter monasteries as novices. They learn about the dhamma and can be ordained as monks in their late teens. Not all monks stay in the monastery for life. In some places, it is traditional for young men to spend anything from a few weeks to several years in a monastery. During this time, they are educated and acquire merit. Other Buddhists dedicate their entire lives to the sangha.

Thai Buddhist monk with two novices

Monks and novices traditionally go barefoot.

97

Continued on next page

The monastic way of life

Buddhist monks and nuns agree to obey more than 200 rules, covering everything from their relations with other people to the clothes they wear and the food they eat. They give up sexual contact, live in monasteries, and practise meditation. Monks and nuns, however, are not isolated from the world. In addition to teaching, some members of the sangha help to run health clinics, look after orphaned children, or care for the elderly and the sick.

"The homeless wanderer ... is content with little, easily pleased ... not addicted to society, energetic, independent, solitary, perfect in his conduct ..."

MILINDAPANHA
Laymen and monks

DAILY DUTIES
Every day, monks like these in Thailand meet to chant verses from the sutras to honour the Buddha. They may also recite the monastic rules to remind them of the discipline under which they live. Buddhist monks also meditate regularly. This trains their minds to become calm and encourages right effort, right mindfulness, and right concentration.

TIME TO TEACH
Buddhist monks spend a lot of their time teaching others about the dhamma. The Buddha depended on his followers to pass on his ideas. This teaching can take different forms. It may involve explaining the texts of Buddhist scriptures or showing people how the Buddha's ideas can help them overcome their problems.

Fans were originally carried to help monks keep cool in hot climates.

The monk sits in the half-lotus position when teaching.

ACCEPTING ALMS

Many monks and nuns accept alms, or gifts.
Alms are donated by lay people – Buddhists
who are not members of the monastic sangha.
In the early days of Buddhism, monks had to
depend entirely on alms for survival. Rich lay
Buddhists then began making gifts of land
to groups of monks. Strictly speaking, this is
against monastic rules, but it allows monks
and nuns to settle down, build monasteries,
and grow their own food.

Rice and
lotus flower
offerings

*The outer robe
is worn outside
the monastery.*

*The alms
bowl is held
out ready to
receive food.*

GIVING AND RECEIVING

In places where monks still rely upon direct gifts
from lay people, they hope for practical alms of
things like food and medicine. Such gifts also help
those who give. By giving, lay people gain merit
that will lead them towards better rebirths and
perhaps membership of the sangha in a future life.

*Monks are not
allowed to take
gifts directly in
their hands.*

MORNING STROLL

In places such as Thailand, monks still spend
part of each day walking through the streets so that
people can place food into their alms bowls. This
daily alms round takes place in the morning so that
the monks can gather enough food for their main
meal, which they have to eat before midday.

Burmese nuns discussing
the scriptures

GROUP STUDY

Monks and nuns study regularly, often meeting to discuss the
scriptures. Members of the sangha have always preserved and
studied Buddhist scriptures. In the early days, they did this by
reciting them aloud; later they wrote out texts by hand. Today
the texts are printed in books and available on the Internet.

Monk
collecting alms

The Buddhist way of life

Stone carving showing two princes and a monk offering flowers to the Buddha

ONE OF MANY
There are a very large number of Buddhist shrines and temples. One reason for this is that putting up a new one is a way for lay people to gain merit. A rich person might pay for a whole temple. Poorer people can join groups to collect funds for building, or build simple shrines like this.

BUDDHISTS REGULARLY visit temples to make offerings, but their faith goes much further than this. It affects their whole lives. When the Buddha described the Noble Eightfold Path, he meant its eight parts to influence every activity. Whether Buddhists are at home, at work, or on holiday they try to live according to their beliefs. Above all, Buddhists try to act in a caring way. They think positively, help others, and promote peace. In doing so, they hope to build up merit to improve their next rebirth. Buddhists also hope to make the world a better place for everyone to live in.

GIVE IT UP
Making offerings to the Buddha is one of the most familiar rituals for lay Buddhists like the princes shown in this carving. It is a symbolic way of following in the footsteps of the Buddha himself, because in his previous lives he gave up his possessions, and sometimes even his life, to help others.

Burning incense sticks

Chinese bronze incense pot

ODOROUS OFFERINGS
One way to make an offering is to do so by burning the aromatic substance incense. Doing this allows lay people to build up merit, which will help to ensure a favourable rebirth. In a similar way, Tantric Buddhists sometimes make offerings of fire.

MERIT SHARING
These vessels are used for a merit-sharing ceremony in which water is poured slowly from one vessel to the other while chanting takes place. Buddhists traditionally consider people to be responsible for their own merit. But it is possible to share merit, for example, by passing it on to a dead person in the hope that a better rebirth will result.

Water vessels used for merit sharing

Pineapple

Papaya

Banana

FRUITFUL GIFTS
Lay people may make offerings of fruit and other foods directly to the Buddha by placing them on a shrine. They can also offer them to monks in the form of alms. Providing that fruit is clean and offered with sincerity, the variety is not important.

Rice offering from a Tibetan Buddhist shrine

REVERED RICE
Rice is a common and welcome gift for Buddhist monks in Asia. It is a nourishing food and a symbol of blessing. Rice is also one of the offerings most often placed on shrines for the Buddha. Buddhists hope that in return for the rice offerings their community will be blessed with enough food. The rice placed on shrines should be changed every full moon. The old rice is taken outside and fed to birds, fish, or other animals.

This elaborate container for rice offerings is made to look like a stupa.

Wash day, Holy Island, Scotland

Gardening, Holy Island, Scotland

Preparing food, Holy Island, Scotland

MERIT IN THE MUNDANE
A Buddhist's beliefs affect every aspect of his or her life. Even everyday tasks like washing, gardening, and cooking should be carried out in a way that is mindful of the Buddha's teachings and does not harm others. Many Buddhists do not eat meat because this involves killing living things. Some Buddhists do not even dig the soil for fear of harming any creatures living in it.

REACHING OUT
This Buddhist monk is working with prisoners in the UK. He tells them about the Buddha's teachings and explains why it is wrong to harm others. Monks also build gardens in prison grounds, creating peaceful spaces for inmates to visit. Some convicted criminals change their way of life as a result of this work.

PEACE PROTEST
These Buddhist monks and nuns are demonstrating against the war in Kosovo in 1999. Buddhists oppose killing and most believe in ahimsa, or non-violence. They will not fight in wars, and often take part in anti-war protests.

Devotion to the Buddha

THE BUDDHA IS an enlightened being, not a god, so he is not worshipped in the way gods are worshipped in other religions. Buddhists do have great respect for the Buddha. They perform rituals of devotion to confirm their commitment to the Buddha, his dhamma, and the sangha. This is known as the Triple Refuge. Buddhists express their devotion in various ways. They make pilgrimages, meditate, give offerings, and prostrate themselves. In each case, the act of devotion also serves to help the devotees. It encourages them to follow the dhamma and reminds them of the Eightfold Path.

FOOTPRINT FOCUS
Images like this one of the Buddha's footprint provide a focus for devotion. The footprint features many key Buddhist symbols and some of the marks of a great man. It reminds Buddhists of the Buddha's remarkable life and teaching.

The case is ornately carved and decorated with jewels.

SPIRITUAL SITES
These Buddhists have made a pilgrimage to Shwedagon pagoda in Burma, where some relics of the Buddha are kept. Buddhists visit places linked with the life of the Buddha, shrines where relics are kept, and other sites with spiritual links. Pilgrimages are especially important to lay people. They allow them to follow in the Buddha's footsteps and to focus on spiritual matters.

JOY AND CONTEMPLATION
This case was used to preserve a relic of a Buddhist saint. Buddhists have always revered the relics of the Buddha and of notable teachers and saints. Pilgrimages to relics of the Buddha can be times of joyful celebration of his life and teaching, but also times of quiet contemplation and spiritual growth.

Prostration and meditation

Prostration is usually performed before a statue of the Buddha. It is repeated three times as a dedication to the Triple Refuge. It is an expression of reverence and helps Buddhists to develop qualities such as humility. Meditation is a vital part of the Buddhist faith. The calm and focused state it provokes brings the devotee closer to wisdom and even enlightenment.

1 DEDICATED BODY
Standing facing a statue of the Buddha, this lama puts his hands together, with the fingers touching and the palms slightly cupped. He raises his hands to his forehead to demonstrate that his body is dedicated to the Triple Refuge.

2 RIGHT SPEECH
Still in the standing position, the lama lowers his hands to just below his mouth to show that he devotes his speech to the Triple Refuge. In doing this, he also recalls the third part of the Eightfold Path – right speech.

The lama clasps his robe to prevent it from falling.

3 DEVOTED HEART AND MIND
Next, the lama lowers his hands further so that they are in front of his chest. This position shows that his heart, and therefore also his mind, are devoted to the Triple Refuge. He then prepares to prostrate himself.

The lama kneels on all fours before sliding to the floor.

The lama is now fully prostrated.

4 PROSTRATION POINTS
The lama kneels down and places his palms on the floor. From this point, he performs a full prostration with his whole body lowered to the floor. Many Buddhists perform a five-point prostration instead. On all fours, they lower their foreheads to the floor so that five parts of their body – their lower legs, their forearms, and their forehead – are in contact with the floor.

A comfortable posture is essential for meditation.

Gong

Hammer

FREEING THE MIND
Meditation clears and purifies the mind. It leads Buddhists to right effort, right mindfulness, and right concentration – three parts of the Eightfold Path. Most Buddhists begin meditation by focusing on their breathing. In some branches of Buddhism, devotees concentrate on an image or object to help them to free their minds from everyday thoughts. Others bang a gong after meditating to spread the merit earned by their act of devotion.

103

Buddhist festivals

Buddhist dancing figure

BUDDHISM HAS adapted to the many different places where it has taken root, so its festivals vary from one country to another. The various schools of the faith also celebrate different festivals. Theravada Buddhists, for example, mark the birth, enlightenment, and death of the Buddha with a single festival. They also have set days throughout the year when lay people join monks in fasting and meditation. Mahayana Buddhists have a variety of festivals, including celebrations at New Year and separate ones for the key stages in the Buddha's life.

JOYFUL JIG
Dance is important in many Eastern cultures, and this tradition has carried over into Buddhism. For lay people, dancing is part of many of the more joyful Buddhist festivals, such as those celebrating New Year and the Buddha's birth. Monks and nuns do not dance.

Monk washing statues of the Buddha in London, UK

The shrine is scattered with petals.

WATER FESTIVAL
Water plays an important part in New Year celebrations in several Buddhist countries. Images of the Buddha are washed and people bathe or are sprinkled with water. This 19th-century painting shows an elaborate New Year water festival in Burma. The use of water helps people start the New Year in a state of spiritual purity and cleanliness.

People fill pots with water in preparation for the festivities.

FREEING THE FISH
This Thai Buddhist is releasing a captive eel into the wild to mark the festival of Vesak, or Buddha Day. Vesak is a Theravada celebration of the birth, enlightenment, and death of the Buddha. It is a time for being especially kind to living things. In Thailand, some people avoid farm work in which living creatures may be harmed and release captive animals to build up merit.

CEREMONIAL CLEANING
In some temples, Vesak is marked by the ceremonial cleaning of statues of the Buddha as a child. People then make offerings of flowers and incense. Lights are lit in temples and trees to symbolize the Buddha's enlightenment. Parades, Jataka readings, and plays re-enacting the Buddha's birth also take place in some areas.

CONVERTING THE KING
In Sri Lanka, monks and lay people gather for a special festival called Poson. This is to celebrate the arrival of Buddhism on the island during the time of the Indian emperor Ashoka. The gathered Buddhists make offerings at Mihintale, where Ashoka's son, Mahinda, is said to have converted the king of Sri Lanka to the faith.

A golden statue of the Buddha is central to the festivities.

Devotees prostrate themselves before the Buddha.

Japanese children preparing paper flowers for Hana Matsuri

FLOWER POWER
The Japanese celebrate the Buddha's birth at the festival of Hana Matsuri. People make whole gardens of paper flowers as a reminder of the lush gardens at Lumbini, where the Buddha was born. In Japan, perfumed tea is poured over statues of the Buddha because it is said that the gods provided scented water for Siddhatta's first bath.

MASKED MONKS
Tibetan New Year is celebrated at the festival of Losar. People wear new clothes and eat special foods, such as cakes called kapse. At the end of the festival, Buddhist monks put on fearsome masks. They then perform a ritual to frighten away any evil spirits that have appeared during the previous year.

The cycle of life

ALL RELIGIONS DEVELOP ceremonies to mark the key stages in a person's life. In Buddhism, two types of ceremonies have special importance. The first are rituals of initiation, in which a child or teenager is welcomed into adult Buddhist society and becomes a part of the monastic community for a short while. The second are funeral rites that mark a person's passing from life and signal their future rebirth. Buddhism has spread so widely around the world that these ceremonies vary greatly. But they are all occasions on which Buddhists meet to share a special moment and celebrate their faith.

BIRTH BLESSINGS
Some Buddhist monks, like this one in the UK, invite new parents to have their babies blessed. But Buddhism does not place great importance on rituals to mark the birth of a child. Parents who wish to mark their child's arrival often use local traditional rituals. Monks are not necessarily involved in these ceremonies.

LITTLE PRINCES
These boys are having their initiation ceremony at the Shwedagon pagoda in Rangoon, Burma. After this, they will join the monastery for a short period. Unlike boys in some other Buddhist countries, they are not immediately given monks' robes to wear. They are dressed in rich clothes, like those Siddhatta wore before leaving his father's palace to seek enlightenment.

The monk uses his razor to shave the boy's head.

Mural from Wat Bowornivet temple, Bangkok, Thailand

COMING OF AGE
Before they can be accepted as full members of the Buddhist community, young boys are taken to their local monastery. Monks shave their heads and give them an alms bowl and robes. They stay at the monastery, sometimes just for one night, but often for several days. At the end of this period the boys are no longer regarded as children.

Buddhist nun blessing a marriage

RELIGIOUS REMINDER
Buddhism stresses the importance of the role and life of monks and nuns, so weddings are not looked on as religious events. Buddhist couples choose to have a civil, or non-religious, ceremony sometimes followed by a blessing from a monk or nun. The blessing reminds the couple that the sangha will remain important in their lives.

Lotus flowers

Candle

FAMILY FAVOURS
When a person dies, relatives usually make offerings such as flowers and candles to the local monks. They gain merit by doing this, and hope that the merit will be transferred to the deceased, helping them on the way to a more favourable rebirth.

FUNERAL TRADITIONS
When Buddhists die, they are usually placed in caskets decorated with cloths and flowers. They are then taken in a procession to the temple, where monks chant scriptures concerning kamma and rebirth. In the Theravada tradition, the deceased person is usually cremated, as the Buddha was, but Mahayana Buddhists bury their dead.

Funeral procession in Burma

Stupa-shaped case for relics from Bihar in India

"Sweet-scented barks and leaves, aloewood, sandalwood, and cassia they heaped on the pyre, sighing with grief all the time. Finally they placed the Sage's body on it."

BUDDHACARITA
The relics

IN THE NEXT LIFE
This ornate stupa-shaped case was probably made to hold the cremated remains of a notable Buddhist saint or teacher. The cremation is the climax of Theravada funeral services. Family members usually keep the ashes in an urn. After the funeral, the relatives may burn the favourite possessions of the deceased so that he or she can enjoy them in the next life.

STAYING POSITIVE
Although it is sad when a friend or relative dies, funerals are positive occasions for Buddhists because they lead to a rebirth. Ceremonies to honour the deceased may involve burning incense. This reminds those present of the Buddha's enlightened teaching that death is merely an interval between two lives.

East Asian Religions

Confucian piety

CONFUCIUS
Confucius, or K'ung Fu-tzu, (551–479 BCE) was China's first great philosopher. His name means "Master King"; a legend says that when he was born it was foretold that he would be "a king without a crown". His discussions and sayings are collected together in *The Analects*.

FOR MANY, CONFUCIANISM is a way of life, a code of behaviour, rather than a religion. Confucians may combine following their master, Confucius, with belief in any god or none. Confucius stressed the importance of li, which means proper or orderly conduct. He taught his followers to be "gentlemen". A gentleman is always courteous, fair, respectful to his superiors, and kind to ordinary people. He also practises "filial piety" – his duty to respect and care for his parents. Because of his belief in filial piety Confucius supported the ancient practice of venerating (giving great respect and honour to) ancestors. He wished to bring order and harmony to society, with everyone doing their duty. He taught that worshipping God and the spirits and honouring one's ancestors means nothing unless the service of other people comes first.

THE THREE WAYS
China is the land of the "Three Ways", Confucianism, Taoism, and Buddhism. For more than two thousand years, they have all played a major role in Chinese life and thought. Confucianism emphasized order and respect, Taoism provided a mystical understanding of the world, and Buddhism offered salvation through compassion and devotion. As they have developed they have merged with each other, and with the age-old folk religion of China, centred on home and family. This painting symbolically shows how the Three Ways mix by representing their three founders together: Buddha (left), Confucius (centre), and Lao-tzu (right).

CONFUCIUS DAY CEREMONY
Confucius did not try to found a religion, but to teach a way of life based on rules of good behaviour. However, after his death, shrines were built in his honour, and Confucianism became the state religion of China.

Modern Confucian temple at Taipei in Taiwan

Priests honour Confucius Day

Bell was hung on a loop so it could vibrate clearly

MUSIC FOR THE MIND
The Chinese people believed that the music of bells calmed the mind and helped clear thinking. It is said that when he heard a piece of ritual bell music, Confucius was inspired to give up worldly comforts and live on rice and water for three months.

Large bronze bell struck like a gong from the outside

What you do not want done to yourself, do not do to others

CONFUCIAN VERSION OF THE *GOLDEN RULE*

Guardian figures often have the look of ferocious animals so they are more effective in frightening away harmful spirits

GUARDIAN FIGURES
On the ridge tiles and at the corners of the roofs of important Chinese buildings, under their eaves and outside tombs, stand figures representing guardian spirits who ward off evil. It is an ancient custom: this guardian figure comes from a tomb of the Tang dynasty, which ruled China from 618 to 907.

Ornate and colourful figures are found in buildings and tombs

Birth and death dates and details of ancestors are inscribed on tablet

ANCESTOR TABLETS
According to Chinese folk religion, ancestors live on in the form of spirits, to whom sacrifices are offered. When a relative is buried, a small stone tablet is taken to the grave. It is then carried back to the house and placed in a shrine.

A man honours his ancestors and places offerings before their tablet so that they will protect and honour him

TOMB STORE
Objects such as this model storehouse were placed in tombs to provide for the dead person's needs in the afterlife. Descendants went to the tomb once a year to perform a ceremony of ancestor veneration at the entrance.

The Tao principle

YIN AND YANG
The Yin-Yang symbol represents the two halves of the Tao, the two opposite, complementary principles Taoists see in nature: Yin – dark, female, passive, soft; and Yang – light, male, active, hard.

TAOISTS BELIEVE THAT THERE IS a principle, or force, running through the whole of the natural world, and controlling it. They call this principle the Tao. Tao means way, or path. To follow the Tao is to follow the way of nature. It is sometimes called the "watercourse way" because Taoists see water as a picture of the Tao at work. Water is soft and yielding, it flows effortlessly to humble places, yet it is also the most powerful of substances, and it nourishes all life. There are two kinds of Taoism: the popular and the philosophical. The followers of philosophical Taoism are likely to be mystical and peaceful. By stilling the inner self, their senses and appetites, they gain an understanding of the Tao, and try to live in oneness and harmony with it. The focus of popular Taoism is different. It includes very many gods, goddesses, and spiritual beings, whose help believers seek, and demons, who are feared. Its followers use magic and ritual to harness Te – virtue or power – in the hope of becoming immortal.

Lu Tung-pin overcame a series of temptations and was given a magic sword, with which he killed dragons and fought evil

Li Ti'eh-kuai used to go in spirit to visit Lao-tzu in the celestial regions; he once stayed so long that his body had gone when he came back, so his spirit had to enter the body of a lame beggar

Ho Hsien-ku lived on powdered mother-of-pearl and moonbeams; her emblem is the lotus

THE FOUNDER
According to Taoist tradition, Lao-tzu lived in central China in the 6th century BCE, at the same time as Confucius, who is said to have visited him as a young man. Lao-tzu worked as keeper of archives for the Chou dynasty. In later life, tired of Chou corruption, he tried to flee to Tibet. But he was stopped at the border and refused permission to leave unless he left behind a record of his teachings. In three days he produced the *Tao Te Ching*, the greatest of Taoist writings. Then he handed it over and rode away on a water buffalo, never to be heard of again.

Ts'ao Kuo-chiu, patron of the theatre, wears a court headdress and official robes, and holds his emblem, a pair of castanets, in one hand

THE EIGHT IMMORTALS
The Eight Immortals are legendary beings believed to have attained immortality, through their practice of the Tao principle. They are said to have lived on earth at various times, and each represents a different condition in life: poverty, wealth, aristocracy, low social status, age, youth, masculinity, and femininity. Here they are shown with a fabulous being called Si Wang Mu who has the power to give away the peaches of immortality, which grow on the peach tree of the genii, beside the Lake of Gems in the West.

THE FAIRY CRANE

The traditional Chinese focus on death, immortality, and the ancestors means that funerals, and the rituals surrounding them, are often very important. A paper fairy crane is often carried at the head of the funeral procession of priests (shown here, with the abbot in his chair). The crane symbolizes a winged messenger from heaven, and when the paper crane is burnt the departed soul rides to heaven on the winged messenger's back.

Chang Kuo-lao, a magician, could make himself invisible

> *To exist means to embrace the Yang principle (of the light) and turn one's back on the Yin (of the dark)*
>
> TAO TE CHING

The magical being Si Wang Mu, here shown as male, more often appears as female

Han Hsiang-tzu is patron of musicians; his emblem is the flute

Lan Ts'ai-ho, patron of florists, holds aloft her emblem, the flower-basket

Chung-li Ch'uan holds a fan with which he revives the souls of the dead

GOD OF LONGEVITY

Chinese people see long life as a very desirable blessing. Therefore Shou-lai, god of longevity, is a popular deity. He is often depicted, either alone or with the Eight Immortals. His image may be carved in wood and stone, cast in bronze and porcelain, or used as a motif in embroidery and porcelain-painting. He is easily identified by his high, bulging forehead and bald head.

RITUAL POWER

Popular Taoism provides for everyday religious needs. Whatever the official philosophy, belief in personal gods and personalized spirits persists, and people still seek their help. Here priests burn incense at a popular ceremony where power (Te) is harnessed through magic and ritual. Priests are mainly concerned with cures for sickness and disease and with the casting out of evil spirits.

Shinto harmony

SHINTO IS THE MOST ANCIENT religion of Japan. The name means "the way of the gods". It is a religion of nature, focused on kami, which are supernatural spirits, or gods, in which the force of nature is concentrated. They include seas and mountains; animals, birds, and plants; even ancestors have the powers of kami. It is said there are eight million kami, worshipped at national, local, and household shrines all over Japan. The force of nature itself is also called kami, and is seen as divine. It inspires a feeling of awe and wonder. The most important shrines are associated with places of natural beauty: on the mountains, in the forests, and near the sea.

SACRED GATE
Since ancient times, Shinto shrines have been marked by entrance gates called torii. Because a beautiful natural setting, such as a sacred open space among trees or rocks, was often sufficient as a shrine, torii stood in such places. The great red torii to the famous island shrine of Itsukushima stands in the waters of the Inland Sea and is one of the great sights of Japan.

SHINTO GODDESS
Kami are rarely represented in the form of images to be worshipped. One exception is Nakatsu-hime, goddess of the Eight-Island Country directly below heaven. In one cult she is seen as an incarnation of the Buddhist goddess Kannon.

The god called Hand Strength Male approaching the cave to bring out the Sun Goddess

The gods decked out the tree of heaven with jewels and a mirror, then made music and danced to attract Amaterasu's attention

THE SUN GODDESS AMATERASU
Amaterasu Omikami, the sun goddess, is the supreme Shinto god. Her shrine at Ise is the most popular in Japan. One myth tells that her brother the Storm god made her so angry that she hid in a cave, bringing darkness to the earth. To persuade her to come out the other gods hung jewels and a mirror on the tree of heaven and danced for her. She looked out to see what was happening, saw herself in the mirror and, while watching, fascinated, was pulled outside. Since then, dawn has always followed night.

MOUNT FUJI
Since ancient times, mountains have been seen as special dwelling places of the gods. Much Shinto art deals with sacred mountains, figures, cults, shrines, settings, or themes. Shinto art also reflects the long interaction between Shinto and Buddhism.

HOLINESS

What is "holy" is separate and different, something "other" – far beyond the ordinary. Either beings or places may be holy or sacred. When we experience the holy, we feel awe and wonder, or blessing, or dread, or peace, or a sense of "wholeness". The word "holiness" also refers to moral or spiritual goodness.

Mallet to grant wishes

SHINTO AND BUDDHISM

Shinto is more a religion of experience than of doctrine (set beliefs), so it easily blended with Buddhism after Buddhism reached Japan in the sixth century. The kami were often seen as local manifestations of buddhas and boddhisattvas, and Buddhist temples existed beside, or inside, Shinto shrines. Buddhist monks such as those above still take part in the great Shinto festivals.

SHRINES AND FESTIVALS

Festivals are important in Shinto practice as the time when all a shrine's worshippers focus on it. One of the greatest is the Gion Festival, held annually since the 16th century. Local people decorate and wheel tall floats through the streets of Kyoto. During the festival this young boy pays his respects to his local god.

Boy taking part in the Gion festival

Wherever the "energy" of the universe attains a particular intensity, revealing itself as beauty, power, wonder, there the ultimate becomes apparent: there is "kami"

FOSCO MARAINI IN *JAPAN: PATTERNS OF CONTINUITY*

The god Daikoku, one of the seven gods of fortune

The god's rat attendant

Sack of rice

THE SEVEN GODS

The seven gods of fortune, or good luck, were originally Buddhist deities and are now worshipped in Shinto too – another example of how Buddhism and Shinto mix. Daikoku is the god of wealth and patron of farmers. He is often pictured with his son, Ebisu, god of honest labour. He is usually shown sitting on sacks of rice, with a bag of jewels on his shoulder, a golden sun disk on his chest, and a mallet with which he grants wishes. His attendant is a rat, sometimes shown nibbling away at the rice sacks. Daikoku is rich though, and always good humoured about it. He is also said to be fond of children.

SIKHISM

Sikh beliefs

Sikhs believe in one God, who is known as Sat Guru (the "true teacher"). Sat Guru is the immortal, invisible creator of the cosmos and for Sikhs his most important aspect is his Word, expressed in the Sikh sacred book, the *Adi Granth*, more popularly known as the *Guru Granth Sahib* (p. 120). The early leaders of Sikhism were teachers of God's Word, so they are known as Gurus. The first, Guru Nanak (1469–1539), founded the Sikh religion in northern India, which is still home to many Sikhs. Nanak was a good teacher and built up a community who shared his beliefs. Before he died he named his successor, Guru Angad. Eight further gurus followed, composing hymns and giving moral guidance that provided the foundation of the Sikh religion.

Kauda holds Mardana above the pot.

Guru Nanak speaks to Kauda.

GURU NANAK SAVES MARDANA
Many ancient stories about Nanak show the power of his teaching. One tells how Nanak's companion Mardana was caught by a cannibal called Kauda. As Kauda was about to lower Mardana into the cooking pot, Nanak cried out to him, "Will you throw yourself into the fire of hell?" Kauda realized that his actions were leading him on a path to hell, so he changed his ways and became a follower of Nanak.

Mardana with his rabab

Followers listen to Nanak

GURU NANAK
Nanak was born near Lahore, in modern-day Pakistan, into a Hindu family. When he grew up he became a government official and met many Muslims, but he was not satisfied by either Hinduism or Islam and decided to follow God in his own way. So he left his job and travelled widely, showing people how they could find God for themselves. He taught that God is present in the heart of every person, whatever their social class or religious faith.

PRAYER BEADS
Beads can be used to help focus the mind on the name of God through the rhythm of the fingers.

This tassle marks the start and the finish of the beads.

NANAK AND THE MUSICIAN
Guru Nanak's friend Mardana was a talented musician, but he was so poor that he could not afford to buy an instrument. Nanak's sister took pity on Mardana and gave him a stringed instrument called a *rabab*, rather like a lute. From then on, whenever Nanak taught by singing hymns, Mardana accompanied him on the *rabab*, creating beautiful tunes that made the guru's words easy to sing and remember.

THE FIVE BELOVED

A key event in the history of Sikhism took place in 1699. Guru Gobind Singh asked for volunteers who were prepared to die for their faith. Five men came forward and went into the guru's tent one at a time. Each time, Gobind Singh emerged with a blood-stained sword. Finally he came out with all five men alive. He explained that these men had been ready to give up their lives for their faith, as all Sikhs should. These men were the first members of the *Khalsa*, a community that unites Sikhs the world over.

Modern British Sikhs re-enact the story of the Five Beloved.

THE TEN GURUS

When Guru Nanak died he chose Guru Angad, who devised the *Gurmukhi* script used for Sikh writings, to succeed him. Later gurus included Guru Ram Das, founder of the sacred city of Amritsar, Guru Arjan, who collected together writings to make the Sikh sacred book, and Guru Tegh Bahadur, who was killed after defending Kashmiri Hindus against the Mughals, who were trying to force them to convert to Islam. Greatest of all after Nanak was Guru Gobind Singh, who ended the line of gurus by passing on their authority to the *Adi Granth* (see p. 120).

Guru Nanak (1469–1539)

Flowers by the body of Guru Nanak stayed fresh after his death, and ever since they have reminded Sikhs of his teachings.

Guru Gobind Singh (1666–1708)

Guru Tegh Bahadur (1621–75)

Guru Angad (1504–1552)

Guru Har Krishan (1656–1664)

The Guru Granth Sahib

From left to right: *Guru Amar Das (1479–1574); Guru Ram Das (1534–1581); Guru Arjan (1563–1606); Guru Hargobind (1595–1644); Guru Har Rai (1630–1661)*

The Sikh scriptures

As the Sikh religion spread, Sikhs needed to collect their hymns in a standard form to keep their teachings consistent. This work was completed by Guru Arjan in the early 17th century, and the volume he produced, the *Adi Granth*, now more popularly known as *Guru Granth Sahib*, became the main sacred text of the Sikh faith. The book contains a series of hymns, grouped according to the musical scale used to sing them. The *Guru Granth Sahib* is at the centre of the Sikh religion and is read regularly both in the temple and at home. Throughout the book, one overall message emerges again and again: salvation for the Sikh depends upon continuous meditation on God's name, so that the individual becomes immersed in his being.

GURU GOBIND SINGH
The tenth guru, Gobind Singh, declared that he would be the last human guru. He passed the authority of the gurus, as religious and political leaders, to the *Adi Granth* and the Sikh community (the *Khalsa*). This is why the book itself is now known as a guru, the *Guru Granth Sahib* (respected teacher of the community). Gobind Singh's own works appear in another sacred book, the *Dasam Granth*.

THE GURU GRANTH SAHIB
Most of the hymns written in the *Guru Granth Sahib* were composed by the gurus themselves, but a few by Hindu and Muslim poets are also included. The hymns portray God as the creator of everything, as eternal and infinite, and as the source of beauty, mercy, and truth.

THE BOOK ENTHRONED
Copies of the *Guru Granth Sahib* are bestowed great respect. Each one is kept under a canopy on a special throne and is covered with protective cloths overnight. People approach the *Guru Granth Sahib* barefoot, with their heads covered, prostrating themselves as they near the book.

READING FROM THE BOOK
There are no ordained priests in Sikhism. When Sikhs worship together the scriptures are usually read by a *Granthi*, an official who looks after the temple and takes a leading role in worship. A *Granthi* may be a man or a woman. He or she must be able to read the *Gurmukhi* script.

This chauri is made from yak tail hair

SACRED CHAURI

The *chauri* is a fan-like object that is waved over the *Guru Granth Sahib* when it is read or carried in a procession. This is a way of showing respect to the book. The *chauri* became a symbol of nobility because servants used to wave it above the heads of kings and noblemen to keep them cool.

Hymns are written in the early Sikh script, Gurmukhi.

The Guru Granth Sahib *has 1,430 pages.*

BOX FOR DONATIONS

Sikhism places a heavy emphasis on giving, encouraging individuals to support the *Khalsa*. The temple is at the heart of every Sikh community, and may offer facilities such as a youth club and library. Donation boxes are placed near the *Guru Granth Sahib*, so that people can give money for the benefit of both temple and community.

FESTIVAL PROCESSION

In India, Sikh festivals that relate to gurus feature a procession in which the *Guru Granth Sahib* is carried through the streets. Set under its canopy and adorned with flowers, the book is accompanied by a number of senior members of the Sikh community. Some of these wear blue sashes, in memory of the Five Beloved (p. 119).

JUDAISM

How it began

JUDAISM IS ONE OF THE oldest world religions, dating back nearly 4,000 years. It has given birth to two other world religions: Christianity and Islam. At the heart of Judaism lies the belief in one God. Jews can trace their origins and faith to a group of people called Hebrews, later known as the Israelites. These people lived a nomadic lifestyle in a region now regarded as the Middle East. Abraham is seen as the first Jew, and together with his son Isaac and grandson Jacob, they are known as the patriarchs, or fathers, of Judaism. Jacob's 12 sons were to become the leaders of the 12 tribes of Israel. Their story is told in the Hebrew Bible (Old Testament to Christians).

ABRAHAM IS CHOSEN
Although Abraham was born into a society that believed in many gods, as a young man he rejected this form of worship and began to worship one supreme God. Abraham believed that this God was asking him to leave his home in Harran (in what is now Iraq), to become the father of a great nation.

Clay goblet

Drinking flask

SUMERIAN POTTERY
Archeological objects such as these provide information about the time in which the stories of the patriarchs are said to have happened. This may have been between 2600 and 1800 BCE (Before the Common Era), with the story of Abraham being the earliest and Joseph's life in Egypt set around 1800 BCE. Excavations of objects help us to understand how people lived and worked in biblical times.

A NOMADIC LIFESTYLE
The Hebrew Bible describes the patriarchs as nomadic people, like the Bedouins today. They lived in large families, or clans, on the edge of the Judaean desert, wandering from area to area in search of water and pasture for their animals.

THE COVENANT
The Hebrew Bible tells how God made a covenant (agreement) with Abraham, promising him children who would live in a special land known as Canaan. In return, Abraham and his descendants would have to show God their faith and obedience. This ancient clay column bears the names of Abraham and his descendants.

Abraham and the
sacrifice of Isaac

ISAAC

Abraham and his wife
Sarah wondered how
God's promise could
be fulfilled – they were
both very old and could
not have any children.
But Sarah did give birth
to a son, called Isaac, just
as God had promised. To
test Abraham's obedience,
God asked him to sacrifice his
son. Just when Abraham was
about to strike, God told him
to sacrifice a ram instead.
Jewish tradition calls this
story the *Akeda*, which is
Hebrew for "binding",
because Isaac was only
bound and not sacrificed.

Statue of a
high-ranking
Egyptian
official

THE STORY OF JACOB

Isaac had two sons called
Jacob and Esau. Jacob
was the third and final
patriarch. One night,
God came to Jacob in
a dream and told him
that the land he lay on
would belong to his
descendants. God
renamed Jacob "Israel".
Later, Jacob had 12 sons,
including Joseph, who
were to lead the
12 tribes of Israel.

Detail showing Jacob
and his 12 sons

JOSEPH IN EGYPT

Jacob's favourite son
was Joseph. One day,
his jealous brothers sold
him to some merchants.
Joseph was taken to
Egypt, where he worked
as a slave. The rulers of
Egypt were called
pharaohs. They built
palaces, temples, and
pyramids for their
tombs and treasure.
Joseph managed to
rise to a position of
importance in the
Egyptian court, and
would have dressed like
an Egyptian official.

Bow

Lyre

*Coloured
tunics were
made of wool*

*Donkeys were used in
biblical times for carrying
goods and people*

INTO EGYPT

Joseph was reunited with his family when they went to Egypt to
avoid famine in their own land. This Egyptian wall painting is from
the tomb of Khnum-hotep, 19th century BCE. It shows Semitic-looking
people going to Egypt, just as Joseph's family had done with their
herds and goods.

The Promised Land

NEARLY 300 YEARS AFTER Joseph's death, the rulers of Egypt turned against the Israelites. So God chose a man called Moses to lead the Israelites out of Egypt, known as the Exodus, and into the Promised Land of Canaan. The Israelites were given a set of laws to follow, which included the Ten Commandments. After 40 years in the wilderness, they reached Canaan. According to the Bible, it was a land flowing with milk and honey, and was later renamed Israel. It was here that the people would build the Temple and live by the *Torah*. They would have their own kings, priests, and prophets. Above all, God promised them peace and prosperity. In return, they made a promise to God to keep all the laws and to show justice and mercy to the inhabitants of Canaan.

RAMESSES II
The Egyptian pharaoh at the time of Moses is thought to have been Ramesses II (c. 1279–1213 BCE). Royal records from his court show that he used slave labour to build his cities.

LIFE IN EGYPT
The Israelites were treated harshly by their Egyptian masters. Along with people from other lands, they were used by the pharaohs as slaves, helping to build their cities and temples.

Slaves are depicted making bricks in this Egyptian wall painting

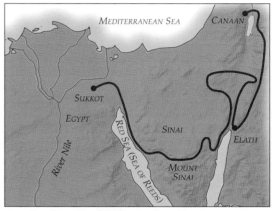

— *Possible route of the Exodus from Egypt*

THE TEN PLAGUES
As instructed by God, Moses left his home in Sinai and went to Egypt. He asked Pharaoh to set the Israelites free. But Pharaoh refused, so God sent a series of terrible plagues. When the tenth plague struck, every first-born Egyptian boy died, including Pharaoh's son, and so he relented. The Israelites were saved because the angel of death passed over their homes. Led by Moses, the Israelites left Egypt in search of Canaan.

CROSSING THE SEA
It was not long before Pharaoh changed his mind and sent his army after the Israelites, who had set up camp by a sea. It is likely that this was the Sea of Reeds – the original Hebrew translation was the Red Sea, but this was south of the Exodus route. For the terrified Israelites, this was their first test of obedience. They turned to Moses, accusing him of bringing them to harm. But God parted the waters so they could cross safely, and when Pharaoh's army followed, the waters flowed back, drowning the army. The people rejoiced, and once again placed their faith in God to lead them to the Promised Land.

Moses leads his people

The sea closes in on Pharaoh's army

> *"I am the Lord your God, who brought you out of Egypt, out of the land of slavery. You shall have no other gods before me."*

ONE OF THE TEN COMMANDMENTS

GOD'S LAWS

Upon reaching Mount Sinai, Moses received from God the *Torah* (all the laws, including the Ten Commandments). These laws were written on stone tablets and later housed in a special chest, called the Ark of the Covenant. When Moses passed on these laws, the Israelites accepted the covenant of the Lord.

THE PROMISED LAND

When the Israelites approached Canaan, they discovered that the inhabitants could not be defeated easily, and so they rebelled. God condemned the Israelites to wander in the wilderness for 40 years because of their lack of faith. When Canaan was conquered by the next generation of Israelites, the land was divided among the 12 tribes of Israel, who were descendants of Jacob. Pictured above is the Jordan Valley, part of ancient Canaan.

CANAANITE GODS

Canaan was settled by people who worshipped many gods. Baal was one of the most popular Canaanite gods. Such pagan worship was seen as a potential threat to the religion of the Israelites.

Fertility goddess

Bronze figure of Baal

14th-century Bible illustration showing Moses on Mount Sinai

The first kings

SAUL IS ANOINTED
For centuries, the Israelites were led by tribal leaders, known as Judges. The Israelites pleaded with the prophet Samuel to ask God to give them a king. Saul, who was known for his bravery, was chosen as the first king to rule and unite the tribes of Israel. During his reign (c. 1025–1004 BCE), Saul organized an army and waged war against many of his enemies. But Saul often disobeyed God. He finally lost his life in battle with the Philistines.

THE RULE OF KINGS in ancient Israel was a gradual process. When the Israelites settled in Canaan, there were many conflicts with the Philistines over land. By the end of the 11th century BCE, the Israelites had been defeated. This led to a call by the people to be ruled by a king, who would unite all the tribes of Israel. Jewish kings were expected to be just and kind, but many were known for their injustice. It was the prophets who criticized both kings and priests when they oppressed the poor and made unjust laws. They also pleaded for moral and religious reform in the country. Often the prophets were regarded as enemies of the state and punished for telling the truth.

THE SEA PEOPLE
The Philistines belonged to a group of people known as the Sea People. From the Aegean area, they sailed to Egypt, finally settling along the coast of Canaan. Findings of Philistine artefacts such as the jug above, dating from the 12th century BCE, indicate a very developed culture.

Jerusalem, from a 15th-century manuscript

Jerusalem is also known as the City of David

"Praise God, all nations, extol the Eternal One you peoples! For God's love for us is strong, and the truth of God is eternal. Hallelujah!"

PSALM 117

King David's harp may have looked like this musical instrument, called a kinnor

KING DAVID
David, Saul's son-in-law, was the second king of Israel. He reigned for 30 years, joining all the tribes together under one central authority. He also defeated the Philistines. Although he was a warrior king, David is often depicted playing the harp. He is said to be the author of many of the Psalms in the Bible. The Psalms consist of poems or hymns praising God.

JERUSALEM
Jerusalem had been a Canaanite stronghold until the Jebusites (a group of people from different origins) had taken over the city. When David captured Jerusalem in 1000 BCE, he made the city the capital of his new kingdom, and housed the Ark of the Covenant there. As a result of this, Jerusalem became the political and religious centre of the kingdom.

THE KINGDOM OF SOLOMON

Solomon, son of David and Bathsheba, was the third king of Israel. His reign was peaceful, and under his leadership the kingdom prospered. Solomon was responsible for constructing many magnificent buildings, including the First Temple in Jerusalem. This provided a focal point of worship for all Israelites, and strengthened the city's religious importance. But soon after Solomon's death in c. 930 BCE, the kingdom was divided between Solomon's son Rehoboam and a military commander named Jeroboam.

This bracelet may have been made from gold stolen by Pharaoh Shishak when he raided the Temple

THE KINGDOM OF JUDAH

In the south was the smaller kingdom of Judah, which was ruled by Rehoboam. The division made Judah vulnerable to attack. The Egyptian Pharaoh Shishak plundered the Temple in Jerusalem, while the Israelites turned to paganism. It was not until the 8th century BCE, under the leadership of King Uzziah (783–42 BCE), that the faith was restored.

Seal belonging to an official in the court of Jeroboam

THE KINGDOM OF ISRAEL

Jeroboam ruled the kingdom of Israel in the north. Israel came into conflict with its neighbours, and it was not until the late 9th century BCE that the kingdom witnessed a more settled and prosperous time. But, like Judah in the south, this prosperity left Israel open to pagan influences.

King Solomon reading the *Torah*, from a medieval manuscript

12th-century detail of Isaiah

THE PROPHETS

The prophets were a group of people who reminded the Israelites of God's ways. They explained what was right and wrong, and did not accept injustice, especially if it came from the king. The prophet Isaiah, for example, protested against those who broke religious law and demanded justice for the poor.

New rulers

JUST AS THE PROPHET AMOS predicted Israel's destruction, the prophet Micah warned of a similar fate for Judah. From the mid-8th century BCE onwards, both kingdoms were conquered by a number of foreign rulers. Each new rule brought changes to the way the Israelites lived and worshipped. Under Assyrian and Babylonian rule, the Israelites were exiled and the Temple was destroyed. Nearly 200 years later, a more tolerant Persian ruler enabled the Israelites to return to Jerusalem to rebuild their Temple. But by the end of Greek rule, Judah was plunged into instability, resulting in a short-lived period of independence under the Hasmonean dynasty.

PERSIAN GUARD
King Cyrus the Great of Persia allowed the conquered peoples to follow their customs.

THE ASSYRIANS
By 722 BCE, Israel had been conquered by the Assyrian army. The Assyrian king, Sargon II, deported many of the Israelites to Mesopotamia and in return brought people from his Assyrian Empire to Israel. In 701 BCE it was Judah's turn to face the might of the Assyrian army. Lachish, which was southwest of Jerusalem, was destroyed, but Jerusalem was spared.

The entire siege of Lachish was depicted in stone – this detail shows people fleeing

BABYLONIAN EMPIRE
During the 6th century BCE, a new power emerged – the Babylonians. They invaded Jerusalem in 586 BCE, destroying the city and Temple. As a means of breaking their national identity and preventing them from organizing into rebellious groups, the Israelites were exiled. The clay tablet above records the fall of Jerusalem.

THE REIGN OF KING CYRUS
In the mid-6th century BCE, the Persian dynasty emerged as a powerful force. King Cyrus the Great of Persia conquered Babylon in 539 BCE. He allowed the Jews to return to Jerusalem and rebuild their Temple. Upon their return, the exiled people did not always get along with the Israelites who stayed. Despite the tensions in the Jewish community and the lack of resources, work on the Second Temple began in 516 BCE, led by two prophets, Haggai and Zechariah. In 458 BCE, the prophet Ezra returned with more exiles. He introduced new laws that helped to ensure the survival of Judaism.

A reconstructed model of the Second Temple

Persian silver coin used during this period – on one side is an eagle, the other side is a lily

THE REBUILDING OF JERUSALEM

In 445 BCE Nehemiah was appointed governor of Judah, and set about rebuilding the walls of Jerusalem. Nehemiah was an important figure in the the Persian court. Not only did he organize the repair of Jerusalem, but he also implemented reforms aimed at strengthening the religion. These included discouraging marriage with non-Jews and prohibiting all work on the Sabbath.

RECAPTURE OF THE TEMPLE

Alexander's early death resulted in a number of conflicts. Judah was eventually conquered by the Seleucids, who ruled over Asia Minor during this period. Heavy taxes were levied, non-Jewish priests were appointed to the Temple, and the people were banned from practising their religion. The latter led to a revolt in 164 BCE organized by a priest called Mattathias. His son Judah the Maccabee recaptured the Temple and restored the Jewish religion. Today, the victory is still celebrated by the festival of *Hanukkah*.

Judah the Maccabee stands triumphant

ALEXANDER THE GREAT

In 332 BCE, Alexander the Great, ruler of Macedonia and Greece, conquered Judah and put an end to Persian rule. He respected the Jewish God and allowed them to run their own affairs. New religious groups emerged at this time, the most notable ones being the Pharisees and the Sadducees. Many Jews accepted Greek culture, called Hellenism, but the Pharisees and the Sadducees did not. The Pharisees observed all Jewish ritual laws and emphasized the importance of the oral *Torah* (the laws given to Moses), while the Sadducees accepted the written *Torah* (the first five books of the Bible).

This bronze coin comes from the reign of Mattathias Antigonus (40–37 BCE) – the last of the Hasmonean kings

THE HASMONEAN DYNASTY

Judah the Maccabee's victory led to a new line of rulers called the Hasmonean dynasty, which was headed by the Maccabees. But to the dismay of the Pharisees and Sadducees, the Maccabees were influenced by the same Hellenistic culture they rebelled against. Over a period of time, the Hasmoneans started fighting among themselves. Rome, the new emerging power, took advantage of the situation, and ended the Hasmonean dynasty.

Roman rule

Roman bronze helmet, dating from the time when Rome occupied Judaea

WHEN THE ROMANS CONQUERED Judaea (as Judah came to be known under Roman rule) in 63 BCE, they installed a new ruler, Antipater, whose son Herod the Great later became king of all Judaea. The Jews were allowed to practise their faith, but after Herod's rule, a number of Roman policies and the introduction of Hellenistic practices led to several Jewish revolts, all of which were brutally crushed by the Roman army. Many Jews were deported as a form of punishment. This was the start of what is known in Jewish history as the Diaspora (dispersion), and was to affect the nature of Judaism.

THE ROMANS IN JUDAEA

Herod the Great was given the title "king of all the Jews" in 40 BCE. Although Judaea prospered under his rule, the Jewish way of life was greatly threatened. Herod had members of the Hasmonean family put to death because they were seen as rivals. He encouraged foreign influences, and placed a golden eagle (a Roman symbol) on the front of the Temple.

PROCURATORS

From CE 6–66 (Common Era), Rome was ruled by a number of officers, called procurators. This was a time of considerable unrest, and Jewish rebels, known as zealots, become active. Pontius Pilate (ruled CE 26–36) was the worst of the procurators. He had images of Caesar carried by Roman legions, used the Temple's money for erecting buildings, and issued coins with a pagan symbol – a curved staff, which was the mark of a Roman official who predicted the future. This was especially offensive to Jewish people.

Pagan symbol

Coin issued by Pontius Pilate

THE FIRST JEWISH REVOLT

In CE 66, when Jews were celebrating the festival of Passover, Roman soldiers marched into Jerusalem and stripped the Temple of its treasure. The Jews rebelled and succeeded in controlling Jerusalem. But under the direction of Roman general Titus, the rebellion was finally crushed in CE 70. Jerusalem was no longer the focus of Jewish life and faith. The great Roman victory was commemorated in a triumphal arch, which stands in Rome, Italy.

Torah scroll

The Menorah *from the Second Temple is carried away by Roman soldiers*

Detail of the frieze from the Arch of Titus

RABBINICAL JUDAISM

Although Jerusalem was destroyed, the faith was given a new direction. Rabbinical schools developed, and the word "rabbi" (master) was used for the *Torah* scholars. With the Temple destroyed, the synagogue became the focus of the faith.

THE BATTLE FOR MASADA

The fall of Jerusalem in CE 70 did not stop the rebels fighting to the bitter end. Herodium, Machaerus, and Masada were still in the hands of the zealots. Herodium and Machaerus were the first to fall. But Masada was recaptured after a year-long battle. Nearly 960 men, women, and children committed suicide when faced with defeat.

This arrow still had its handle intact

Arrowhead

THE EVIDENCE

Excavations at the fortress of Masada have unearthed a number of objects that would have belonged to the rebels. Among the findings have been prayer shawls, leather sandals, and these arrows, providing evidence of the fighting that took place.

"Masada shall not fall again."

THE OATH TAKEN TODAY BY ISRAELI SOLDIERS

The mountain-top fortress of Masada is located in the Judaean desert, overlooking the Dead Sea

KING HADRIAN

Tensions arose once more during the reign of Emperor Hadrian (117–138 BCE). He introduced many changes that angered the Jewish people. Hadrian banned the Jewish practice of circumcision, and embarked upon turning Jerusalem into a Roman city, changing its name to Aelia Capitolina.

Relief of Emperor Hadrian

Coin issued by the Bar Kokhba rebels

THE SECOND JEWISH REVOLT

Emperor Hadrian's policies led to the Bar Kokhba Revolt of 132 BCE. The revolt was led by Simeon bar Kokhba, and was supported by some of the important rabbis of the time, such as Rabbi Akiva. The revolt lasted three years. Thousands of Jewish rebels died, while others were sold into slavery. Jerusalem was now devoid of any Jewish inhabitants, who were forbidden to even enter the city. Just as Jerusalem's name was changed, Hadrian embarked upon changing the name of Judaea to Palaestina.

The Middle Ages

15th-century woodcut entitled *Massacre of the Jews*

FALSE ACCUSATIONS

In 1144, Jews in Norwich, England, were accused of murdering a Christian child in order to make unleavened bread for Passover. This slander came to be known as the Blood Libel, and prevailed for centuries. Jews were also accused of causing the deadly Black Death of 1348 by poisoning wells and rivers. Jews were usually not affected by the Black Death, because they lived in ghettos and maintained higher standards of hygiene. But their good health cast suspicion on them. Many Jews were attacked or murdered.

JEWS OFTEN FACED GREAT religious hostility during the Middle Ages (7th–15th centuries), because Christians blamed Jews for the death of Jesus. This led to hatred and expulsion from Christian countries. England was the first country to expel Jews in the 13th century, followed by France. In Spain and Portugal, attacks against Jews reached a peak in the 15th century. Wherever they lived, Jews had to pay special taxes, were forced to wear certain clothing to single them out, and were often housed in ghettos (segregated areas). Generally, life for Jewish people was better under Muslim rule than it was under Christian rule.

The bell-shaped hat was a mark of disgrace

THE MARK OF DISGRACE

In some countries, Jews were forced to wear clothes with a badge depicting the stone tablets or the Star of David. Some Jews even had to wear pointed hats. All this was done to single them out from Christians and humiliate them.

Muslim soldiers

Crusaders

MONEY-LENDING

Jews were not allowed to own land and many other forms of livelihood were closed to them. Since the Church forbade Christians to lend money and charge interest, Jews were forced to become the money-lenders of Europe. Thus a new stereotype emerged: the Jew as a greedy money-lender.

THE CRUSADES

By the 11th century, Muslims had conquered many lands: Syria, Palestine, Egypt, and Spain. Life for Jews living in these countries improved. But by the end of the 11th century, this was to change with the Crusades – a series of holy wars waged by Christians, one of which was to free the Holy Land from Muslim rule. When the first Crusaders left Europe for the Holy Land in 1096, they destroyed the Jewish communities along the way. In 1099, they attacked Jerusalem, killing Jews as well as Muslims.

CHRISTIANITY VERSUS JUDAISM

The Church was a major force in medieval Europe, affecting every aspect of daily life. It held the view that the only hope for Jews and other non-Christians was to convert to Christianity. This supremacy of the Church over Judaism was a popular subject in Christian art at the time. The figure of Synagoga, downcast and holding a broken lance, represented the Jewish faith. The Church, represented by Ecclesia, was always crowned and standing triumphant.

Interior of the synagogue of Toledo – one of ten synagogues in Spain by the end of the 14th century

The humbled figure of Synagoga

The proud figure of Ecclesia

THE "GOLDEN AGE"

Between the 10th and 12th centuries, Jewish communities in Spain and Portugal flourished under Muslim rule. Some cities, such as Granada and Tarragona in Spain, had such a large Jewish population that they came to be known as Jewish cities. A unique Jewish culture developed, giving rise to poets, philosophers, and theologians who co-existed happily with their Islamic and Christian counterparts. But by the end of the 13th century, the status of the Jew changed for the worse. The Christians regained control of Spain, and although tolerant at first, they forced Jews to convert to Christianity or be expelled.

Martin Luther preaching

French manuscript illumination, 13th century

PROTESTANT REFORMATION

Martin Luther (1483–1546), who led the Protestant Reformation, was at first sympathetic to the plight of Jews. But in later years he preached against them, advocating the burning of synagogues and Jewish schools. Luther also repeated the Blood Libel charges and the poisoning of wells slander.

Life in the Diaspora

SHABBETAI ZEVI
Jews believe in the coming of the Messiah, who will pave the way for God's rule. The most famous of the false messiahs was Turkish-born Shabbetai Zevi (1626–76). He became popular with Jews, especially those from Eastern Europe, who were facing great hardship. When he converted to Islam, many of his followers became disillusioned.

SEPHARDI JEWS
Sephardi Jews (descendants of Spanish and Portuguese Jews) first settled in Amsterdam during the 16th century. The Dutch operated a tolerant policy towards Jews, and news of this soon spread. Within a short period of time, large numbers of Jews from Spain and Portugal had moved to the Netherlands. Many of the settlers were educated men – doctors, writers, scientists, and lawyers. Soon, both the Jewish community and the Dutch economy flourished.

18th-century Torah *mantle used by Amsterdam's Sephardi Jews*

The Ark of the Covenant is woven on the mantle

BETWEEN THE 16th and 18th centuries, Jewish communities were founded in a number of European countries, including the Netherlands, Italy, France, England, and Poland. Jews living in these countries enjoyed varying degrees of prosperity and freedom. In Amsterdam, for example, the Jewish community was the richest and largest in Western Europe, and had an enormous impact on the economy. But in Poland, the story was different. There was very little interaction with Polish society, and the majority of Jews earned a meagre living – many turning to false messiahs in the hope of salvation. Polish Jews were also denied equal rights, which were granted to Jews of Western Europe.

The crown symbolizes the glory of the Torah

GHETTOS IN ITALY
The policy towards Jews in Italy, which had generally been favourable, changed during the 16th century. The segregation of Jews was made compulsory. In cities such as Venice and Rome, Jews had to live in filthy, overcrowded ghettos, which were a health hazard. Despite this, they were able to follow their faith, and Jewish culture flourished. The picture above shows the Jewish ghetto of Rome, c. 1880s.

Ashkenazi Jews outside their synagogue

ASHKENAZI JEWS
The number of Jews arriving from Eastern Europe, known as Ashkenazi Jews, increased in the 1620s. At first they were dependent on the Sephardi community. Many came from poor backgrounds and lacked the wealth and education of the Sephardi Jews. The artist Rembrandt van Rijn (1606–69), who lived near the Jewish quarter of Amsterdam, took an interest in its life, and often portrayed Jews in his work, as shown above.

MERCHANTS
During the 17th century, Amsterdam became an important centre for international trade. As well as being allowed to practise their faith, Jews were allowed to participate freely in economic matters. Merchants were involved with banking, overseas trade, businesses, and with the diamond industry. The latter was to become a Jewish area of expertise – from trading raw diamonds to cutting and polishing the precious stones.

Diamonds

EQUAL RIGHTS FOR JEWS

By the end of the late 18th century, the granting of equal rights was debated across Europe. In 1789, revolutionary France was the first European country to grant equal rights to Jews. The Netherlands, under the influence of the French Revolution, soon abolished all laws that discriminated against Jews. In other European countries, the call for equality and freedom continued into the 19th century.

Napoleon is shown granting religious freedom

Oliver Cromwell

THE JEWS OF ENGLAND

Jews had been expelled from England since 1290. In 1653 a few Portuguese Jews, who had been forced to convert to Christianity, settled in England. These so-called converts continued to practise their faith secretly. Manasseh Ben-Israel (1604–57), a Sephardi scholar from Amsterdam, petitioned Oliver Cromwell (1599–1658) to readmit Jews. Cromwell, ruler of England after the Civil War, realized that Jews could be of value as they had been for the Dutch economy, and permitted their readmission in 1656. It was not until 1829 that English Jews were granted citizenship.

LIFE IN EASTERN EUROPE

Many of the persecuted Jews fled to Poland during the 1500s. By the mid-1600s, nearly 500,000 Jews lived in this tolerant country. The majority of the inhabitants were poor – peddlers, tailors, and cobblers – living in close-knit communities known as *shtetls*. The synagogue, the rabbi, the *yeshiva* (study-house), and the home were all important features of the *shtetl* community.

Scene from the film *Fiddler on the Roof*, based on the life of a *shtetl* community

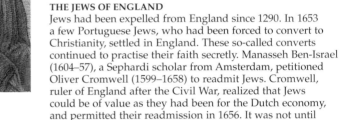

The pogroms

DURING THE 18TH CENTURY, Poland was conquered by three powerful neighbours: Russia, Austria, and Prussia. Its territory was divided among these powers. Nearly all Polish Jews came under Russian rule – which meant over half the world's Jewish population now lived in Russia. These Jews were confined to living in an impoverished area called the Pale of Settlement. Denied freedom of movement, very few options were open to them. The Russian tzars (kings) were not sympathetic towards their plight. At first the tzars tried to force them to change so that they would follow a Russian way of life. Tzar Alexander II (1818–81), however, was more tolerant than his predecessors, and gave hope to Jews. He permitted them to live outside the Pale and lifted some of the legal requirements imposed on them. But his assassination marked a turning point in the history of Russian Jews. It led to attacks on them, known as the pogroms (Russian word meaning "devastation"), and thousands of Jews fled in panic.

THE RUSSIAN TZARS
Alexander II reigned from 1855 to 1881. His assassination was blamed on Jews, but it is more likely that he was murdered by his own people. With a new tzar in place, Alexander III (1845–94), Jews were once again at the mercy of an unsympathetic ruler. Anti-Jewish attacks broke out, which were both organized and often encouraged by the authorities.

START OF THE POGROMS
The first wave of pogroms (1881–84) resulted in the deaths of hundreds of Jews. Their homes and synagogues were also looted and vandalized, while the police just stood by. In 1882, Alexander III passed the May Laws, which imposed restrictions on Jews. These laws also helped to reinforce the view among many Russians that Jews were responsible for the assassination of the tzar. The second wave of pogroms (1903–06) followed a similar pattern of death and destruction.

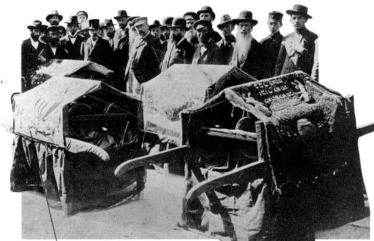

Torah scrolls vandalized during the pogroms are buried by Jews

Frightened Jews start to leave Russia

THE JEWISH RESPONSE
There was very little Jews could do to protect themselves during the pogroms. One course of action was to escape from Russia. Others rallied behind the socialists, who wanted to change the way Russia was ruled. Many of the socialist leaders were Jewish, and this fuelled further attacks on Jews.

Jewish migration, 1880–1914

- ▦ The Pale of Settlement
- ▦ Region with Jewish emigration
- ▦ Region with Jewish immigration
- ✻ Region where pogroms occurred
- • Gateway city
- ➔ Sephardi Jews
- ⇒ Ashkenazi Jews

NEW LANDS
More than 2 million Jews left Russia between the start of the pogroms in 1881 and the Russian Revolution of 1917. The Revolution signalled the end of tzarist government and the restrictions imposed on Jews. While some resettled in Europe and Palestine, many Jews fled to countries as far away as South America, Canada, the USA, and South Africa.

Citrus crops were commonly grown in Palestine

PALESTINE
Nearly 70,000 Jews went to Palestine during the First *Aliyah* (a Hebrew word used to describe the immigration of Jews to Palestine). However, faced with difficult conditions, only half this number remained. Those that did stay received help from the French Jewish benefactor Baron Edmond de Rothschild (1845–1934). He bought land for the settlement of Jews, and introduced new crops in addition to those being grown.

Jewish immigrants arriving in the USA

UNITED STATES OF AMERICA
The first few Jews to settle in the USA in 1654 were those escaping persecution in Spain and Portugal. With the on-going attacks on Russian Jews in the late 1800s, thousands arrived at the docks of Manhattan, hoping for a better life. The USA accepted more Jews than any other country, and by 1929, nearly 5 million Jews had moved to the safe haven of the USA.

THE NEW LIFE
The immigrants settled in cities such as New York, where they lived in crowded neighbourhoods. Most were employed by Jews who ran clothing factories. New York's East Side was a typical Jewish neighbourhood – nearly 350,000 Jews lived in this small area.

The Jewish market on New York's East Side, c. 1900s

Zionism

THE WORD ZION, a biblical word, is often used as an alternative name for the Land of Israel. Zionism is the political movement that gained momentum in the 19th century as a result of the pogroms and the resurfacing of anti-Semitic views witnessed during the trial of a French Jew, Alfred Dreyfus. The Zionists believed that the only way to avoid persecution was to have their own homeland – the Land of Israel. This cause was taken up by Theodor Herzl, a journalist covering the Dreyfus trial. Herzl was instrumental in setting up the First Zionist Congress in 1897. Later, the Jewish National Fund was established to buy land in Palestine. The Zionists were further helped when Britain took control of Palestine during World War I (1914–18), and made a promise to back Jewish settlement in Palestine.

THE CALL FOR A HOMELAND
In 1882 Leon Pinkser (1821–91) wrote his pamphlet *Autoemancipation* (above). He described anti-Semitism as a disease and said the only cure for it was to allow Jews to create a homeland. The idea of Zionism dates back nearly 2,500 years, when the exiled Jews of Babylon yearned to return to their homeland. In the 1800s, Zionism became an important political force.

Alfred Dreyfus had his stripes removed and his sword broken as part of a military humiliation

THE DREYFUS AFFAIR
Alfred Dreyfus (1859–1935), a captain in the French army, was wrongly accused of treason in 1894. He was found guilty and imprisoned for life. A victim of anti-Semitism, Dreyfus was supported by important members of French society, such as the writer Emile Zola (1840–1902). However, it was not until 1906 that Dreyfus was finally cleared of all blame.

THE SOLUTION
Theodor Herzl (1860–1904), a Hungarian-born Jew, was shocked by the anti-Semitic treatment of Alfred Dreyfus. Herzl realized the need for a solution to the anti-Semitism still faced by Jews, even in countries where they had been granted equal rights. In 1896, he published his book, *The Jewish State*. Herzl called for the establishment of a Jewish state in Palestine – this was the only solution.

Theodor Herzl, who helped to found the Zionist movement

Herzl's suggestion for a Jewish flag was adopted by the Zionist Congress

THE FIRST ZIONIST CONGRESS
Not all Jews, especially those living in Western Europe, agreed with Herzl's solution. Many felt that his views would lead to further anti-Semitism. Nonetheless, the First Zionist Congress took place in 1897. The Congress called for the resettlement of Jews in Palestine, and set up the World Zionist Organization to put its goals into practise.

גאולה תתנו לארץ
ע"י קרן קימת לישראל

אל תאמר מחר נגאל. שמא נאחר את
המועד.
אוסישקין

...יה ושערה וגפן ות
ת שמן ודבש

*Poster issued by the Jewish
National Fund, calling for a
return to the Land of Israel*

RESETTLEMENT

The Jewish National Fund, established in 1901 to buy land for Jews, helped the immigrants who made up the Second *Aliyah* (1904–14). Many resettled in the cities, while others tried to farm the land. One group of immigrants set up a farming community, where all the work and produce was shared equally. This laid the foundations of the *kibbutz* – unique to Israel then as it is now.

Tel Aviv in the 1920s

DEVELOPMENT OF THE CITIES

In 1909 the town of Tel Aviv was founded to house the increasing number of immigrants. It was the first all-Jewish city. The settlers were provided with funds for the building work, which they carried out themselves. By 1914, the flourishing city had over 1,000 people. In the same year, the number of Jewish inhabitants in Jerusalem totalled 45,000. The Zionists planned to build the first Hebrew University in Jerusalem, a goal finally realized in 1925.

THE BALFOUR DECLARATION

During World War I, Britain hoped to win Jewish support for its war efforts. In 1917 the Balfour Declaration was drafted by Lord Arthur Balfour (1848–1930), the British foreign secretary. The Declaration recognized the right of Jews to live in Palestine. This was a major landmark for the Zionists. In 1918, Britain conquered Palestine, which had been part of the Turkish Ottoman Empire since 1516. With a mandate to rule Palestine, Britain was now responsible for implementing the Declaration.

*Lord Balfour is shown
on this commemorative version
of the Balfour Declaration*

A new nightmare

I<small>N</small> 1933 A<small>DOLF</small> H<small>ITLER</small> (1889–1945) became
chancellor of Germany. This was the start of a
slowly unfolding tragedy for Jews throughout
the world. Hitler's right-wing Nazi Party
was driven by its programme of hate – the
elimination of Jews. Step by step, the Nazis
put this policy into practice. A campaign of
lies (propaganda) was launched against Jews.
School children were taught Nazi policies,
while their parents were told to boycott Jewish
shops. Anti-Jewish laws were passed, and
many Jews were attacked or murdered.
By 1937 over a hundred thousand Jews had
fled from Germany, while Hitler marched
into neighbouring countries, signalling the
same fate for their Jews.

ECONOMIC STEPS
In April 1933, a one-day boycott
of Jewish shops was organized by
the Nazis. The people were led to
believe that Jews were greedy
capitalists, and the best way to
strike back was not to buy from
them. Nazi guards stood outside
some Jewish shops, and signs were
also placed outside warning people
not to enter. The sign above reads,
"Germany! Resist!
Do not buy from Jews!"

SPREADING LIES
Propaganda played a crucial part in the success of
the Nazi regime. All forms of media, such as leaflets,
radio, films, and posters, were used to show Jews as
an inferior race and the cause of Germany's economic
problems. A minister of propaganda was also appointed
to promote the lies. By changing the minds of the
people, the Nazis believed that they could then put
their policies into action with very little resistance.

*Detail from a Nazi leaflet
designed to imply that Jews
had built walls to divide people*

BURNING BOOKS
In 1933 and 1936, the Nazis raided
libraries and bookshops. Thousands
of books were taken away. Many were
written by Jews, but there were also
books by non-Jewish writers, such as
the American Ernest Hemingway,
who did not agree with Nazi policies.
The German people were encouraged
to show their anti-Semitic feelings
by burning the books.

Passport of a Jewish woman

ANTI–SEMITISM IN SCHOOLS

The Nazis realized that it was important to win the minds of young children for the future survival of the Nazi Party. In schools, books were rewritten to further the cause of anti-Semitism. German children were taught that they belonged to the Aryan race (the superior fair-skinned, fair-haired race). By 1939, all children under the age of 18 years had to join the Nazi Youth Organization. Eventually, both Jewish teachers and children were forced out of German schools.

This detail from a Nazi school book shows German children as the superior race

THE "J" STAMP

By the end of 1933, nearly 38,000 Jews had left Germany, mainly bound for England or the USA. Between 1934 and 1939 a further 210,000 left, all having to pay large sums of money for their freedom. Their travel documents were stamped with the letter "J". The Hebrew name of Israel was added to every Jewish man and Sarah to every Jewish woman in an attempt to humiliate them. But these people were the lucky ones. After 1939, Jews were not able to leave Germany.

KRISTALLNACHT

In 1938, the Nazis launched their first full-scale attack on Jewish communities. Synagogues were set on fire, and Jewish homes were vandalized, as were Jewish shops and factories. This destruction was known as *Kristallnacht* (meaning "night of the broken glass"). Thousands of Jews were arrested and many were murdered. Soon, neighbouring countries were invaded by the Nazi army. Jews in these countries were subjected to the same brutality and persecution faced by German Jews. The invasion of Poland in 1939, home to nearly 3 million Jews, sealed the desperate fate of European Jews.

A burning synagogue in Berlin

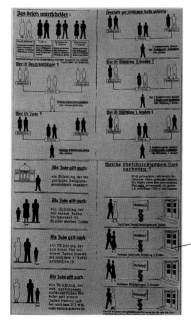

Detailed charts were issued to show how to implement the Nuremberg Laws

THE NUREMBERG LAWS

During Nazi rule, laws were introduced to restrict the freedom of Jews. The worst of the anti-Jewish laws were known as the Nuremberg Laws of 1935. Jews were banned from marrying non-Jews and from taking up professional jobs such as teaching. The aim was to isolate Jews from all walks of German life, socially and economically. These laws were also introduced in countries occupied by the Nazis.

The charred remains of a synagogue – one of 600 to be reduced to ashes

The Holocaust

THE TERM HOLOCAUST is used to describe the worst genocide that took place during World War II (1939–45). This mass extermination was the attempt by the Nazis to eradicate all Jews. Six million Jews were murdered, along with other people considered to be undesirable. The steps taken to wipe out the Jewish population of Europe varied from one Nazi-occupied country to another, but were more brutal in Eastern Europe. For Jews living in countries under direct Nazi rule, their prospect for survival was bleak. They were rounded up and confined to ghettos until they could be transported to the labour or death camps. Despite the hopelessness of their situation, Jewish resistance groups emerged. There were also many non-Jewish people who risked their lives to protect Jewish people.

THE YELLOW STAR
From 1942 onwards all Jews in Nazi-occupied Europe had to wear the yellow Star of David. This was designed to degrade all Jews (an act that can be traced back to the Middle Ages). The yellow colour symbolized shame. Every Jew over the age of ten years had to wear the badge or face being shot.

Auschwitz concentration camp

THE WARSAW GHETTO UPRISING
The best-known example of Jewish resistance was the Warsaw ghetto uprising (nearly 445,000 Jews were crammed into this filthy ghetto in Poland). The rebellion started in 1943 when a group of Jewish fighters obtained arms and attacked German soldiers. But it was not long before the Germans forced the people out of their bunkers by burning the buildings. It has been estimated that 7,000 Jews in the ghetto were killed. Those who survived were sent to the death camps.

Survivors are rounded up by the Nazis

CONCENTRATION CAMPS
At first, the Nazis set up mobile death units to carry out their extermination plans. These death squads moved from area to area, killing Jews. Later, concentration camps were built for mass killings. The main death camps were in Poland, notably Auschwitz and Treblinka. Auschwitz was by far the largest of the death camps, where up to 12,000 Jews a day were killed.

This tin from Auschwitz contained cyanide gas crystals

THE GAS CHAMBER
It was from Auschwitz that the Nazis perfected their extermination method. In 1941, gas crystals were used to kill some of the victims in a makeshift gas chamber. But by the end of 1942, the Nazis converted two farmhouses into gas chambers, which worked day and night. These gas chambers could kill several hundred people each time. Then, in 1943, the Nazis built four gas chambers that could kill 2,000 people at once.

PRISONERS AT AUSCHWITZ
Upon arrival, men, women, and children were forced to wear ill-fitting, filthy uniforms. Conditions at the camp were so inhumane that many prisoners died as a result.

THE STORY OF ANNE FRANK
Anne Frank was a young girl when her parents decided to leave Germany to escape Hitler's anti-Jewish policies. They moved to Amsterdam, in the Netherlands. In 1942, when Anne was 13, the family hid in an annexe above her father's business premises. She was given a small book that she used as a diary. Most of the Frank family, including Anne, perished in Auschwitz when they were discovered by the Nazis. After the war her diary was found and published in 1947. Since then the diary has been translated into more than 50 languages.

Anne Frank

The diary kept by Anne Frank

THE UNIFORM
The prisoners of Auschwitz had numbers tattooed on their left forearms for identification. Names were not used because the aim was to dehumanize the victims. Prisoners wore uniforms that had a triangular badge sewn on the front: yellow for Jews, red for political prisoners, green for criminals, brown for gypsies, and pink for homosexuals.

"If I just think of how we live here, I usually come to the conclusion that it is a paradise compared with how other Jews who are not in hiding must be living."

ANNE FRANK

The remains of Schindler's factory, Poland

Oskar Schindler

ACTS OF HEROISM
Thousands of individuals risked their lives to help save the lives of Jews. Those who were well-connected, such as the Swedish diplomat Raul Wallenberg (1913–45), used their position to issue false documents and passports. But many of the individuals who helped came from ordinary walks of life. In France, Father Pierre-Marie Benoît (1895–1990), a monk from Marseilles, helped to smuggle thousands of Jewish children out of France and into Switzerland or Spain. Oskar Schindler (1908–74), a factory owner, employed Jewish prisoners. By doing so, he saved over a thousand people from certain death.

The aftermath

WORLD WAR II ended in May 1945 and so did the Holocaust. The aftermath revealed that one-third of the world's Jewish population had been killed as part of Hitler's plan. The war also displaced millions of Jewish people throughout Europe, and fearing repercussions, many did not want to return to their homes. Displaced Persons' (DP) camps were set up to provide shelter for them, while the perpetrators of the Holocaust were put on trial. Once again, the call for a Jewish homeland gathered momentum, resulting in the creation of the State of Israel in 1948. Sadly, this did not bring the peace and security that was hoped for.

THE SURVIVORS
It has been estimated that about 200,000 Jewish people survived the Holocaust by either hiding or pretending to be non-Jews. Children were often left with Christian families to be looked after, while others were taken to convents. The picture above is of Henri Obstfeld, who survived because he was hidden from the Nazis. Henri's parents did not see him for nearly three years.

This story book was sent to Henri by his parents when he was hiding

DISPLACED PERSONS
The war left over 1.5 million people without homes. Known as Displaced Persons, nearly 250,000 of these were Jews. Some returned to their homes to rebuild their lives. But this was not to prove easy – anti-Semitism did not end with the war. For example, Jews returning to Poland found their homes occupied, and many were attacked. The majority of the survivors found refuge in Displaced Persons' camps, where they were provided with much-needed food and medicine.

Mother with her children at a Displaced Persons' camp

Zionist poster calling for survivors to go to Palestine instead of other countries

NEW HOMES
Five years after the Holocaust, there were still survivors with nowhere to go. The Zionists hoped to resettle as many of the Displaced Persons in Palestine as was possible. But Britain, which still had a mandate to govern Palestine, would only admit 13,000 of them. As a result, many of the Holocaust survivors were smuggled into Palestine, often through dangerous routes. Nearly 70,000 Jews entered Palestine in this way.

NUREMBERG TRIALS

In 1945, the Allied Forces (Britain, USA, France, and the Soviet Union) agreed to bring 22 high-ranking Nazis to trial in Germany. In what became known as the Nuremberg Trials, the Nazis were charged with committing crimes against humanity. The trials lasted 11 months, and judgements included death sentences, imprisonment, and acquittals. To this day, trials against the perpetrators continue. Many may never be found, since they changed their names and fled to other countries to avoid being caught.

THE STATE OF ISRAEL

The pressure to find a homeland for the survivors was considerable. Many wanted to return to Palestine, but were unable to do so. In 1948, Britain withdrew its forces from Palestine, thus ending its mandate. Despite fierce opposition from Arab governments, the United Nations decided that Palestine was to be divided to create the State of Israel. Almost 50 years on, Theodor Herzl's dream had been realized.

Children wave the new flags of the State of Israel in England, 1948

NEW CONFLICTS

Thousands of Jews made the journey to the new State of Israel. The people included survivors of the war and Jews from countries outside Europe who wanted to return to their ancient homeland. Between 1948 and 1951, nearly 700,000 immigrants settled in the new state. However, since 1948, Israel has survived many wars, including the War of Independence (1948), the Six-Day War (1967), and the *Yom Kippur* War (1973). In the war of 1967, East Jerusalem was captured by the Israeli army, giving Jews access to one of the holiest places, the Western Wall. This important victory is celebrated on Jerusalem Day.

Israelis celebrate the first Jerusalem Day, 1968

THE PAST

Memorials have been built in many countries as a reminder of the millions of lives lost during the Holocaust. For many people, it is important to remember the horrors of the past. In Israel, people remember the tragedy on *Yom Hashoah* (Holocaust Day).

Holocaust memorial of a hand reaching to the sky, South Beach, Florida, USA

The synagogue

THE SYNAGOGUE IS AN IMPORTANT place of worship and centre of Jewish life. Derived from the Greek word meaning "place of assembly", the synogogue was essential to the survival of the Jewish faith. When the Second Temple was destroyed in 70 CE, the rabbis developed the idea of a house of worship in order to keep the faith alive among the people of the Diaspora. The importance of the Temple has never been forgotten. Even today, when a synagogue is built, a section of a wall is sometimes left unplastered and this serves as a reminder of the Temple's destruction. Unlike the Christian church, there is no set style for the exterior design of the synogogue. Often the architecture reflects the culture of the country in which they are built. The layout inside, however, follows a common pattern.

Each minaret stands 43 metres (141 feet) tall

A PLACE FOR STUDY AND PRAYER
Another name for a synagogue is *Bet Hamidrash*, meaning "House of Study". This is a reminder of the close relationship between prayer and *Torah* study. Synagogues hold classes, where older boys and young men can study rabbinic texts.

AN ORNATE SYNAGOGUE
The Dohany Synagogue in Budapest, Hungary, is the largest synagogue in Europe, accommodating up to 3,000 people. Built in 1859, the synagogue reflects Islamic influences with its decorative features and minaret-like towers.

Model of the Kaifeng Synagogue

THE PAGODA SYNAGOGUE
One of the most unusual houses of worship was the Kaifeng Synagogue of China. It was first built in 1163 by the descendants of Jewish silk merchants from Persia (modern Iran). The synagogue was rebuilt several times, but by the mid-1800s, the Jewish community in China had declined, and the synagogue was demolished.

Hechal Yehuda Synagogue

A MODERN SYNAGOGUE
This Sephardi synagogue in Tel Aviv, Israel, was designed with the hot climate in mind. Built from concrete, the white shell-like exterior reflects the heat, while cool air circulates around the cavernous interior. In Israel, there is a mixture of ancient and modern synagogues existing side by side.

There is always an Eternal Light in front of the Ark

Women can watch the service from this room

The bimah (a raised platform) from where the Torah is read

The Ark holds the Torah scrolls

INSIDE A SYNAGOGUE
All synagogues have the same internal features. This cross-section of the Old-New Synagogue of Prague, in the Czech Republic, shows the typical layout and features of a synagogue. As in all Orthodox synagogues, there is a separate section for women – in Reform synagogues, men and women sit together.

RELIGIOUS MOTIFS
The decorations used in synagogues reflect the wealth of the Jewish communities. Often they take the form of religious symbols. Shown above is a stained-glass window with the Star of David and the *menorah*.

A pair of lions represent the tribe of Judah

Eagle wearing a crown is another popular motif

Stone tablets depict the Ten Commandments

A CONTEMPORARY INTERIOR
The Beth Shalom Congregation in Pennsylvania, USA, was designed by Frank Lloyd Wright in 1953. Many contemporary synagogues, especially American ones, have the feel of a large, modern auditorium flooded with natural light.

THE SACRED FEATURE
The main feature of any synagogue is the cupboard to house the *Torah* scrolls. This cupboard is called the Ark and is always positioned on a wall that faces Jerusalem. The *Torah* is the holiest object in Judaism, so the design is given the greatest attention to detail, like this ornate Ark found in a synagogue in New York City, USA.

Prayer

PRAYER IS CENTRAL TO JUDAISM, as it is in other religions. Jews are supposed to pray three times a day – morning, afternoon, and night. Prayers can be recited alone, but it is preferable to pray with a group of at least ten people (or ten men in an Orthodox community), called a *minyan*. The prayers are contained in a book called a *siddur*, and the most famous prayer is the *Shema*, which declares the supremacy of God. Although there is no Jewish law dictating the dress code, male Jews normally wear a head covering, known as a *kippa* or *yarmulka*, and a *tallit* (prayer shawl) to pray. For morning services, other than those on *Shabbat* or a festival, a *tefillin* (two small boxes containing sacred text) is also worn. Women may wear some or all of these items in non-Orthodox communities.

TALLIT
A *tallit* may be beautifully embroidered and decorated, but the most important part are the tassels (*tzitzit*) on each of the four corners. The Book of Exodus mentions the wearing of these tassels as a visible sign of obedience to God. Jewish men, and in some cases women, wear a *tallit* to pray.

MEZUZAH
The *mezuzah* is a small container holding a piece of parchment on which the words of the *Shema* are written. It can be made of any material and is often highly decorated. The *mezuzah* is placed on the front door of a Jewish house and sometimes on all the internal doors of the house, except the bathroom.

"Hear, O Israel, the Lord is our God, the Lord is one."

FIRST LINE OF THE SHEMA

KIPPA
Some Jewish men only wear a *kippa* to pray, while others wear one all the time. It is considered respectful to cover one's head because it reminds the wearer that God is constantly present.

WESTERN WALL
The only remaining part of the Second Temple in Jerusalem, Israel, is known as the Western Wall. It is Judaism's holiest site and dates back to the 1st century CE. People come to pray at the wall, and frequently leave written messages in the spaces between the stones. The Western Wall used to be known as the Wailing Wall because it was the scene of so much weeping.

154

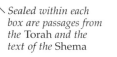

Sealed within each box are passages from the Torah *and the text of the* Shema

Tefillin strapped around the forehead

A right-handed person wears the tefillin on their left arm

The siddur

TEFILLIN
During morning services, Orthodox men wear the *tefillin*. One box is attached to the forehead, and this is said to make the wearer think of his faith. The other box is strapped around the left arm, because this is closest to the heart.

The leather straps are from a kosher *animal*

PRAYERS
In Judaism, there are prayers for all occasions. Many prayers are formal (based on verses in the *Torah*) and have to be said on special occasions, such as on the holy day of *Yom Kippur*. One of the most important prayers is called the *Shema*. This is generally the first prayer a Jewish child learns, and says every night before going to sleep. But it is also important for Jewish people to recite their own daily prayers, bringing them closer to God.

Each tassel has five knots to serve as a reminder of the Five Books of Moses

SIDDUR
In addition to all the prayers, the *siddur* contains many blessings to be said as part of daily life. The word *siddur* means "order", because the prayers are written in the order they are said for the services during the course of the year. It also reflects the fact that God created the world in a certain order.

Sacred books

THE HEBREW BIBLE consists of three books: the *Torah* (Hebrew word meaning "teaching"), *Nevi'im* (the Prophets), and *Ketuvim* (the Writings). The *Torah*, also known as the Five Books of Moses, is the most important in everyday Jewish life. Jews believe that the words of the *Torah* are the words of God as revealed to Moses on Mount Sinai 3,000 years ago. As well as the early history of Jewish religion, it gives instructions on every aspect of daily life, and religious Jews show their obedience to God by following these laws. The *Torah* is always treated with reverence, from the moment a scroll is written by a skilled scribe to its use in synagogue services.

THE FIVE BOOKS OF MOSES
Genesis is the first of the five books found in the *Torah*. It tells the story of how the world was created and covers the stories of Adam and Eve (shown above) and the patriarchs – Abraham, Isaac, and Jacob. Exodus, Leviticus, Numbers, and Deuteronomy form the rest of the *Torah*.

Sample parchment with Hebrew letters and signs

Kosher quill

TOOLS OF THE TRADE
Certain tools are used when writing a *Torah* scroll. The ink has to be specially prepared, and only a quill from a *kosher* bird can be used to write the text. The parchment for the scroll also has to come from a *kosher* animal, which cannot be killed just for its hide.

Special ink

The text is written in columns

THE SCRIBE
The *Torah* has always been written by hand, even to this day. It can take a scribe, or *sofer*, over a year to copy accurately every word. A scribe has to be a religious Jew and must train for seven years. When the *Torah* scroll is completed, it has to be checked several times before it can be used in the synagogue.

THE DEAD SEA SCROLLS

In 1947, fragments of ancient manuscripts were discovered in the caves of Qumran, near the Dead Sea, Israel. They consisted of text from almost every book of the Hebrew Bible. Written between 150 BCE and CE 68, the manuscripts would have belonged to the Essene community – an ancient Jewish sect. The discovery of the Dead Sea Scrolls shows that the Hebrew Bible has changed very little since Roman times.

This inkpot was found in Qumran and may have been used by the scribes

THE TORAH

The *Torah* is the holiest book in Jewish life. It contains 613 commandments. These are instructions for Jews on how to live a good and pious life. From the time of Moses, the laws were passed by word of mouth. Later they were written down so they would not be forgotten. Orthodox Jews adhere strictly to all the laws of the *Torah*. But there are also many Jews who only follow those laws that they feel apply to modern life.

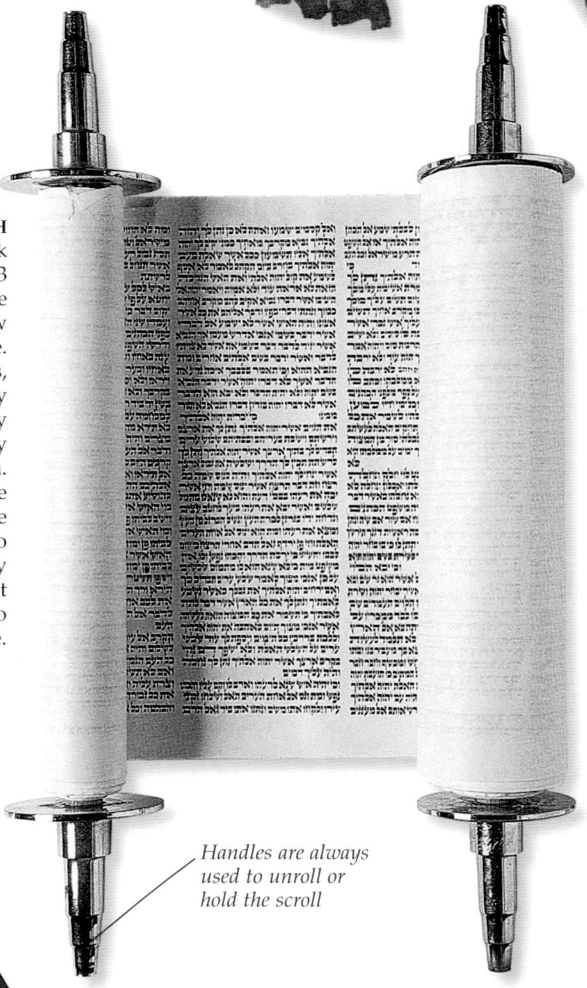

Handles are always used to unroll or hold the scroll

THE YAD

The *yad*, meaning "hand" in Hebrew, is used by the person reading from the *Torah* to point to the words. This is to preserve the handwritten text and prevent it from being damaged. If a single letter of the *Torah* is smudged, the scroll is no longer considered fit to be used unless it is repaired by a scribe.

The Torah *scroll is raised after the service and shown to the congregation*

READING THE TORAH

The *Torah* scroll is read over the course of a year with a section chanted each *Shabbat* in the synagogue. Everyone in the congregation stands up as a mark of respect when the *Torah* is taken out of the Ark.

Writings and thinkers

Noah's ark

THE IMPORTANCE OF learning has always been valued in Judaism, and the compilation of the *Talmud* and the *Midrash* illustrate this point. After the *Torah*, the *Talmud* has become the most important religious book. It was created over the years as thousands of rabbis studied the *Torah* and recorded their interpretations. Notable scholars also added comments to the wealth of religious thought and practices. One such figure was Maimonides, who was known for his theological and philosophical works. Scholars of a more mystical nature recorded the oral traditions that became the *Kabbalah*. Another book, the *Haggadah*, recounts the story of the Exodus from Egypt and has become an integral part of Jewish life.

THE MIDRASH
The *Midrash* is a collection of writings that helps to explain the stories of the Hebrew Bible, such as Noah's ark and Jonah. Written by rabbis, their goal is to teach moral lessons.

THE TALMUD
The *Talmud* is a compilation of Jewish laws with explanations provided by Jewish scholars. Completed in the 5th century, the writings cover every aspect of Jewish life, from prayers to business disputes. Subsequent rabbis added their own commentaries. One of the most famous was French-born Rabbi Rashi (1040–1105).

The main text is always in the centre of the page

Commentaries from various rabbis appear around the page

"What is hateful to you do not do to your neighbour. That is the whole Torah – the rest is commentary."

TRACTATE SHABBAT 31A, THE TALMUD

MAIMONIDES
Rabbi Moses ben Maimon (1138–1204), known as Maimonides, was a distinguished philosopher and physician. Born in Spain, Maimonides settled in Egypt, where he wrote the *Mishnah Torah*, a review of all Jewish religious laws based on the *Talmud*. He also attempted to reconcile Jewish faith with reason, based on the teachings of Greek philosopher Aristotle.

> *"Before God manifested Himself, when all things were still hidden in Him He began by forming an imperceptible point – that was His own thought. With this thought He then began to construct a mysterious and holy form – the Universe."*
>
> **THE ZOHAR**

THE HAGGADAH
Dating from the time of King Solomon's reign (c. 10th century BCE) the *Haggadah*, meaning "narrative", recounts the story of the Exodus from Egypt. It also contains blessings and psalms, and is always read before the Passover meal. The illustration above is from a children's *Haggadah*, showing the ten plagues sent by God to punish the Egyptians.

This is one of the earliest examples of an Ashkenazi Haggadah

THE BOOK OF SPLENDOUR
In Judaism, the term *Kabbalah* (meaning "tradition") represents an alternative mystical view of the world based on the *Torah*. The ideas were passed on by word of mouth and kept secret. The *Zohar*, or *Book of Splendour*, is the most important text for followers of the *Kabbalah*, introducing new rituals. The book is attributed to Moses de Leon, a *Kabbalist* who lived in Spain during the 13th century.

SEFIROT
In the *Zohar*, the *Kabbalah* is explained in terms of ten creative forces, known as the *sefirot*. These are the ten attributes by which God has created the Universe. The *sefirot* are shown as branches of a tree, and include love, wisdom, power, intelligence, and beauty.

Diagram representing the ten *sefirot*

BIRD'S HEAD HAGGADAH
This famous *Haggadah* from 13th-century Germany is illustrated with biblical scenes. As the name suggests, most of the human figures are drawn with birds' heads. Today, a *Haggadah* may illustrate contemporary events such as the creation of the State of Israel, or convey the socialist ideas of the *kibbutz*.

159

Values

Prophet
Jeremiah

JUSTICE AND EQUALITY
Over 2,000 years ago, Jewish people were already governed by a system of checks and balances. Power to govern was not vested in the hands of the king. It was left to the *Sanhedrin* (the Jewish Supreme Court) to interpret the laws of the *Torah* and apply them fairly. The prophets also rebuked those who were seen to act against the interests of the people.

For observant Jews, the *Torah* is more than just learning about the early history of Judaism and following a set of religious beliefs. It provides a moral blueprint on how to live good and honest lives. Not only are there laws governing a person's relationship with God, but there are also laws about how to treat other people. Several fundamental values are addressed in the *Torah* – the sanctity of life, justice and equality, kindness and generosity, the value of education, and social responsibility. One of the most frequent commands in the *Torah* is the *mitzvah* (commandment) of showing kindness to strangers. Jews have lived without a homeland for thousands of years, and they know what it is like to be a stranger in a foreign land. However, it is the value of human life that takes precedence, to the extent that many of the commandments may be broken to protect life. Such values are as relevant today as they were in biblical times, and are seen as an essential part of any democracy.

RESPECT FOR LIFE
Judaism emphasizes the value of human life. The life of one person is no less important than the life of another. This concern for life also extends to animals. One of the oldest laws prohibiting cruelty to animals is found in the *Torah*. In many Jewish homes, the creation of the world is remembered during *Shabbat*.

HOSPITALITY
The obligation to look after travellers and strangers is central to Judaism. Abraham, regarded as the first Jew, and his wife Sarah were always hospitable and set the tone for future generations. During the Middle Ages many Jewish villages had a guest house where travelling beggars could stay for free. One rabbi in the *Talmud* even voiced the opinion that welcoming guests is more important than welcoming God by studying the *Torah*.

Stained-glass detail of Abraham

Charity boxes are often seen in Jewish homes

REPAIRING THE WORLD
Loving your neighbour as yourself is a biblical instruction. Man was created in the image of God, and so individuals must be treated with the utmost respect and honour. Ignorance and intolerance darken the world, but understanding and love bring light and help to restore the world.

Hanukkah menorah symbolizes the triumph of good over evil

CHARITY
The Hebrew term *tzedakah* is used to describe charitable acts, and it is seen as the duty of every person to share what God has given them. Every week, before the start of *Shabbat*, coins are dropped into a charity box, and on festivals such as *Purim*, collections are taken for various charities. According to Maimonides, the best act of *tzedakah* is helping someone to help themselves by teaching them a skill.

Torah scroll and yad

EDUCATION
The importance of knowledge is stressed by the *Torah*. Education is not only seen as a means of achieving a worthwhile career, but also as a way of teaching children how to behave correctly. The *Torah* says it is the duty of every individual to pursue a good quality of life, while being respectful to others and not following the path of greed.

SOCIAL RESPONSIBILITY
One of the commandments of Judaism is to look after the welfare of others, just as God had done by visiting Abraham when he was sick. The illustration above shows the biblical figure of Job, who endured much suffering, being visited by friends. The obligation to care for one another has prevailed in Jewish communities.

Kosher food

THERE ARE LAWS GOVERNING every aspect of Jewish life, and this extends to food. The dietary laws are known as *kashrut*, and they outline the foods that can be eaten and how they should be prepared. The word *kosher* (meaning "fit" or "proper") is used to describe food that complies with these laws. Religious objects, too, have to be made in accordance with the rules. Many of the dietary laws are mentioned in the *Torah*, and others come from rabbinic interpretations. As well as being a biblical command, the food laws also serve a hygienic function and form a strong source of group identity. The degree of observance varies among Jews, with some adhering to all the laws, while others only follow certain rules.

THE KOSHER SHOP
The laws of *kashrut* are complex, so it is far easier and safer for observant Jews to buy their food from *kosher* shops. The majority of the packaged foods have a *kosher* label to show that a rabbi has visited the factory and certified that the food has been prepared correctly.

MEAT AND DAIRY
Animals that have cloven hooves and chew the cud, such as lamb, are regarded as *kosher*, but pork is not. Animals have to be slaughtered by a trained person to minimize the amount of pain. Blood also needs to be drained from the meat, because it contains the life of the animal. Meat and dairy products cannot be eaten together, and a *kosher* household must have two sets of utensils and plates to keep meat and dairy products separate.

This kosher food stall only sells meat products, such stalls are found in areas where there is a large Jewish community

Lentils

PARVE FOOD
Foods that are neither dairy nor meat are known as *parve* and can be eaten with both kinds of meals. These foods include fruit, vegetables, rice, eggs, and lentils. But fruit and vegetables have to be checked thoroughly before consumption to make sure that there are no insects – the *Torah* considers all insects to be non-*kosher*.

SEAFOOD
Only fish with both fins and scales, such as salmon, trout, and cod, are considered *kosher*. This means that all shellfish and other seafoods are not permitted. These forbidden foods are known as *treifah*.

Crab

Salmon

Shofar

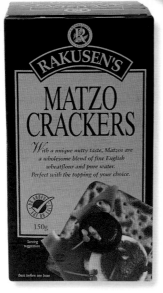

PASSOVER

There are certain ingredients, that cannot be eaten during Passover. For identification purposes, some food packages have a "*Kosher* for Passover" label, such as the package above that contains unleavened bread.

THE VINEYARD

Considerable care must be taken when managing a *kosher* vineyard. The *Torah* instructs that grapes from a new vineyard cannot be used until the fourth year, and every seven years the vineyard has to be left fallow.

RELIGIOUS OBJECTS

The laws of *kashrut* are also applicable to ritual objects. These include the *shofar*, which has to be made from the horn of a *kosher* animal. The parchment found inside a *mezuzah* or used for the *Torah* scroll also has to come from a *kosher* animal.

WINE PRODUCTION

In ancient times, Jews were forbidden to drink wine that may have been part of pagan worship, so they produced their own. Today, strict regulations apply to the production of *kosher* wine. For example, only observant Jews are allowed to oversee the production. The winery also has a supervising rabbi to make sure that all the requirements have been met before issuing a *kosher* certificate.

Torah scroll

Kosher wine

The faces of Judaism

THE MAJORITY OF JEWS TODAY are descendants of the Ashkenazi (Eastern European) or the Sephardi (Spanish). Within these two main cultural groups, there are several religious branches, which have developed over a period of time to meet the demands of contemporary life. The branches of Judaism differ in the strength of their beliefs, ranging from extreme Orthodox to those adopting a more liberal approach to life and religion. But because Judaism is more than just a faith, various customs and traditions have developed in the communities that exist around the world. For example, there is a considerable difference between the Jews of Ethiopia and those of Yemen. Essentially, what all Jews share is a common history and language, no matter what beliefs and customs they follow.

CONSERVATIVE
Solomon Schechter (1847–1915) (above) was the driving force behind the Conservative movement. Known as *Masorti* (meaning "tradition") in Israel, Conservative Jews take the middle ground between Orthodox and Reform Judaism.

REFORM
The movement known as Reform Judaism began in Germany during the 19th century. Reform Jews believe that the *Torah* and *Talmud* do not contain the literal words of God, but were written by people who were inspired by God. This means they can adapt their faith to suit modern life, such as improving the status of Jewish women. Reform Judaism is also known as Liberal or Progressive Judaism. This is the largest group of Jews in the USA.

Female rabbi

Samaritan *Torah* scroll

An ultra-Orthodox Jew praying

ORTHODOX
Orthodox Jews follow their traditional practises and faith closely. The majority of Jews who live in Europe are Orthodox. But ultra-Orthodox Jews are one of the fastest-growing groups. Uncompromising in their religious beliefs, these Jews tend to live in separate communities with their own schools and courts of law. Generally, they feel it is wrong to mix with the outside world, even with less observant Jews. Within the ultra-Orthodox movement, there are various sects, each with their own leadership, such as the Lubavitch sect in the USA.

Children in a *kibbutz*
school, Israel

JEWS IN ISRAEL

Israel is home to over 4 million Jews, the
second-largest community outside the USA.
The Law of Return, which was passed by
the Israeli government in 1950, allowed
thousands of Jews to become citizens.
Jews from countries throughout the
world were all welcomed. At the same
time, the immigrant communities in
Israel have maintained the traditions of
their country of origin. Today, a majority
of Israelis consider themselves secular
(non-religious) Jews.

SAMARITANS

The Samaritan community
in Israel can be traced back
to the 7th century BCE. Although
they do not consider themselves
to be Jews, they practise a form
of Judaism. Samaritans accept
the authority of the Five Books of
Moses, observe the *Shabbat*, and
perform circumcision. Today,
the Samaritan community
living in Israel numbers
up to 500 people.

ETHIOPIAN JEWS

The origin of Jews from
Ethiopia, known as *Beta Israel*
("House of Israel"), is a source
of debate. Some Ethiopian
Jews believe that they are
the descendants of the son
of King Solomon and the
Queen of Sheba. Others believe
that they belong to a lost tribe
of Israel. Whatever their
origins, the existence of
Ethiopian Jews only came
to light during the 1850s.
To escape the famine
in war-torn Ethiopia,
almost the entire Jewish
population was airlifted
to Israel in the
1980s and 1990s.

Ethiopian Jews take part in a blessing for Passover

JEWS OF INDIA

The Jewish community of
India is thought to have been
founded over 2,000 years
ago. There were three distinct
groups: Bene Israel ("Jews of
Israel"), the Cochin Jews, and
those from European countries
such as Spain. All groups
followed Sephardi practises
and had their own synagogues.
Today, there are only a few
thousand Indian Jews.

*Copper plate granting privileges to
a Jew, Joseph Rabban, dating from
the 11th century, Cochin, India*

Observant Yemenite
Jews study the *Torah*

YEMENITE JEWS

There is evidence of
Jews living in Yemen
from the 1st century CE.
Yemenite Jews have a
very strong scholarly
tradition and their own
prayer book, called the
tiklal. Most now live
in Israel or the USA,
though a small number
remain in Yemen.

Through a Jewish lifetime

In JUDAISM, KEY LIFE EVENTS are marked with special ceremonies. The circumcision of baby boys is a universal Jewish custom, dating back to biblical times. More recently, people have also begun to welcome baby girls with a baby-naming ceremony. *Bar* and *Bat Mitzvah* mark the point at which children become adult members of the community. Some Reform Jewish communities also celebrate a coming of age for both sexes at 15 or 16 in a ceremony called confirmation. There are specific Jewish customs marking marriage, and also surrounding death and mourning. All these life-cycle events are celebrated publicly, stressing the communal nature of Jewish life.

BAR AND BAT MITZVAH PRESENTS
This *siddur* is designed to be given to a girl on her *Bat Mitzvah*. Although gifts are often given to mark the occasion, a *Bar* or *Bat Mitzvah* is not about presents, but about taking on the responsibilities of a Jewish adult.

Birth

In addition to an English name, every Jewish child is given a Hebrew name, which will be used for the rites of passage. Often, the Hebrew name will be the same as that of a relative who has recently died. The Hebrew name of a baby boy is announced at his *Brit Milah* (circumcision) ceremony, while that of a baby girl is announced in the synagogue on the first *Shabbat* after her birth or, alternatively, at a special baby-naming ceremony.

CIRCUMCISION CEREMONY
Brit milah is carried out on the eighth day after the birth of a boy. It dates back to God's promise with Abraham that every male child be circumcised to show that he is a member of the Jewish people. A trained *mohel* (circumciser), who is often a rabbi or a doctor, performs the operation.

Paper amulet, Morocco, 20th century

CIRCUMCISION AMULETS
In former times, circumcision amulets were used by some communities to protect newborn babies against evil. These small pieces of parchment, paper, or metal were inscribed with magical signs, combinations of letters, names of angels or of God. They were worn or placed on a wall near the baby's cot. Many rabbis, including Maimonides, opposed such amulets as mere superstition.

Amulet from Germany, 19th century

Coming of Age

At the age of 13, a boy is considered to be *Bar Mitzvah* ("son of the commandment"), and becomes responsible for his religious actions. For example, he must fast on *Yom Kippur*, and he may be counted as part of the *minyan* in the synagogue. A girl is considered to be *Bat Mizvah* ("daughter of the commandment") at 12 years old. Depending on her community, she may or may not participate in a *minyan* or read from the *Torah*.

This woman wears a tallit and a kippa for her ceremony

BAT MITZVAH

Bat Mitzvah ceremonies for girls did not develop until the beginning of the 20th century. Today, this rite of passage can be marked in different ways, ranging from one in which the girl reads from the *Torah*, exactly the same as boys do, to an Orthodox *Bat Chayil*, where the girl gives a sermon in the synagogue. Some Orthodox communities do not publicly mark *Bat Mitzvah*.

Tefillin

TEFILLIN

An Orthodox boy will be given a set of *tefillin* for his *Bar Mitzvah*. From then on he is expected to pray every weekday morning wearing the *tefillin*. When not being worn, they are kept in a bag, which may be decorated with the owner's name in Hebrew.

Tefillin case with the boy's name in Hebrew

A boy reads from the Torah during a weekday ceremony

BAR MITZVAH

At a *Bar Mitzvah* ceremony, the boy is called to read a section from the *Torah*, which he has prepared in advance. This symbolizes his acceptance of the commandments. In very observant communities, a boy may read the entire *sidra* (portion) for that week – normally four to six chapters long. The *Bar Mitzvah* is celebrated after the synagogue service, where most boys also give a speech called a *dvar Torah* ("word of *Torah*").

Continued on next page

The huppah *is depicted in this ancient* Torah *binder*

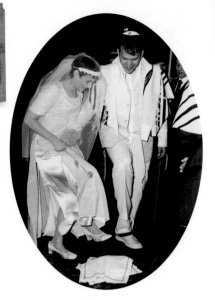

Marriage

Observant Jews see marriage as a gift from God, and it is an important religious occasion. The marriage is the start of a new home, and, often, a new family to ensure that the practices and traditions of Judaism continue. Ceremonies vary depending on whether the service is Orthodox or Reform, and there are also different local customs. Generally, Jewish weddings can take place anywhere – in a synagogue, at home, or in the open air.

BREAKING THE GLASS
The end of the ceremony is marked by the groom breaking a wine glass. This symbolizes the destruction of the Temple and the fragility of marriage. The picture above shows a Reform service, where both the bride and groom share the symbolic gesture.

THE HUPPAH
The main service is conducted by a rabbi under the *huppah*, a cloth canopy supported by four poles. In some Jewish communities, a prayer shawl is held over the bride and groom. The *huppah* symbolizes the couple's new home.

The ketubah *is beautifully decorated with motifs or biblical scenes*

THE KETUBAH
The Jewish marriage contract, which details the obligations of the groom towards his bride, is called a *ketubah*. It is signed by the groom at the start of the ceremony, although in modern weddings both the bride and groom sign the document. The *ketubah* is read during the marriage service, and decorative ones are often displayed at home.

The ornate head-dress contains the herb rue to ward off evil

WEDDING CUSTOMS
In many Jewish weddings, it is customary for the bride to wear white and sometimes also the groom. In contrast, Yemenite Jews dress in highly ornate clothing, as illustrated.

Ornate Italian wedding ring

WEDDING RING

The exchange of wedding rings was a Roman practice adopted by various faiths, including Judaism. In traditional Jewish weddings the groom places a ring on the bride's finger and blessings are recited. In the past, some Jewish communities would loan the bride a magnificent ring, often decorated with a miniature house and inscribed with the words *Mazel Tov* ("Good Luck").

AN OLD CUSTOM

Traditionally, a father would begin saving almost from the time his daughter was born so he could give her a dowry. In the case of orphans or girls from very poor families, the Jewish community would pool together to provide basic items for a dowry. In modern families, this is not considered necessary.

This necklace belonged to a Jewish bride from Bokhara, Uzbekistan, and dates from the 19th century

BRIDAL CASKET

In the past, the bride would be given gifts by the groom. The *ketubah* contained a clause saying that if the couple divorced, the woman would be able to claim these possessions as her own. This made Judaism an enlightened religion, because for centuries, Christian or Muslim wives had no formal right to any property in the event of a divorce. This bridal casket was a gift to a Jewish bride by her wealthy groom.

15th-century bridal casket, Italy

Death customs

The traditional customs associated with the last rite of passage have two purposes: to show respect for the dead and to help the grieving process. Mourners usually express their initial grief by making a tear in their clothing. It is also important for the deceased to be buried promptly (usually within three days). However, some Jews today prefer cremation. The funeral services are simple affairs, so that there is no distinction between a rich and a poor person's ceremony.

MARK OF RESPECT

From the time of the death to the burial, the body is not left alone. A special candle is also lit and placed next to the body as a sign of respect. On the eve of the anniversary another candle is lit, known as *yahrzeit* (meaning "year time"). The candle is left burning for 24 hours, the flame symbolizing the soul of the deceased.

Yahrzeit candle

An old Jewish cemetery in Worms, Germany

MOURNING CUSTOMS

A seven-day mourning period begins on the day of the burial. This is known as *shiva* (meaning "seven") and usually takes place at the home of the deceased. All mirrors in the house are covered, and mourners sit on low stools, reciting the *kaddish*, a prayer in praise of God and affirming life. For close family of the deceased, the mourning continues for 12 months, during which all parties and celebrations are avoided.

Shofar

High Holy Days

THE THEMES OF forgiveness and repentance are reflected in the most important holy days in Judaism – *Rosh Hashanah* (the Jewish New Year) and *Yom Kippur* (the Day of Atonement). These High Holy Days are commemorated in September or October, depending on the Hebrew calendar. Synagogues are filled to capacity, with many running overflow services for those who don't normally attend during the year. *Rosh Hashanah* is followed ten days later by a day of prayer and fasting called *Yom Kippur*. For Jews, this entire period is a critical time when God not only decides their fate but also shows mercy to those who want to mend their ways.

Rosh Hashanah

This festival marks the creation of the world. It is also seen as a time of judgement when God balances a person's good deeds against their bad deeds, and decides what will be in store for them in the coming year. His judgement is noted in one of three books: one for the good, one for the wicked, and one for the average person. During the next ten days, known as the Days of Awe, people are given a chance to repent, since God's final judgement is sealed at *Yom Kippur*.

THE SHOFAR
During *Rosh Hashanah*, synagogue services are longer and more solemn than usual, and include a confession and prayers of repentance. An important ritual associated with the occasion is the sounding of the *shofar*, often made from a ram's horn as a reminder of the ram that was sacrificed by Abraham. The sound of the *shofar* is also intended to be a wake-up call, inspiring people to reflect on the year that is ending and resolve to lead a better life in the coming year.

TASHLIKH
On the afternoon of *Rosh Hashanah*, some people go to a river or the sea and recite prayers. As a symbolic gesture, they empty their pockets and throw breadcrumbs into the water to represent their sins. This custom is called *tashlikh*, which means "casting away".

A Happy New Year!

Rosh Hashanah card

NEW YEAR CUSTOMS
In some communities, people send New Year cards. Unlike secular New Year celebrations, this is a time for Jewish people to ask forgiveness from God and from those who have been wronged.

Kiwi fruit

Papaya

Honey

Apple

A SWEET NEW YEAR
On the eve of the festival it is customary to eat a piece of apple dipped in honey in the hope that the new year will be sweet. People also eat an exotic fruit they have not eaten for some time or wear new clothes.

Tzedakah (charity) box

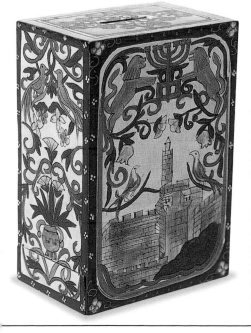

Yom Kippur

The holiest day of the Jewish calendar is *Yom Kippur*. Apart from the ill or those taking medicine, everyone above the age of *Bar* or *Bat Mitzvah* fasts for 25 hours, and most people spend the entire day praying in a synagogue to make amends with their creator. The *Yom Kippur* service ends with a single blast of the *shofar*, and everyone returns home feeling cleansed and with a new sense of purpose.

GIVING TO CHARITY
The High Holy Day prayers say that those who sincerely repent, pray, and give charity will be granted a good year. Although no money is handled on *Yom Kippur* itself, in many synagogues, the rabbi will make an appeal encouraging people to donate money to a particular charity.

Jonah being cast into the sea for disobeying God

THE BOOK OF JONAH
On *Yom Kippur* the Book of Jonah is read in the synagogue. It recounts the story of Jonah, who is asked by God to tell the people of Nineveh to repent. At first, Jonah refuses, but God forces him to deliver the message. The people ask for forgiveness and are saved, demonstrating God's compassion.

Festivals

THERE ARE MANY IMPORTANT religious festivals throughout the Jewish year. Some mark key events in the history of Judaism, while others have an agricultural significance. The festivals are celebrated not only in synagogues but with various rituals at home, too, each one marked with a different type of food. In addition, the Sabbath, or *Shabbat* in Hebrew, provides a weekly structure for the year. Each festival starts on the evening before the event and then continues on the next day, because in biblical times a day began at sunset, since that was a way of marking time.

THE SUKKAH
The *sukkah* is a temporary shelter. It is built with three walls and a small gap left in the roof so that people can see the stars – a reminder that God is looking after them. Although some families build a hut in their gardens, some synagogues also have a communal *sukkah* for people to use after the service.

Sukkot

The week-long festival of *Sukkot* (meaning "huts") is celebrated five days after the solemn High Holy Days. *Sukkot* commemorates the time when the Israelites lived in temporary dwellings during the Exodus from Egypt, and also celebrates the gathering of the final harvest. A ritual associated with *Sukkot* is the blessing over the four plants – a palm branch, an *etrog* (citrus fruit), myrtle, and willow. These are known as the Four Species, or the *Lulav*, and represent the agriculture on which we all depend.

Etrog

Willow

Myrtle

FOUR SPECIES
During the synagogue service, the four plants are are waved in all directions. This is to show that God is everywhere.

Palm branch

Blessings are recited on the Four Species

DECORATING THE SUKKAH
It is customary for children to help decorate the *sukkah* with pictures, paper chains, and seasonal fruit, representing the autumn harvest. Meals are eaten in the huts, and sometimes, people sleep there too.

THE PROCESSION
On each day of the festival a blessing is said while holding the Four Species. On the seventh day of *Sukkot*, followers end the morning service by walking seven times around the synagogue. The figure seven is symbolic of the seven processions made by the priests around the Temple during biblical times.

Simchat Torah

Immediately after *Sukkot* comes *Simchat Torah* (meaning "rejoicing over the *Torah*"). The festival marks the end of the *Torah* readings and the start of a new cycle of readings. This shows that God's words are continuous. Amid dancing and clapping, all the *Torah* scrolls are taken out of the Ark and paraded several times around the synagogue or in the streets.

A *Torah* procession at the Western Wall, Israel

Sweets are given to children in the synagogue on Simchat Torah

Chocolate coins

HANUKKAH TRADITIONS
During *Hanukkah*, people usually eat food cooked in oil, such as *latkes* (potato pancakes) and doughnuts. This serves as a reminder of the miracle of the oil. In some communities children also receive money or chocolate coins.

Latkes

Hanukkah

The festival of *Hanukkah* commemorates an important historical event. Nearly 2,000 years ago, Jews in ancient Israel were not allowed to practise their faith. A monumental battle was won when they rebelled against their foreign rulers. Judah the Maccabee, leader of the revolt, rededicated the Temple, which had been used for pagan worship. The eternal lamp was relit, and although they only had enough oil to last one day, miraculously the oil lasted for eight days.

LIGHTING THE MENORAH
On each night of *Hanukkah*, the family gathers to recite blessings, light the candles, and sing *Hanukkah* songs. The *hanukkiya*, or *menorah*, holds eight candles as well as a servant candle to light the others. The newest candle is lit first, then the others are kindled. By the end of the week, all eight candles are lit, symbolizing the miracle of the oil in the Temple.

A candle is lit on each night

THE DREIDEL
While the candles burn, children play with a special spinning top called a *dreidel*. On each of its four sides is a Hebrew letter standing for the words "a great miracle happened there".

Continued on next page

Omer

In ancient Israel, the 49 days between Passover and the festival of *Shavuot* were counted. This period was known as the *Omer*. It marked the end of the barley harvest and the start of the wheat harvest. A sheaf (*omer* in Hebrew) from the new season's barley crop was offered at the Temple in Jerusalem.

LAG BAOMER
Day 33 of the *Omer* calendar is known as *Lag BaOmer*. A rabbi, Shimon bar Yochai, is said to have revealed mystical secrets contained in the *Kabbalah* on this day. Another tradition tells the story of Rabbi Akiva, a noted *Torah* scholar who lost 24,000 of his students in an epidemic during the *Omer* period. However, on the *Lag BaOmer*, no one died. Some people light bonfires to mark the occasion.

OMER CALENDAR
Although there is no Temple or *omer* offering today, some observant Jews still count down the days between Passover and *Shavuot*. They use a special calendar to help them keep track of the days.

Omer calendar for children

SEVEN SPECIES
As well as the commandments, *Shauvot* celebrates the bringing of the first fruits (shown below) to the Temple in Jerusalem. These fruits have always been identified with the land of Israel.

Shavuot

The Greek name for the festival of *Shavuot* is *Pentecost*, from the word for "fifty", because it begins after the 49 days of the *Omer* period. *Shavuot* celebrates the giving of the *Torah* by God to Moses on Mount Sinai and the beginning of a new wheat harvest. During the synagogue service, the Ten Commandments and the Book of Ruth are read. The festival lasts for two days.

Barley

Dates

Grapes

Wheat

Figs

Olives

Children in a kibbutz school celebrate Shavuot *as a harvest festival*

Pomegranates

TRADITIONS
On *Shavuot*, some people eat dairy foods. This is a reminder of the time when the Israelites ate only dairy food while waiting to hear the commandments – they wanted to avoid eating meat forbidden in the dietary laws. Synagogues are also decorated with flowers to celebrate the giving of the commandments, and very observant Jews stay up all night learning the *Torah*.

Cup for
washing
hands

Shabbat

The Jewish day of rest, the Sabbath is
known in Hebrew as the *Shabbat*. It begins
every Friday at sunset with the lighting of
the *Shabbat* candles and ends the following
Saturday night. In Jewish communities,
the *Shabbat* is observed in various ways.

CHALLAH
The two *challah* loaves on the *Shabbat*
table recall the time when the Israelites
wandered in the desert. God gave them
manna to eat every day, but on Friday
they received double the amount.

*"Remember the Sabbath
day and keep it holy. On
the seventh day you shall
do no work."*

ONE OF THE TEN
COMMANDMENTS

WASHING HANDS
Before the start of *Shabbat*, some
Jews wash their hands three times
with a special two-handed cup.
Only when this is done can the
Shabbat meal begin.

*Shabbat
table*

HAVDALAH
The ceremony marking
the end of *Shabbat* is called
havdalah, which means
"separation". It features
a plaited candle, wine,
and sweet-smelling spices.
Havdalah emphasizes
the separation
between the holy
Shabbat and the
other days of
the week.

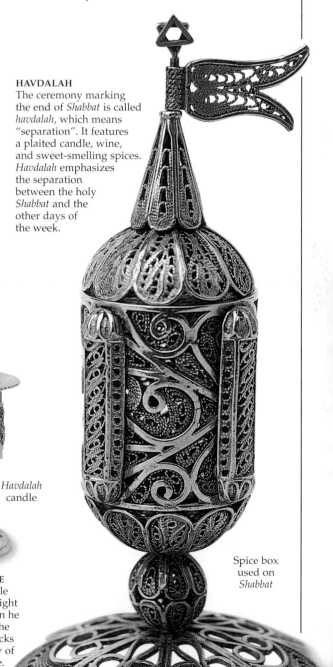

Havdalah
candle

Spice box
used on
Shabbat

THE MEANING OF SHABBAT
Just as God rested on the seventh day after creating
the world, observant Jews do not work at all on *Shabbat*.
It is traditional to invite guests home for the *Shabbat*
evening meal, especially those without families.
Essentially, *Shabbat* is seen as a time to worship,
rest, and be with the community.

PLAITED CANDLE
The *havdalah* candle
brings to mind the light
created by God when he
brought order to the
world. Its many wicks
symbolize the unity of
the Jewish people.

Jewish contribution

Despite the prejudice that existed against the Jewish people – which lasted well into the 20th century and beyond – their contribution to all aspects of life has been remarkable. Always driven by the desire to excel and inspire, both intellectually and academically, the Jewish people have felt motivated to make their mark – from the lasting legacy of music and painting to pioneering breakthroughs in science and medicine and cutting-edge technology to improve people's lives. The prejudice and hostility faced by Jews over the years, however, has often been incorporated into the emotion of their work, whether a painting, a novel, or the desire to negotiate a more tolerant and peaceful world.

The arts

From pianist to poet and author to artist, Jews have enriched the world through their passion for music, painting, literature, and design. A combination of drive and imagination, bravado and brilliance have kept them at the forefront of everything that is exciting in the arts. It was immigrants to the USA who, almost single-handedly, set up the early film studios in Hollywood – including Metro-Goldwyn-Mayer (MGM), 20th Century Fox, and Warner Brothers.

DESIGN
Arne Jacobsen (1902–71), a Danish architect, achieved fame in 1958 with his modern SAS Hotel in Copenhagen, constructed using tinted glass. This revolutionary design influenced architects the world over. During World War II, however, Jacobsen had to leave Denmark for Sweden, but returned after the war. His 1950s and 1960s furniture designs, such as the egg chair, are still selling today.

The egg chair

PAINTING
Marc Chagall (1887–1985) was born into a devoutly Jewish family in Russia, where he was first exposed to anti-Semitism. In 1910, he moved to Paris, France, to further his career as an artist, but left for the USA following German occupation. His life in Russia, together with the experiences of World War II and the revelation of the death camps, had a profound impact on his work.

MUSIC
One of the greatest violin virtuosos, Yehudi Menuhin (1916–99) impressed audiences from the age of seven, when he performed with the San Francisco Symphony Orchestra. He was world-famous for his technical ability and sensitive interpretation.

LITERATURE OF THE MIND
Sigmund Freud (1856–1939) studied medicine in Austria, and went on to develop a new science of the mind – psychoanalysis. He popularized his ideas in books such as *The Interpretation of Dreams*. Freud left Austria for England in 1938 to escape the Nazi occupation.

Community by Marc Chagall

Film poster for *Schindler's List* (1993)

FILM-MAKING
After success with films such as *Jaws* and *ET*, director Steven Spielberg gave millions of people their first insight into the Holocaust with *Schindler's List*. As part of the film-making process, Spielberg recorded the memories of more than 50,000 Holocaust survivors.

Politics

A history of a people in turmoil, together with the Jewish teaching that demands concern for less fortunate people, has led many Jews to become involved in politics. The ideal of a tolerant people living in a peaceful world continues to be a driving force at both local and national levels.

President Bill Clinton witnesses the historic handshake outside the White House, Washington, DC, USA, in September 1993

Yitzhak Rabin

PEACEMAKERS
After heading the armed forces in the Six-Day War, Yitzhak Rabin (1922–95) became Ambassador to the USA. In 1992, as Prime Minister of Israel, he put the Israeli-Arab peace process on his political agenda and, in 1995, won the Nobel Peace Prize. However, some people opposed his ideas, and he was assassinated at a peace rally in Tel Aviv, Israel.

DIPLOMACY
Henry Kissinger (b. 1923) was a refugee from Nazi Germany who went on to teach at Harvard University, USA. He later became US Secretary of State. In 1972, Kissinger organized President Nixon's historic visits to Russia and China. The following year, he was awarded the Nobel Peace Prize.

Yasser Arafat, joint winner of the Nobel Peace Prize

CHRISTIANITY

In the beginning

THE BIBLE BEGINS WITH stories of the creation of the world and the early Jewish people. These books, which make up the Old Testament of the Christian Bible, and which are also sacred to the Jews, were written by Jewish scribes long before the birth of Jesus. For the Jews they are important because they describe the covenant, or special relationship, between God and the Jewish people. For Christians the Old Testament has added significance because many of the stories seem to prefigure, or mirror, events that happened later when Jesus came to save humankind from sin.

4th-century depiction of Adam and Eve in Eden

FORBIDDEN FRUIT

Genesis, the first book of the Bible (p. 198), tells how God created Heaven and Earth, land and water, animals and birds, and finally Adam and Eve – the first man and woman. God put them in the Garden of Eden, and told them that the only fruit they must not eat was the fruit of the Tree of Knowledge.

ENEMY IN EDEN

Satan, who lived in Hell (pp. 204–205), was God's archenemy. Early Jewish writers said that the serpent in the Garden of Eden, a cunning tempter, was Satan in disguise. In the Book of Genesis, the serpent tempts Eve to eat the forbidden fruit, just as Satan later tempted Jesus in the New Testament.

The serpent is often pictured as a snake like this red spitting cobra

The forbidden fruit is often imagined to have been an apple

ORIGINAL SIN

The serpent tempted Eve to eat the forbidden fruit, and Adam followed suit. God was angry at their disobedience and threw them out of the Garden of Eden. Christians believe that Adam and Eve, and their descendants, were tainted with this "original sin". Only the coming of Jesus Christ would eventually offer humankind a way of escaping sin and achieving everlasting life with God.

This 12th-century painting of Satan shows him with Saint Michael

Saint Michael is weighing souls to determine whether they should go to Heaven or Hell

Satan

The dove brought Noah a leaf to show that the flood waters were going down

THE GREAT FLOOD

Another story in Genesis tells how God became disenchanted with all the evil in the world, and sent a great flood to destroy much of the wickedness. Only one good man, Noah, was allowed to escape with his family. He built a great boat, the ark, in which he, his sons and their wives, and all the birds and animals took refuge. Christians think of Noah as the second father of the human race, after Adam.

Mosaic of Noah and his family in the ark

"Don't hurt the boy or do anything to him. Now I know that you honour and obey God."

GENESIS 22:12
Angel of the Lord to Abraham

God provided a ram for Abraham's sacrifice

Moses window from Augsburg Cathedral in Germany

SACRIFICIAL RAM

God ordered Abraham to kill his son Isaac as a sacrifice. Abraham was about to obey when an angel told him to stop and kill a ram instead. Christians see this story as a prophecy of the way in which God would sacrifice Jesus.

Daniel window from Augsburg Cathedral in Germany

Isaiah window from Augsburg Cathedral in Germany

PROPHETS AND LEADERS

The Old Testament contains stories about Jewish ancestors such as Abraham and the great leader Moses, who guided the Jews from slavery in Egypt back to their homeland. The Old Testament also includes writings about and by prophets such as Isaiah and Daniel, who told of the coming of a Messiah, or saviour.

The birth of Jesus

THE GOSPELS (p. 199) tell how a virgin called Mary gave birth to Jesus Christ in Bethlehem. Followers of Christ (Christians) believe that Jesus was God's son, and that the prophets of the Old Testament had predicted he would come and save humankind from sin. The idea that God became human in this way is called the incarnation, meaning that God's spirit was made into human flesh. The birth of Jesus marked the origin of the Christian religion.

HUMBLE BEGINNINGS
Mary and Joseph were staying in Bethlehem at the time of the nativity, or birth, of Jesus. All the inns in the town were full, so Jesus had to be born in the humblest of surroundings – a stable.

The angels play instruments that were popular in the 16th century, when this altarpiece was made

Mary is traditionally shown wearing blue

MADONNA AND CHILD
Statues of Mary, or the Madonna, and the infant Jesus are a reminder of Mary's vital role in the Christian story. She is a link between the human and spiritual worlds.

The Holy Spirit is shown in the form of a dove

Modern mosaic from Old Plaza Church in California, USA

THE ANNUNCIATION
Luke's Gospel describes how the angel Gabriel appeared to Mary to tell her that, even though she was a virgin, she was about to become pregnant. Gabriel announced that Mary would be visited by the Holy Spirit (p. 204) and would give birth to God's son, who would be a king whose rule would last for ever. Mary was told to call her son Jesus.

John carries a banner bearing Latin words meaning "Behold the Lamb of God"

John wears camel-hair clothes, the typical garments of a prophet

JOHN THE BAPTIST
John led the life of a prophet and preacher, encouraging people to repent their sins and be baptized. John's preaching prepared the way for Jesus, and when Jesus grew up he asked John to baptize him in the River Jordan.

Statue by Donatello, 1386–1466

GLAD TIDINGS
Luke's account of the nativity describes how angels appeared to shepherds in the fields just outside Bethlehem. The angels told them the good news of Jesus' birth and the shepherds came down from the fields into the town to worship the newborn king. This story shows that Jesus is important to everyone, even "outsiders" like the shepherds.

*God looks down
from Heaven*

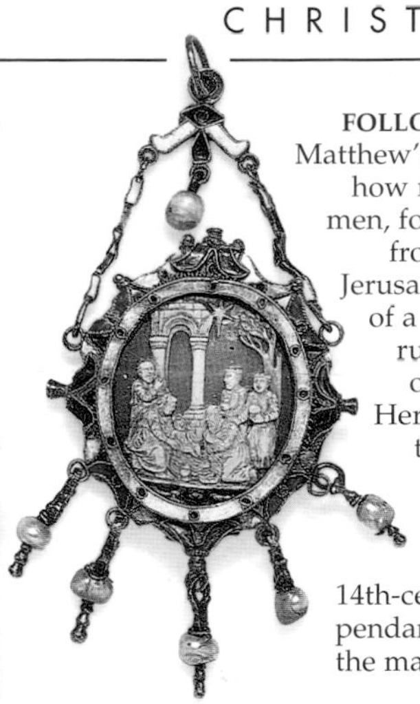

FOLLOW THE STAR
Matthew's Gospel tells how magi, or wise men, followed a star from the east to Jerusalem in search of a child born to rule the people of Israel. King Herod sent them to Bethlehem, where they found Jesus.

*14th-century
pendant showing
the magi with Jesus*

Gold

Frankincense

Myrrh

FIT FOR A KING
The magi worshipped Jesus and gave him three gifts: gold, frankincense, and myrrh. The symbolism of these gifts may be interpreted in different ways. One interpretation is that gold represents riches, frankincense kingship, and myrrh a special spiritual calling.

*The shepherds
watch their
flocks of sheep*

*15th-century
stained glass
from Ulm
Cathedral in
Germany*

ROYAL RIVALRY
King Herod ruled the Holy Land on behalf of the Romans. According to Matthew, he tried to destroy Jesus, whom he saw as a rival to his throne. Herod told his men to kill all the children in Bethlehem who were less than two years old. God warned Joseph of this, and he escaped with Mary and Jesus to Egypt.

*Mary, her husband Joseph,
and the baby Jesus*

Glazed earthenware
altarpiece made by
Giovanni della Robbia, 1521

The teachings of Jesus

JESUS' MINISTRY – his period of teaching – probably lasted no more than three years, but it had an enormous impact. During this short time he preached, taught, and performed miracles in the Holy Land, especially in the villages around the Sea of Galilee. Jesus was a brilliant teacher who could explain things in ways that everyone could understand. His teachings attracted many followers because they revealed a new way of looking at God's kingdom. He said it was open to all believers who would turn away from their sins, including the poor, the sick, and social outcasts.

FISHERS OF MEN
As this Italian mosaic shows, Andrew and Simon were fishermen. Jesus called them to be his disciples, telling them that, if they followed him, he would teach them to catch people (enlist new followers of Christ) instead of fish.

GOD'S OWN SON
The Gospels describe how, when Jesus was baptized (p. 58), the Holy Spirit came down like a dove and God's voice was heard saying, "This is my own dear Son". This momentous event, shown here in a 5th-century mosaic from Ravenna in Italy, marks the beginning of Jesus' ministry.

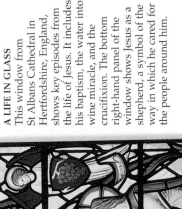

A LIFE IN GLASS
This window from St Albans Cathedral in Hertfordshire, England, shows key episodes from the life of Jesus. It includes his baptism, the water into wine miracle, and the crucifixion. The bottom right-hand panel of the window shows Jesus as a shepherd, a symbol of the way in which he cared for the people around him.

Jesus on the cross surrounded by Roman soldiers and the two Marys

Jesus turns water into wine at Cana

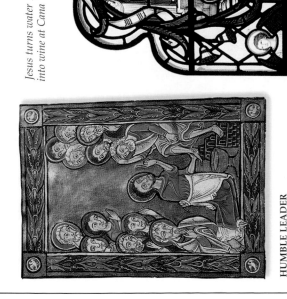

HUMBLE LEADER
Jesus called 12 disciples to be his special companions. They were expected to leave their families and possessions to follow and help Jesus, and carry on his work after his death. When he washed the disciples' feet, as shown on this French manuscript, Jesus was showing them that they should be as humble as their leader.

FEEDING THE MULTITUDE
This is the only miracle described in all four of the Gospels. After a long day's preaching, Jesus and the disciples wished to rest, but they were followed by a vast crowd who wanted to hear Jesus speak. Jesus felt sorry that the crowd had no food, and produced enough for all of them from the only available foodstuffs – five small loaves and two fishes.

Continued on next page

Terracotta jars for storing water

TAX COLLECTORS
Some members of a Jewish group called the Pharisees tried to trick Jesus into criticizing the Roman authorities. They asked him whether it was right that they should pay taxes to the Romans. Jesus showed them the emperor's portrait on the coins and said that they should give the emperor what belonged to him.

Paying the tax collector

The miracles

The Gospels describe more than 30 of Jesus' miracles. Some of these involved feeding the needy, others were "nature miracles", such as calming the storm or walking on the water. But the majority involved some sort of healing – either curing people of physical diseases like leprosy and paralysis or "casting out demons" to rid people of mental illness. The Gospels record three occasions when Jesus even raised people from the dead.

WATER INTO WINE
Jesus' first miracle, which is described in John's Gospel, took place at a wedding that he attended at Cana in Galilee. When the wine ran out, Jesus told the servants to fill six large pots with water, and when they poured the liquid out of the pots it had turned into wine. The wine was so good that the guests thought the bridegroom had kept the best until last.

CALMING WATERS
Jesus grew up in Nazareth, but moved to Capernaum, on the banks of the Sea of Galilee, where he began his ministry. Jesus did much of his teaching in this region, and one of his miracles was the calming of a storm on the lake's waters. When he wanted a quiet place to pray, Jesus travelled into the local hills, which can be seen in the background of this photograph of the Sea of Galilee's northern shore.

Continued from previous page

Parables and lessons

Jesus' favourite way of teaching was to use parables –
short stories that make their point by means of a simple
comparison. Jesus used these parables to talk about the
kingdom of God, and to illustrate how people should
behave towards each other. Jesus also preached moral
lectures called sermons. The most famous of these was
the Sermon on the Mount, in which he explained the key
features of the kingdom of God (p. 204) and the Christian
way of life. Above all, Jesus said that you should "Do for
others what you want them to do for you".

THE LOST SON
This parable tells of a man who divided his wealth between his two sons.
The younger son went off and spent his share, while his brother worked
hard at home. When the younger son returned, his father killed his prize
calf for a celebratory feast. The elder son objected, but his father said,
"He was lost, but now he has been found". These Chinese illustrations
show the story from the handing over of the money to the family feast.

SERMON ON THE MOUNT
In this sermon Jesus said that members
of God's kingdom should try to achieve
the perfection shown by God. For
example, he explained that it is
not enough simply to obey the
commandment, "Do not commit
murder". Christians should
avoid anger completely.

*The disciples have
haloes, to indicate
their holiness*

19th-
century
window of
the Good
Samaritan

THE GOOD SAMARITAN
Jesus taught that you should love your neighbour. When someone asked
Jesus, "Who is my neighbour?" he told this story: A man was robbed and
left for dead. A Jewish priest and a Levite passed, but did not help. Then a
Samaritan – a member of a group scorned by the Jews – came by. He helped
the injured man and took him to safety. The Samaritan was the true neighbour.

PLANTING WORDS
Jesus compared his words to seeds
scattered by a farmer. Some of the
seed fell on the path and was stepped
on. Some fell on rocky ground or
among thorn bushes, where seedlings
could not grow. Finally, some fell on
good soil and grew into corn. Jesus said
that people who heard and
understood his words
were like the good soil.

Sower's bag
and seeds

Figs and
fig leaf

LESSON OF THE FIG TREE
Jesus told people to think of a
fig tree. When its leaves start to
appear, people know that summer
is on its way. Similarly, they should
look out for signs of Jesus' second
coming. When strange things happen
to the moon and stars, when whole
countries are in despair, and people are
faint from fear, then they will know that
the kingdom of God is about to come.

Jesus would probably have sat down to deliver the sermon

THE LORD'S PRAYER

Jesus gave his most important lesson about prayer in the Sermon on the Mount. He told his listeners not to pray ostentatiously with long, elaborate prayers – God knows what you need before you ask. Instead, he gave them the *Lord's Prayer* beginning, "Our Father in Heaven, hallowed be your name…". It has been translated into languages as diverse as Spanish and Chinese, and is repeated in Christian churches the world over.

Horn book with the text of the *Lord's Prayer* in Latin

15th-century fresco by Fra Angelico

Common poppies

FLOWERY FINERY

During the Sermon on the Mount, Jesus told his listeners that they should not care too much about everyday things like food and clothes. Wild flowers do not have fine garments, but they are still beautifully dressed. People should be concerned with God's kingdom, not with possessions or finery.

"Happy are those who are merciful to others; God will be merciful to them! Happy are the pure in heart; they will see God!"

MATTHEW 5:7–8
Jesus' Sermon on the Mount

The crucifixion

JESUS WARNED HIS DISCIPLES several times that he would soon die. He told them that the Jewish chief priests would reject him, that he would be killed, and that he would rise again after three days. The disciples failed to understand these warnings, and were unprepared for what happened when Jesus went to Jerusalem. Jesus was put on trial and condemned to death on the cross. This is the most solemn part of the Christian story, but it is also the major turning point – Christians believe Jesus' blood was spilt so that they could be granted eternal life with God.

ENTRY INTO JERUSALEM
Jesus rode into Jerusalem on a donkey, as shown in this painting from the Oratory of Saint Pellegrino in Italy. Many people laid down palm leaves, or even their coats, to cover the dusty path in front of him. They were happy because the prophet Zechariah had predicted that their king would arrive on a donkey.

Jesus is shown with the marks of the nails in his palms

BODY AND BLOOD
At the last supper with his disciples, Jesus broke the bread and told them to eat it, saying, "This is my body". He then gave them the wine, saying, "This is my blood". When Christians celebrate Communion (pp. 52–53) they remember or recreate these events.

Christ looks triumphant, not suffering

ON THE CROSS
In Jesus' time crucifixion was the normal way in which the Romans imposed the death sentence. Jesus was crucified between two criminals, and the Gospels recall that his death took about three hours – much faster than usual. At the point of Jesus' death the curtain in the Temple in Jerusalem was torn in two and an earthquake shook the ground.

10th-century crucifix from Denmark, made of gilded carved oak

Rosary medal showing Jesus carrying his cross

A modern reconstruction of the crown of thorns

Rosary medal showing Jesus wearing the crown of thorns

THE ROAD TO CALVARY

Jesus was flogged and mocked before his death. Because he had been called King of the Jews he was forced to wear a crown of thorns. He was made to carry his heavy cross along the steep road to Calvary, the place of crucifixion. Jesus tried but he was too weak, so a spectator, Simon of Cyrene, carried it for him.

A CONDEMNED MAN

The council elders took Jesus to Pontius Pilate, the Roman governor, who had the power to impose the death penalty. Jesus was accused of setting himself up as King of the Jews but, when asked about this, Jesus simply said, "So you say". Pilate was unwilling to condemn Jesus, and said the crowd could choose one prisoner to be set free. But they refused to release Jesus.

IN DENIAL

Jesus was taken to the High Priest, Caiaphas, and was put before the supreme Jewish council. As the disciple Peter sat outside he was accused three times of being one of Jesus' followers, but he denied it each time. A cockerel crowed as Peter made his third denial. Jesus had told Peter that this would happen.

Many churches have a cockerel weather vane to remind us of the denial

THE LAST SUPPER

At the time of Jesus' arrest it was Passover – the festival that celebrates the freeing of the Jews from slavery and looks forward to the coming of the Messiah. Jesus told his disciples to arrange a Passover meal. He said that this would be the last meal he would share with them and that one of them would soon betray him.

The Kiss of Judas by Giotto di Bondone

13th-century Syriac manuscript

JUDAS KISS

After the last supper, Jesus went to the Garden of Gethsemane. His disciple Judas Iscariot arrived with Roman soldiers and the Jewish Temple guard. Judas greeted Jesus with a kiss – a signal he had agreed with the soldiers. The soldiers arrested Jesus, who told his disciples not to resist but to accept God's will.

The resurrection

CHRISTIANS BELIEVE that on the third day after his crucifixion Jesus rose from the dead. The Gospels (p. 199) describe how, when he appeared to his disciples after the resurrection, some of them did not recognize him. Jesus' body seemed to have changed, and he apparently was able to appear and disappear at will. Christians believe in the resurrection in different ways. Some are convinced that the risen Jesus was literally alive on Earth. Others believe his presence was a spiritual one, seen only in the ways in which his followers behaved. Most Christians believe that Jesus joined God in Heaven, where he will stay until the last judgement (p. 264).

STRONG SYMBOL
The resurrection is one of the most important parts of the Christian story. It is often depicted symbolically, as in the case of this embroidered decoration from a priest's clothing.

John, whose symbol is an eagle

Matthew, whose symbol is a man

THE EMPTY CROSS
An empty cross is a reminder of Jesus' resurrection. The lamb at the centre is a familiar symbol of Jesus, who is often referred to as the Lamb of God. The lamb is an innocent creature that is easily killed, so it reminds Christians of the sacrifice made by God in order to redeem humankind from sin.

Mark, whose symbol is a lion

ROCK TOMB
Joseph of Arimathea, a disciple of Jesus, offered his own tomb for Jesus' burial. This tomb was probably similar to the one above. Called an arcosolium, it has been cut into the rock of a cliff face and sealed with a large, round stone.

RISEN FROM THE DEAD
Pontius Pilate ordered soldiers to guard Jesus' tomb in case the disciples came to take away his body. But the Gospels tell how, on the third day after the crucifixion, Jesus rose from the dead while the guards slept. This set of three 15th-century Italian paintings (see also opposite) shows Jesus rising from a Roman-style sarcophagus, or tomb, set into the rocks.

SUPPER AT EMMAUS

Shortly after the resurrection, Jesus met two of his disciples near a village called Emmaus. The pair did not recognize him, but invited him to supper with other disciples. It was only when Jesus broke the bread and blessed it that they recognized him. Then he disappeared from their sight.

Illustration from a 15th-century Italian Bible

DOUBTING THOMAS

The disciple Thomas said that he would believe in Jesus' resurrection only if he saw the wounds that Jesus had received when he was crucified. John's Gospel recalls that, when Jesus met the disciples, he showed Thomas his wounds.

Mural from the Holy Trinity Church in Sopocani, Serbia, c. 1265

Jesus is shown surrounded by clouds and angels

"The Messiah must suffer and must rise from death three days later."

LUKE 24:46
Jesus to his disciples

Luke, whose symbol is an ox

THE ASCENSION

The Gospels and another New Testament book called Acts record that, after telling his disciples to spread the word (pp. 196–197), Jesus joined his Father in Heaven. He was raised up into the sky and then vanished behind a cloud.

12th-century stone relief from Saint Dominic's Abbey in Silos, Spain

THE EMPTY TOMB

A group of women, probably including Jesus' follower Mary Magdalene, went to the tomb to anoint his body with spices. When they arrived, they found the tomb open and empty. An angel appeared to them and told them that Jesus had risen from the dead. In Matthew's account of this story, the amazing news was accompanied by an earthquake.

LOOKING FOR JESUS

John's Gospel contains a moving account of Mary Magdalene's search for Jesus' body. As she wept at his disappearance, a man appeared whom Mary believed to be a gardener. But when he spoke her name, she realized immediately that it was Jesus. He said, "Do not hold on to me, because I have not yet gone back up to the Father".

God's book

THE CHRISTIAN BIBLE consists of more than 60 separate books written over many centuries. These books are divided into two main groups. The Old Testament contains the history and sacred writings of the Jewish people before the time of Jesus, which are sacred to Jews as well as to Christians. The New Testament deals mainly with Jesus and his early followers. The original texts (the Old Testament written in Hebrew and Aramaic, and the New in Greek) were translated into modern languages by biblical scholars in the 20th century (pp. 212–213).

WHO WROTE THE BIBLE?
The Bible was actually written by many different people. The books of the Old Testament were written by unknown scribes over hundreds of years. The authors of the New Testament were early Christians. Scribes later made copies of these original texts by hand using quill pens.

Quill pens and ink horns

Mosaic of the creation of the birds, Monreale Cathedral, Sicily

THE FIRST FIVE
The first five books of the Bible describe the creation of the universe and tell stories of the earliest Jewish ancestors. One of the most important stories relates how the Jewish leader Moses received the tablets of law, or ten commandments, from God. It is sometimes claimed that Moses was the author of these books.

GETTING HISTORICAL
Many of the Old Testament books are historical, following the fate of the Jewish people over hundreds of years. These historical writings describe events in the lives of notable kings, such as Solomon, who was famously visited from afar by the Queen of Sheba and her entourage.

HOLY PLACE
Built by King Solomon, the Temple in Jerusalem was the holiest of all places to the Jews. It was destroyed by the Babylonians, but the Jews eventually restored it. In the Roman period, the Temple was rebuilt again by Herod the Great. Luke's Gospel describes Jesus visiting this temple as a boy.

Artist's impression of Solomon's Temple in the time of Christ

2,500-year-old carved head of a woman from Sheba

13th-century illustration of David playing a harp

THE WORDS OF THE PROPHETS

A large number of Old Testament books contain the sayings of prophets, such as Jeremiah, Isaiah, and Ezekiel. These men brought messages from God, telling people about God's will in relation to everything from everyday life to the future of the Jewish people. To early Christians, many of the prophets' words seemed to predict the coming of Jesus.

Depiction of Jeremiah from a 12th-century wall painting from Cyprus

Illustration of Paul's death from a 12th-century manuscript

WORDS OF WISDOM

The wisdom books are a group of Old Testament books written in various styles and on a range of subjects. The Psalms (originally said to have been written by King David) contain poetry praising God; the Proverbs consist of pithy, instructive sayings; and other books, such as Job, discuss human suffering.

13th-century illustration of Jonah and the fish

STORY WITH A MORAL

God told the prophet Jonah to visit the city of Nineveh to persuade the people to repent their sins. When Jonah refused, God sent a storm. Jonah was thrown overboard from his ship, and was swallowed by a great fish. When the fish finally spewed Jonah onto dry land, the prophet went straight to Nineveh.

WORK OF GOD

The later books of the New Testament are concerned mostly with the work of Jesus' followers, who carried on his mission after the resurrection. This work is described both in the book of Acts and in the various epistles (letters) written by early church leaders such as Saint Paul.

SEEING TOGETHER

The first four books of the New Testament – the Gospels – tell the story of Jesus' life, crucifixion, and resurrection. The Gospels of Matthew, Mark, and Luke are very similar and are known as the "synoptic" (seeing together) Gospels. These were probably written soon after A.D. 65. John's Gospel is thought to have been written at the end of the 1st century.

Luke, the winged ox

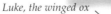

John, the eagle

The symbols of the evangelists, or writers of the Gospels, by modern artist Laura James

Matthew, the angel

Mark, the lion

Continued on next page

Continued from previous page

Later Bible texts

From the 4th to the 15th centuries, monks translated the Bible into Latin, the language of the western church. But the Reformation (pp. 212–213) brought a new demand for vernacular (local or current language) Bibles. People have been translating the Bible ever since, and today's translators try to be as accurate as possible while using words and phrases that are familiar to ordinary people.

Illuminated Bible with Latin text

THE ONE AND ONLY

Several Latin translations of the Bible were made, but the most famous was the one called the Vulgate, made by Saint Jerome in the late-4th century at the request of the pope. In 1546, the Council of Trent, a meeting of church leaders, declared the Vulgate to be the only authentic Latin text of the Bible.

The text of the Gutenberg Bible is the Latin Vulgate translation

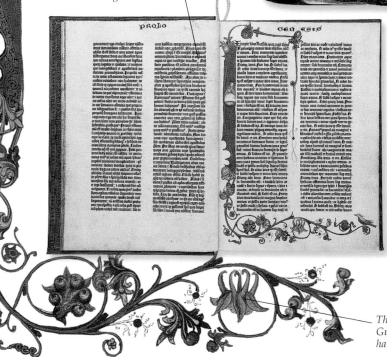

HANDY WORK

In the days before printing, monks wrote out the Latin texts of the books of the Bible by hand, often decorating the pages with beautiful illustrations. Psalters, which contain the words of the Psalms, were in great demand for use in services. This one includes an Old English translation between the lines of Latin text.

IN PRINT

Johannes Gutenberg (p. 212) produced the first printed edition of the entire Bible in Germany in 1455. Suddenly, it became possible to produce large numbers of Bibles quickly, bringing knowledge of the actual words of the Bible to more people than ever before.

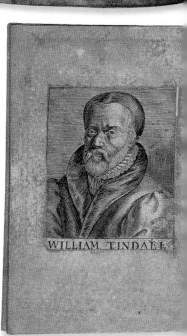

WILLIAM TINDALL

The coloured decorations in the Gutenberg Bible were added by hand after the text was printed

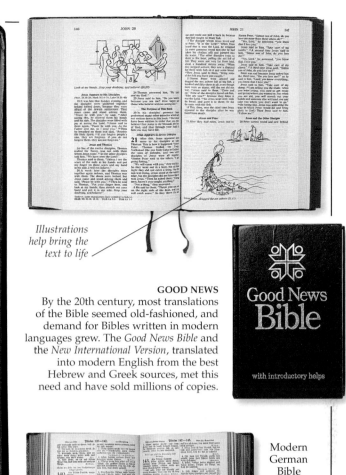

Illustrations help bring the text to life

GOOD NEWS
By the 20th century, most translations of the Bible seemed old-fashioned, and demand for Bibles written in modern languages grew. The *Good News Bible* and the *New International Version*, translated into modern English from the best Hebrew and Greek sources, met this need and have sold millions of copies.

Modern German Bible

AHEAD OF THEIR TIME
German theologians translated parts of the Bible into their native language throughout the Middle Ages. The whole Bible was translated by about 1400, but the church frowned on vernacular Bibles, and these were not widely available until after the Reformation (pp. 212–213).

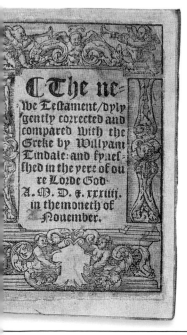

The different languages are divided into columns and blocks

A GOOD INFLUENCE
In the early-16th century, reformer William Tyndale wanted to translate the Bible into English. The English church would not allow this, so Tyndale moved to Germany, where he published his New Testament in English in 1525. This copy is a revised version, printed in 1534. It greatly influenced later Bible translators.

LOTS OF LANGUAGES
The interest in Bible translation, and the need to compare different texts, led to the production of polyglot Bibles, in which the text is printed side-by-side in several different languages. These pages come from an early polyglot Bible of 1516, with the text in Hebrew, Greek, Latin, and Arabic.

Heaven and Hell

12th-century icon from Saint Catherine's Monastery in Sinai, Egypt, depicting the last judgement

ALL CHRISTIANS believe in one eternal and almighty God, who exists as three beings – the Father, the Son, and the Holy Spirit. They believe that Jesus is the Son of God, that he lived on Earth as the son of the Virgin Mary, and that he was crucified and rose from the dead. Christians have faith that if they follow the teachings of Jesus and repent their sins they will be rewarded after death with everlasting life in Heaven – the traditional name for God's eternal kingdom. Its opposite, the place or state without God, is known as Hell.

14th-century painting of the Holy Trinity by Andrei Roublev

THREE IN ONE
The idea of the Holy Trinity, the one God who exists as three beings, is one of the deepest mysteries of Christian faith. God the Father is the almighty creator of the universe. God the Son is Jesus, God made human. God the Holy Spirit is God's power on Earth. The Bible describes Jesus as sitting at God's right hand in Heaven.

This medieval illustration shows angels blowing their trumpets as the dead rise from their graves

Angel carrying a golden censer

LAST JUDGEMENT
Christians look forward to a time when Jesus will return to Earth. They believe that he will come again in glory to judge the living and the dead. Jesus will reward the righteous with eternal life, and the kingdom of God will truly exist and have no end.

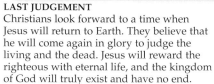

Ivory counter showing human figures fighting off the demons of Hell to ascend to Heaven, 1120

IN HEAVEN
For some, Heaven is a literal place, a paradise where God dwells. Others emphasize that Heaven is not a place, but a state of being with God for ever. Catholics (pp. 206–209) believe that a person's soul goes first to a third place, called Purgatory, where it is purified before entering Heaven.

WINGED MESSENGERS
The Bible refers to angels as spiritual beings who live with God in Heaven. They act as messengers, bringing God's words and judgements to people on Earth and providing spiritual guidance. The Bible gives few clues about what angels look like, but they are traditionally portrayed as winged beings with human bodies.

JACOB'S LADDER

The life of Jacob, one of the ancestors of the people of Israel, is described in the Book of Genesis. Jacob had a dream in which he saw a ladder connecting Heaven and Earth. As Jacob watched angels passing up and down the ladder, God spoke and promised that the land where he slept would one day belong to him and his descendants.

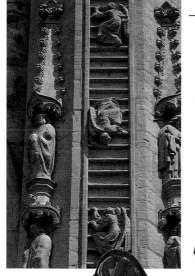

Relief of Jacob's ladder, west front of Bath Abbey, England

Angel carrying a casket that may contain saintly relics (pp. 220–221)

Angel carrying a model church

Angels are often portrayed with shining, golden wings

THE FALL OF SATAN

According to the Book of Revelation, Satan – a member of the highest rank of angels, the archangels – started a war with God. As a result he was thrown out of Heaven and started his own evil kingdom in Hell. Some Christians believe Hell to be a place of pain, where Satan and his demons torture the souls of the damned, forcing them to endure everlasting fire.

DEVILISH DEPICTIONS

Since medieval times, artists have portrayed Satan and his demons as grotesque creatures, human in form but with horns, tails, and cloven hoofs. Most Christians today are less concerned with the appearance of Satan and Hell, and are more likely to think of the torture of Hell as the agony of an existence without the love of God.

Modern Mexican stamp depicting a devil

LOTERIA DE
MEXICO 1998-99
20¢
EL DIABLITO
G. NORMA / C. VERGARA   T.I.E.V.

The Orthodox church

T HE FORM OF CHRISTIANITY that is strongest in eastern Europe and western Asia is known as the Orthodox church. It developed between the 9th and 11th centuries as a result of a split between eastern and western Christians, and claims to be closest to the faith as originally practised by Jesus' disciples. Like the Catholics, Orthodox Christians recognize several sacraments and venerate the Virgin Mary, but they do not recognize the authority of the pope. They place a heavy stress on holy tradition as revealed through the Bible and the collective decisions and teachings of the early church leaders.

ORTHODOX CHURCHES
The Orthodox church is a group of individual churches, each led by a patriarch, or senior bishop. Saint Basil's Cathedral in Moscow, Russia – with its striking onion domes – is under the leadership of the Patriarch of Moscow and all Russia.

Orthodox priests often have long beards and long hair

Greek icon showing three saints

HOLY FOCUS
Icons – usually small paintings of Jesus, Mary, or the saints – play a key part in Orthodox worship. Orthodox Christians see icons as reminders that God became human in the form of Jesus. They use them to help focus their prayers and devotions.

Russian annunciation icon

Portable icon designed to be worn as a pendant

The nails in Christ's hands are clearly visible

Crucifix icon from the Crimean War

THE HEART OF THE MATTER
Orthodox priests must be more than 30 years old, and they are allowed to be married. The celebration of Holy Communion (pp. 230–231), usually referred to as the Liturgy, is at the heart of their work. Orthodox Christians believe that, during the Liturgy, God is especially present in the wine.

ROYAL DOORS
In Orthodox churches, the sanctuary (the area containing the altar) is hidden by a screen called the iconostasis. The screen has a pair of doors called the royal doors, which are frequently beautifully decorated. These royal doors from the Russian Orthodox church in London, England, are decorated with images of the annunciation and the evangelists.

PORTABLE ICONS
Although the main place to display icons is in church, Orthodox Christians also use portable icons. These can be carried in processions, hung at shrines by the roadside, or used at home to help concentrate the mind during private prayer. Portable icons and similar items like this crucifix are especially popular in Russia.

OIL OF GLADNESS
When infants are baptized in the Orthodox church the priest immerses them three times in the font before anointing them with the "oil of gladness". The priest then performs the ceremony of chrismation, anointing the child on the head, eyes, nose, ears, and mouth. Chrismation in the Orthodox church is the equivalent to the western ceremony of confirmation (p. 236).

ORTHODOX MONASTICISM
Monasticism (pp. 222–223) began in the east, in areas such as Egypt and Syria, and is still an important part of Orthodox religious life. Orthodox Christians believe that the presence of the Holy Spirit is revealed in the lives of monks and nuns. The most famous Orthodox monasteries are on Mount Athos in Greece, a monastic republic where monks have lived since the 10th century.

Stoles were originally made of wool to symbolize the flock for which priests are responsible

The crozier symbolizes the priest's power over his flock

Cuff symbolizes the power of God's right hand

BISHOP'S BUSINESS
All bishops are equal in the Orthodox church. They do have an overall leader – the Patriarch of Constantinople (Istanbul) – but he has no authority over the others. The main authority comes from synods, or meetings, of bishops held in each of the Orthodox churches to make decisions on matters affecting the church as a whole. Orthodox bishops are not permitted to marry, so bishops begin their calling as monks not priests.

Orthodox bishop's vestments

The Reformation

During the 14th and 15th centuries, many people in Europe were worried that the Catholic church was becoming corrupt. In the early-16th century three men – Martin Luther from Germany, Ulrich Zwingli from Switzerland, and John Calvin from France – spearheaded the reform of the church across Europe. In the movement now known as the Reformation, they and their followers founded new, Protestant churches. These churches rejected the control of the pope and bishops and stressed the importance of the Bible and preaching God's word.

Medal from the 1500s depicting the pope as Satan

CHURCH ABUSES
Reformers objected to several practices in the Catholic church. One of the most widespread abuses of the church was the use of indulgences – the payment of money instead of doing penance for sins. Even some popes were corrupt, and objectors often portrayed them as devil-like figures.

Bar, to screw down the platen

Platen, used to press the ink onto the paper

The coffin is pushed beneath the platen

Ink ball, to spread the ink evenly

AGAINST CORRUPTION
This coin was made in honour of Jan Hus, a Czech priest who became a reformer in the early-1400s. He spoke out against the corruption of the church but, despite support from ordinary people, was prevented from preaching, excommunicated, forced to leave Prague, and eventually burned at the stake.

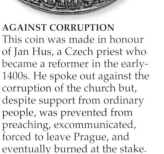

EARLY IDEAS
Englishman John Wyclif, a theologian and politician, began to demand church reform in the late-14th century. Many of his ideas – such as the denial of the pope's authority and the call for the Bible to be translated into modern European languages – were taken up by later reformers all over Europe. In this painting by Ford Madox Brown, Wyclif is reading from his translation of the Bible.

PRINTING PRESS
In the 1450s, craftsman Johannes Gutenberg of Mainz in Germany invented a new method of printing. It enabled books to be printed quickly and cheaply. This major advance allowed the ideas of the Reformation to travel around Europe at great speed.

VOICE OF REASON
Education developed rapidly at the time of the Reformation through the work of teachers like Desiderius Erasmus, shown here in a painting by Hans Holbein. His methods were different from Luther's passionate, revolutionary approach – he hoped to reform the church through reason and scholarship. Erasmus edited the Greek New Testament, which was a great help to the scholars who would later translate the Bible into modern European languages.

MOTHER TONGUE
In 1549, the Archbishop of Canterbury, Thomas Cranmer, published the *Book of Common Prayer* – a church service book in English. It enabled English people to hold services in their own language for the first time. When England briefly returned to Catholicism, under Queen Mary I in 1553, Cranmer was executed.

FAMOUS THESES
In October 1517, Martin Luther posted 95 theses (arguments against indulgences) on a church door in Wittenberg, Germany. He followed this with several books about reform. He argued that salvation came from God's grace through the individual's faith in Christ, and could not be bought.

Full- and pocket-sized copies of the Book of Common Prayer

Tympan, where the paper is put

CHURCH LEADER
In 1534, King Henry VIII forced the English church to break from Rome because the pope would not allow him to divorce his wife, Catherine of Aragon. Henry himself became leader of the English church although, apart from his rejection of the pope, he remained Catholic in his beliefs. Despite this, he began the process that brought Protestantism to England.

Gallows, to support the tympan

Bolton Abbey, England

16th-century portrait of Henry VIII by Hans Holbein the younger

DISSOLUTION OF THE MONASTERIES
Henry VIII ordered his chief minister, Thomas Cromwell, to compile a report on the monasteries in England. Cromwell concluded that many were rich and corrupt, so Henry ordered all the monasteries to be dissolved (closed). He seized the wealth of the monasteries and gave many of their lands to his lords. Most of the monastery buildings, like Bolton Abbey, were left to become ruins.

Continued from previous page

Lemon balm

Marjoram

Lungwort

Feverfew

HEALING HERBS

In the Middle Ages, monks grew plants like feverfew, lungwort, lemon balm, and marjoram to make medicines for ailments such as headaches and respiratory disorders. The monks wrote down their discoveries about the healing powers of plants in books called herbals. Herbs are still grown alongside other food plants in many monastery gardens today.

Everyday life and work

Although the divine office and prayer are at the heart of monastic life, monks and nuns are also expected to work hard to support themselves and their community. Monasteries often try to be as self-sufficient as possible, with many producing their own food, and some making items for sale. With their atmosphere of quiet contemplation, monasteries have always been centres of learning. In the Middle Ages, they provided Europe's only education and health services, and today many monks and nuns still teach in schools. They may also work in the wider community, giving aid to the sick, poor, and needy.

Benedictine monks in the refectory

FOOD FOR THOUGHT

In most monasteries, the monks or nuns eat together at long tables in a large communal refectory, or dining room. The food is simple but nourishing. Religious devotion even continues at meal times – everyone is expected to eat in silence while one of their number reads passages from the Bible.

SCENTED SERVICES

Incense – a substance that makes a sweet scent when it is burned – is used widely during services in both the Catholic and Orthodox churches. Some monasteries make incense, both for use in their own church and for sale to raise money.

Raw olibanum gum

Ground raw olibanum gum

Finished incense

Rubber gloves provide protection from the highly concentrated oil

1 NATURALLY SWEET
The naturally sweet-smelling raw olibanum gum is ground into smaller pieces. The monk then measures out a small amount of concentrated perfume oil and mixes this thoroughly with the ground gum.

2 DRYING OUT
The monk places shovels of the scented, ground gum into a large, wooden tray with a wire bottom and spreads it out evenly. He leaves the incense mixture until it is dry and then packs it up ready for sale.

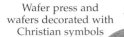
Wafer press and wafers decorated with Christian symbols

FLAT BREAD
In many churches, specially made wafers – traditionally manufactured in monasteries – are used instead of ordinary bread during Communion (pp. 230–231). The process starts with a bread dough mix. This is pressed into thin sheets, often marked with a Christian symbol, and cut into small discs. The finished wafers are then packaged and supplied to churches all over the world.

FAR FROM HOME
Many monks and nuns travel long distances to take part in aid programmes in areas that are affected by drought, war, famine, or other disasters. Members of monastic orders help to save lives and bring education to areas where there are no state schools.

Nun distributing cooking oil in Rwanda

The text is in Latin and is beautifully decorated

The desk slopes to make writing for long periods more comfortable

The nun studies the honeycomb to see if it is ready for harvesting

llelu   ya.

ursus.

om   nis tr

WRITING FOR GOD
In the Middle Ages, monks and nuns were among the few people who produced books. They wrote out each page by hand and decorated them to produce results like this beautiful music manuscript. Today, some monks preserve these ancient skills, while others are notable scholars. They write books on subjects such as the Bible, theology, and the history of the church.

Monastic scribe's desk

Wax tablet for writing holy passages on

SWEET AND SYMBOLIC
Honey is an ancient Christian symbol that reminds the faithful of the sweetness of Jesus' words. This Franciscan nun has learned the valuable skill of beekeeping, providing a nutritious food source for her sisters and beeswax for making candles. Many monks and nuns sell any honey and wax they do not use themselves to members of the public.

The angel's banner says "With the Lord a thousand years is a single day"

Plate made to commemorate the year 2000

CHRISTIAN CROCKERY
The pottery founded by the Benedictine monks of Prinknash Abbey in England produces simple wares for everyday use, and more decorative ceramics that are especially attractive to visitors. Their millennium plate bears a picture of an angel, a reminder that the year 2000 was, above all, a Christian event – the 2,000th anniversary of Jesus' birth.

The church

PRAYER IN PRIVATE
The earliest churches were often small and very simple in design. This 6th-century building in Ireland is an oratory, a place where someone can pray in private rather than a church for a large congregation. It has sloping stone walls, a single door, and no windows.

The WORD CHURCH means a community of Christian believers, but it is also used to refer to a building in which Christians worship. Churches vary widely, but most have a large main space – often called the nave – for the congregation. Many churches also have a chancel or sanctuary, which houses the altar (p. 230); side chapels, used for private prayer; a vestry, where the priest prepares for services; and a space in which baptisms take place.

Ornate holy water stoup

HOLY WATER
In many churches there is a stoup, or basin, near the door. This contains holy water with which people can cross or sprinkle themselves as they enter the building, as a way of affirming their baptism (p. 236).

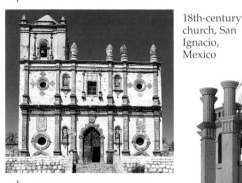

ALL SHAPES AND SIZES
There are many different church designs. The mission church at San Ignacio (above) and Saint George in the East (right) are in the baroque style, which uses decorative features adapted from buildings in ancient Rome. Both have a bell tower and a large door leading to the nave. Elaborate architecture like this is common in Catholic churches, but Protestant buildings tend to be plainer.

18th-century church, San Ignacio, Mexico

MAKING AN ENTRANCE
Church doorways are sometimes surrounded by statues of saints and biblical scenes, which remind people that they are entering a sacred building. This doorway is topped by a carving of the baby Jesus and the magi.

Carving of a bishop

Doorway to a 12th-century church at Loches in France

Bell tower

Main entrance

Model of Saint George in the East church, London, England

Carving of Saint Peter

A WORLD OF HORROR
In the Middle Ages, builders often placed carvings of ugly faces, monsters, and other weird beasts on the outside walls of churches. People looking at these grotesque carvings knew that when they went inside the church they were leaving behind the world of horror and the evil that went with it.

GOSPELS IN GLASS
In ancient churches, stained glass was a way of teaching Bible stories to ordinary people, most of whom were not able to read or write. Christian symbols like this fish from Prinknash Abbey in Gloucestershire, England, are particularly popular in modern churches.

15th-century
German
altarpiece

FOCAL POINT

Behind the altar in many churches there may be an altarpiece. This is a screen, painting, or carved relief that focuses attention on the altar itself. An altarpiece may be decorated with scenes from the Bible, images of saints, or representations of everyday life, as in this example that shows a family caring for a newborn child.

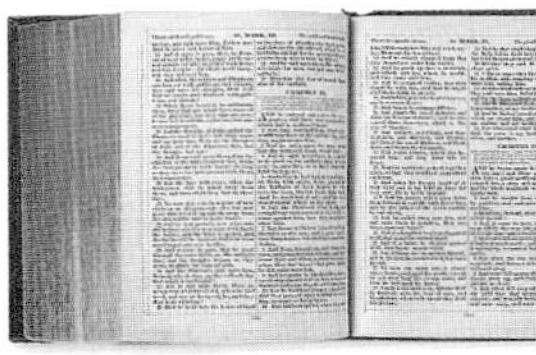

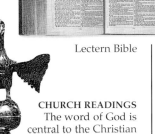

Lectern Bible

CHURCH READINGS

The word of God is central to the Christian faith and Bible-readings are part of almost every service. Most churches keep a large Bible open on a stand called a lectern. Lecterns are often made in the shape of an eagle, the emblem of Saint John the Evangelist.

Medieval lectern

ELEVATED POSITION

The structure in which the priest or minister stands to preach the sermon (p. 232) is called the pulpit. It is generally raised so the preacher can be seen and heard by everyone in the congregation. In Catholic churches the pulpit is usually set to one side, but in Protestant churches it is often central – reinforcing the emphasis on the importance of God's word.

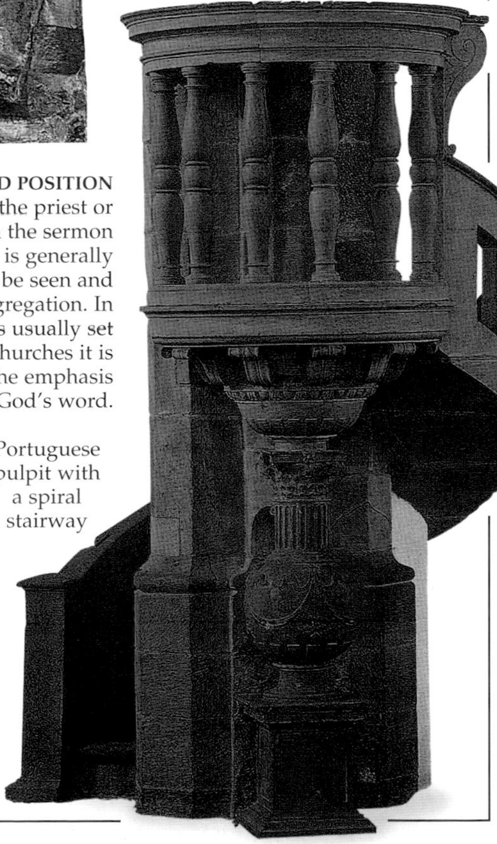

Portuguese
pulpit with
a spiral
stairway

SITTING COMFORTABLY

In a Catholic church like this English monastic chapel, the congregation sits in pews in front of the altar, which is the main focus. In Orthodox churches the altar is hidden behind a screen and there are few seats, so most of the worshippers stand. Congregations in Protestant churches tend to sit facing the pulpit.

ACTING WITH PASSION

In some parts of Europe, local people put on traditional plays enacting the story of the Passion – the events leading up to Jesus' crucifixion. In the village of Oberammergau in southern Germany, the Passion play has been staged regularly ever since the people escaped the plague in 1633. The play is now produced every ten years.

This scene is set in the disciple Simon's house

The performing arts

Music has been a part of Christian worship for centuries, and many composers in the Middle Ages were monks who spent their lives writing and singing church music. But from the beginning, religious music influenced other types of music, from extravagant choral pieces to dances and popular songs. Drama has also been influenced by Christianity for hundreds of years, and there are numerous famous films and plays with religious themes.

The parting of the Red Sea

Moses

Rameses II

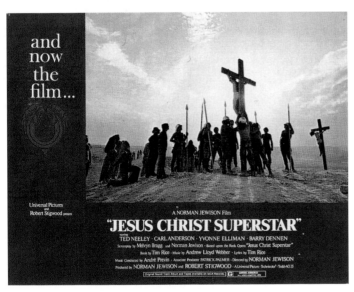

FROM STAGE TO SCREEN

The "rock opera" *Jesus Christ Superstar* was first staged in 1970, and made into a film in 1973. With music by Andrew Lloyd Webber and words by Tim Rice, the production was one of the most popular 20th-century treatments of the Christian story.

EPIC MOVIE

The Ten Commandments – a film created in 1956 by Hollywood director Cecil B. de Mille – tells how Moses led his people out of slavery in Egypt to their promised homeland. It features a huge cast, with Charlton Heston as Moses and Yul Brynner as Rameses II, and spectacular special effects, such as the parting of the Red Sea to let the Israelites pass.

> *"Sing to the Lord, all the world!*
> *Worship the Lord with joy;*
> *come before him with happy songs!"*
>
> PSALM 100:1–2
> A hymn of praise

SACRED SONGS
Sacred oratorios (a blend of solo and choral music) became popular in the 18th century. Among the most famous are J. S. Bach's two settings of the Passion story and G. F. Handel's *Messiah*. Handel wrote the piece in less than four weeks in 1741, and its portrayal of Jesus' life is still enjoyed by audiences today, especially around Christmas time.

Handel's original score of *Messiah*

Gospel choir performing in Washington D.C. in the USA

MUSICAL CONVERSATION
Baptist churches in the USA are the original home of gospel music, in which the preacher and congregation create an emotional musical conversation. The excitement of gospel music – with its sliding melodies, joyful shouts, and other vocal effects – has had a huge influence on singers in many diverse areas of modern music, from soul to rock.

THE KING
Rock and roll legend Elvis Presley learned to sing in his local church choir, and was influenced by gospel music. He combined this with rhythm and blues and country music to create a unique style. Later in his career, he recorded unique versions of a number of hymns and carols.

GRACEFUL GOSPEL
Soul singer Aretha Franklin is the daughter of a preacher and a gospel singer from Detroit in the USA. She sang with her father's choir before starting to make her own records. Her music is powerfully emotional and full of strong vocal effects, showing her roots in gospel music. Her album *Amazing Grace* is a collection of reworked gospel songs.

ISLAM

Early Arabia

THE ARABIAN PENINSULA is home to the Arab people. There had already been advanced cultures in this area before the birth of Muhammad, the Prophet of Islam, in the sixth century. Arabia's position at a crossroads between Asia, Africa, and Europe allowed many Arabs to make fortunes trading. Although most of the Arab tribes worshipped their own idols, Christians, Jews and followers of Abraham worshipped one God. When Muhammad told them that the religion of the One God had been revealed to him and that at last they had a message, the Qur'an, in their own language and a religion called Islam, some were enthusiastic.

SOUTH ARABIC INSCRIPTION
The Sabaeans, who ruled southern Arabia between the eighth and second centuries BCE, used a script called South Arabic. Archaeologists have found many inscriptions in this angular script, which passed out of use after the Sabaeans lost power.

DATE HARVEST
Settlements grew up at the small oases that are dotted around the Arabian Peninsula. Here there was a reliable water supply and date palms grew, providing a succulent harvest for the local people.

DESERT DUNES
Much of Arabia is desert – either vast expanses of sand with rolling dunes or the desert of black volcanic rocks around the city of Mecca. The name Arab means "nomad" because, in such an environment, many Arab people adopted a nomadic way of life in order to survive.

PETRIFIED FOREST
The Arabian Peninsula is, for the most part, an inhospitable terrain of desert and harsh landscapes, such as these jagged rocks. The most fertile area is Yemen, which gets monsoon rains from the Indian Ocean.

WOMAN FROM PALMYRA
The city of Palmyra in the Syrian desert was built where several trade routes met. Its people became rich because they charged merchants a tax when they passed through. This Palmyra woman is displaying her wealth in the form of gold jewellery.

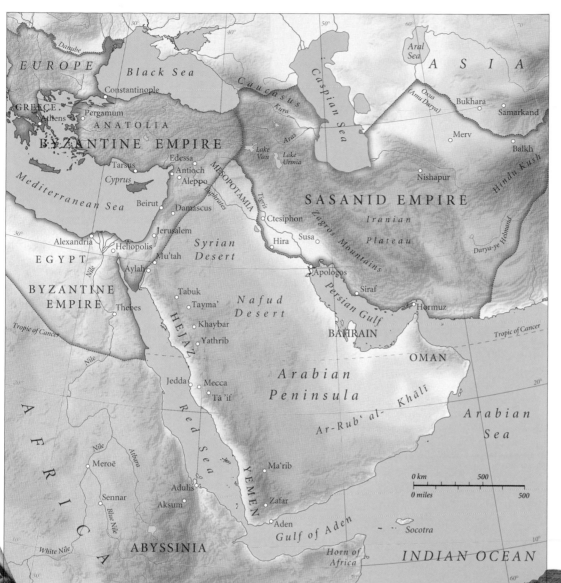

The Arab world at the time of the birth of the Prophet Muhammad in 570

THE ARAB WORLD

The Arabian Peninsula lies between the Red Sea and the Persian Gulf. The Arab peoples built towns in the fertile area of Yemen, at oases, and on the coasts. To the northeast, the Sasanid empire of the Persians occupied Iran. To the northwest, lay the Christian Byzantine empire.

Altar for burning frankincense

PRECIOUS PERFUME

Frankincense was one of Arabia's most prized products, and it was widely traded. Trade routes criss-crossed the peninsula and many of the area's early cities, such as Ma'rib and the Nabatean town of Petra (in modern Jordan), grew up along the roads. Trade has been vital to the area ever since.

WALLS AT MA'RIB

Ma'rib, in Yemen, was the capital city of the Sabaeans, and some of its ancient walls survive. Ma'rib was built on a trade route and grew into a large, thriving city, with a palace (home of the Queen of Sheba) and many houses. There was also a famous dam, an amazing feat of engineering for the seventh century BCE.

The Prophet Muhammad

MUHAMMAD WAS BORN IN 570 in the city of Mecca (in what is now Saudi Arabia). He was a member of the Quraysh tribe. Orphaned as a boy, he was brought up by his grandfather and uncle. His mission as Prophet of Islam began in 610, when the Qur'an was first revealed to him. Three years later, Muhammad began to preach. He attracted some followers, but his teachings about the one God were not widely welcomed in Mecca, where most of the people worshipped idols, many different pagan gods. Eventually he moved to the city of Medina, which became the centre of a great Islamic civilization.

ARCHANGEL GABRIEL
The Qur'an (pp. 248–249) was revealed to Muhammad by the archangel Gabriel, the angel of revelation. On an occasion known as the Night of Destiny, the revelation began. Then the Qur'an was communicated in small parts over a number of years.

WRITTEN OR SPOKEN
This calligraphy represents the name of the Prophet, Muhammad. According to tradition, he actually has 200 names, including Habib Allah (Beloved of God) and Miftah al-Jannah (Key of Paradise). When referring to Muhammad, and other prophets, Muslims usually add the phrase *'alayhi-s-salam* (peace be upon him).

The word "Muhammad" written in calligraphy

THE LIFE OF A TRADER
As a young man, Muhammad became a merchant, working for a wealthy widow called Khadija. Arabia was criss-crossed with trading routes linking the peninsula with the Mediterranean and the Indian Ocean. Muhammad travelled with camel caravans along these routes and made several trading journeys as far as Syria. Khadija was impressed with Muhammad, and, although she was considerably older than him, the two married.

JABAL AN-NUR
Jabal an-Nur (the Mountain of Light) a few kilometres from Mecca, is the place where Muhammad went to meditate. Every year, during the month of Ramadan (p. 253), Muhammad retired to the mountain to pray, fast, and give to the poor. It was on one of these retreats that the Prophet received the first revelation of the Qur'an.

THE PROPHET
Muhammad, whose name is shown here in stylized form, is the Prophet of Islam. Muslims see him as the last of a series of prophets, including Abraham, Moses, and Jesus, all of whom were mortal.

ON THE MOUNTAIN
When visiting Jabal an-Nur, Muhammad stayed in a cave called Hirah, at the top of the rocky peak. The cave, with an opening that faced towards Mecca, was quite small, but there was enough space for Muhammad to pray. One of the Prophet's daughters used to climb the mountain to bring him food so that he could stay at the cave for the whole month of Ramadan.

Star pattern based on "Allah" in Arabic script

ALLAH

Allah is the name of the one God in whom Muslims believe and upon whom all life and all existence depends. He is unique and infinitely greater than any thing He has created. The Qur'an says that He is "unbegotten". In other words, He is eternal, having no origin and no end. He is and always will be.

The Prophet's mosque

MEDINA

Muhammad was persecuted in his native Mecca and some of his followers took refuge in Abyssinia (present-day Ethiopia) under the Christian ruler there. In 622, people from the city of Yathrib, later called Medina, to the north of Mecca, invited Muhammad to go and live there. The Prophet and his followers took up the invitation. Their migration, known as the *hijrah*, forms the start of the Islamic era. Eventually Muhammad defeated the pagans and cleared the idols from the Ka'ba, so Islam could flourish in Mecca, too.

Muhammad's face is veiled because Islam does not allow him to be depicted.

The archangel Gabriel

The Buraq

THE NIGHT JOURNEY

One night the archangel Gabriel woke Muhammad and led him to a steed called the *Buraq*, which the Prophet mounted (p. 293). The *Buraq* carried Muhammad to the "Furthest Mosque" in Jerusalem, from where he ascended to heaven.

MUHAMMAD'S TOMB

The Prophet died in the lap of his favourite wife, 'A'isha, in her apartment near the mosque at Medina. His tomb was built where he died. Later, his close Companions Abu Bakr and 'Umar, the first two caliphs, were buried on either side.

Pattern based on names of the Companions

COMPANIONS

The Prophet's Companions were his closest followers. They listened carefully to his teachings, memorized the Qur'an, and passed it on to others before it was written down.

The Qur'an

I<small>N THE YEAR</small> 610, the archangel Gabriel appeared to the Prophet Muhammad and through Gabriel, Allah began to reveal the Qur'an, the holy book of Islam. This continued for 22 years. Muslims believe that the Qur'an, Allah's final revelation to humanity, completes the sacred writings of the Jews and Christians, but is on a higher level because its text consists of Allah's actual words. Ever since the Qur'an was revealed, Muslims have preserved its words, first learning them by heart, and later also writing them down. They aim to live by the Qur'an.

QUR'AN CONTAINER
This beautiful inlaid box is designed to contain a copy of the Qur'an divided into 30 sections. One section is read on each night of Ramadan, the month of fasting, a time when the Qur'an is read intensively.

DECORATED QUR'AN
This copy of the Qur'an is open at the beginning of one of its 114 chapters, or *suras*. Each *sura* has a name that comes from a notable word that occurs in its text.

This box gives the number of verses in the sura. The box at the top gives the name of the sura.

Bold *Kufic* script

KUFIC SCRIPT
Arabic can be written using several different types of script, the earliest of which is called Kufic, from the town of Kufah (in modern Iraq). This example of eastern Kufic is from a copy of the Qur'an written out before the year 1000. The script has an angular but elegant appearance with long upright and horizontal strokes.

Eastern *Kufic* script

"Praise belongs to Allah, the Lord of the worlds, the Merciful, the Compassionate, the Master of the Day of Judgement. Thee only do we serve; to Thee alone we pray for help. Guide us on the straight path, the path of those whom Thou hast blessed, not of those against whom Thou are wrathful, nor of those who are astray."

SURA AL-FATIHA, OPENING CHAPTER, THE QUR'AN

ON A GEMSTONE
In the eyes of a Muslim, this gemstone (below) has been made far more valuable as it has a Qur'anic inscription on it, which is translated below.

"Allah – there is no god but He, the Living, the Everlasting. Slumber seizes Him not, neither sleep; to Him belongs all that is in the heavens and the Earth..."

AYAT AL-KURSI, THRONE VERSE, THE QUR'AN

TILE AND TEXT
All over the Muslim world, beautifully written quotations from the Qur'an are used for artistic decoration. Muslims everywhere learn Arabic, the language of the Qur'an. This shared knowledge brings together Muslims from all countries and backgrounds.

The text on this page is the opening chapter, Sura al-Fatiha, which is translated below to the left.

MUSHAF
When people talk about "the Qur'an", they are usually referring to a book that has the Qur'an written in it. However, originally the Qur'an was recited only and Muslims learned it by heart. Later, it was written down and the written version was called a *mushaf*, which means a collection of pages. A *mushaf* will usually indicate whether each *sura* was revealed at Mecca or Medina.

WRITING IT DOWN
Copying the text of the Qur'an is something that must be done with care and reverence – none of Allah's words must be altered. To make a hand-written copy of the Qur'an like this is an activity of great religious devotion.

The Five Pillars of Islam

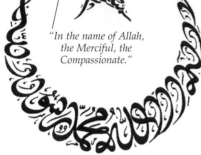

"In the name of Allah, the Merciful, the Compassionate."

CRESCENT MOON AND STAR
A crescent moon with a star above it was used as a symbol by the Turks in the 15th century. Since then it has become the symbol of Islam. The words of the *Shahada* in Arabic calligraphy have been used here to form the shape of the moon. The words, "In the name of Allah, the Merciful, the Compassionate", make the star.

SHAHADA
The Muslim profession of faith is called the *Shahada*. The English translation of it is: "There is no god but God; Muhammad is the messenger of God." Muslims use the Arabic word for God, which is "Allah". When Muslims use the term Allah, they are referring to the same God that is worshipped by Christians and Jews. The words of the *Shahada* are heard often in the Muslim world because they are repeated during the call to prayer. The *Shahada* is normally whispered in a Muslim baby's ear at birth and at the time of death.

THERE ARE FIVE FUNDAMENTAL requirements of Islam, called the Five Pillars of Islam. The first and most important is the profession of faith. Islam, which means "submission" and comes from the word "peace", is considered by Muslims to be a restating of the same truth – belief in the one God – that was revealed to the Christians and the Jews. This faith was revealed through all God's prophets, including Moses and Jesus, or Musa and 'Isa as they are known in Arabic. Muslims believe that God's final and most universal message was revealed to the last of the prophets – the Prophet Muhammad. Faith in this one God is the basic belief of the Islamic religion. The remaining four Pillars of Islam require all Muslims to be committed to prayer, almsgiving, fasting, and the pilgrimage to Mecca.

Prayer

Muslims must pray at five set times during the day. These regular prayers, known as *salah*, make up the second Pillar of Islam. Muslims may pray on their own or in a group, but every Friday at midday, Muslim men are required to gather together for *salat al-juma'a*, or Friday prayers. Friday prayers are led by an imam (literally "one who stands in front"), who will also give a sermon, or *khutba*.

All members of the community are considered equal in the eyes of Allah so they all perform the same rituals of ablution and prayer.

RISE UP FOR PRAYER
Five times each day the *adhan*, or call to prayer, is heard in Muslim communities. The times for prayer are between first light and sunrise (*fajr*), just after noon (*zuhr*), in late afternoon (*'asr*), after sunset (*maghrib*), and evening (*'isha*). The traditional practice is for someone to make the call from the minaret. The first muezzin was Bilal, a freed black slave, chosen for his fine voice.

PREPARING FOR PRAYER
Before prayer, a Muslim must prepare by ridding the mind of distracting thoughts and by cleansing the body. Ritual washing is normally done using running water – either at the fountain at the mosque or using a tap and basin in the home. In places where there is no water, such as the desert, Muslims may use sand or a stone for ritual cleansing.

IN THE DIRECTION OF MECCA
Because Muslims face the Ka'ba in Mecca during prayers, they need to know the direction, *qibla*, of the city. In the Middle Ages, people made instruments to work out the direction. In mosques, a niche, *mihrab*, in the wall indicates the direction of Mecca.

Qibla indicator

PRAYER BEADS
Allah is referred to in many different ways, known as *al-asma al-husna*, meaning the 99 beautiful names. Many Muslim names, such as 'Abd al-Rahman, servant of the Merciful One, are based on one of these names. The string of 99 beads, like a rosary, that a Muslim uses in private prayer, is a reminder of the 99 Divine names.

PRAYER MAT
The majority of Muslims pray on a mat, and some people take this with them wherever they go, so that they are always able to use it. Prayer rugs are often beautifully made, but any mat, from a silk rug to a piece of reed matting, may be used. It is also quite permissible to pray on the uncovered ground, provided that it is clean.

Prayer beads may be used to repeat the 99 beautiful names, or to repeat other phrases used in prayer.

Iranian prayer mat

1 THE RAK'A BEGINS
The words Allahu Akbar – Allah is greater (than all else) – open the *rak'a*. Then Allah is praised, and the first *sura*, or chapter, of the Qur'an, called *al-Fatiha* – the Opening – is spoken, together with a second *sura*.

3 PROSTRATION
This position, known as *sujud*, shows the Muslim's humility. The worshipper says silently, "Glory to my Lord the Most High. Allah is greater."

4 SITTING
This seated position, called *julus*, gives the opportunity for a short silent prayer. Then the prostration is repeated. The sequence concludes with a short prayer for the community of Muslims and for the worshipper's sins to be forgiven.

5 PEACE
The final stage is called *salam*, or peace. The person looks to left and right, and then says, "Peace be with you and the mercy of Allah". These words are addressed to all present, seen and unseen.

2 BOWING DOWN
When another passage from the Qur'an has been recited, the worshipper bows down, to show respect for Allah. This motion, called *ruku'*, is followed by *qiyam*, standing and praising Allah.

Stages of prayer

Prayer is performed following a precise order of words and motions. Each unit of this order is called a *rak'a* and is composed of several stages. During prayers the *rak'a* is repeated two, three, or four times – the exact number depends on which of the five daily prayers is being performed.

Continued on next page

Almsgiving

The giving of alms (gifts) to the poor and needy is very important in Islam. Of all the ways in which one can give to the poor, the most formal is by paying a tax called *zakat*, which is one of the Five Pillars of Islam. The amount of *zakat* that a person has to pay is worked out as a percentage of their wealth. The tax is distributed among the poor and may also be used to help other needy members of society.

WATER SUPPLY
In addition to paying *zakat*, a person may make other personal donations to help the community. These can provide useful facilities such as this public drinking fountain in Istanbul, Turkey. Many Muslim countries are in dry areas where water can be hard to come by, so giving money for a fountain is especially useful.

PUBLIC BATHS
Hygiene is very important in Islam, and baths are a common sight in towns in Muslim countries. They are often paid for by donations. A typical public bath has a changing room, often roofed with a shallow dome, connected to a series of rooms at different temperatures. The hottest of all is the steam room, where the bather works up a sweat before being cleaned and massaged.

HOSPITALS
The places where the sick are treated are another group of facilities that have been paid for by almsgiving. This beautiful latticed window is part of a hospital originally financed with almsgiving contributions. Medicine was one area where the Muslim world made many advances before the West (p. 268).

MONEY OR GOODS
Zakat is commonly paid in money but may also be given in the form of goods. In both cases, rates of payment are laid down, starting at 2.5 per cent of a person's wealth. A person's home and other essential items are not counted when working out what they will pay. The word *zakat* means "purification", because it is believed that giving up part of your wealth purifies what remains.

FOR LASTING GOOD
This document details a gift made to the state for good works. This type of gift is known as a *waqf*, and once given, it cannot be reclaimed. Gifts like this go towards the upkeep of mosques and buildings such as hospitals.

FOOD FOR THE POOR
In some parts of Muslim India, large cooking pots, or *deghs*, are used to prepare food outdoors. At the shrine of Ajmer, two *deghs* are used to make food for the needy, and people visiting the shrine make charitable gifts of food for the pots.

A PROPER MEAL
During Ramadan, Muslims break their fast after sunset with a light snack, which may consist simply of a few dates with water. Sunset prayers are followed by the main meal. This is a bigger meal, but should not be too large because Muslims are not encouraged to eat heavily after the day's fast. In addition, the snack should have already taken the edge off a person's hunger, so a simple dish, such as vegetable soup with bread, is eaten.

JOYFUL PROCESSION
When the great solemnity of the month of Ramadan comes to an end, there may be a procession. This illustration, from a 13th-century book from Baghdad, shows a procession accompanied with trumpets and banners.

Fasting

Muhammad received the first revelation of the Qur'an during the month of Ramadan, and this month has a special significance in Islam. Every day during Ramadan, Muslims fast from dawn to sunset, avoiding food, drink, and sexual relations. Although this fast, or *sawm*, is one of the Pillars of Islam, not everyone has to go without food. For example, those who are too sick to fast, women who are pregnant, and very young children may be excused.

SIGNALLING RAMADAN
In many Muslim countries, it is the custom to fire cannons before the first day of Ramadan, to signal the beginning of the month. Cannons are also used to signal the beginning and end of each day of Ramadan.

ENDING RAMADAN
The end of Ramadan is marked by the festival of *'Id al-Fitr* – the feast of the breaking of the fast – (p. 292). At the beginning of this festival, the whole community gathers at an outdoor prayer area (or at a mosque) to perform the *'Id* prayer. Celebrations last for three days, during which time alms are given to the poor, and friends may exchange gifts.

Continued on next page

Continued from previous page

Pilgrimage

The final Pillar of Islam is pilgrimage, or *hajj*. All Muslims aim to perform this "greater pilgrimage" once in their lives. *Hajj* involves a series of rites that take place annually over several days at the Sacred Mosque at Mecca and the nearby areas of Mina, Muzdalifa, and Arafat. A shorter pilgrimage to Mecca, known as *'umrah*, forms part of the *hajj*, but may be performed by itself at any time of the year.

AT THE KA'BA

Upon arrival in Mecca, the pilgrims perform *'umrah*, when they circle seven times around the Ka'ba and then pray near the Station of Abraham. In memory of Hagar, the mother of Abraham's eldest son, Ishmael, the pilgrims then run back and forth between two small hills known as Safa and Marwa after drinking water from the well of Zamzam.

HAJJ

After performing *'umrah*, the pilgrims leave Mecca and travel to the valley of Mina. On the second day, they go to Arafat and pray for forgiveness. This is said to give pilgrims a foretaste of the Day of Judgement, when they will rise from the dead, have their souls judged by Allah, and enter paradise if they are worthy. On their way back, they stop at Muzdalifa, where they spend part of the night resting, praying, and gathering small pebbles before returning to Mina. On the third day, they throw seven of the pebbles at the largest of the three stone pillars, which represents the temptations of Satan. For the following two days, the pilgrims stay at Mina and throw further pebbles at the pillars. They must also make an animal sacrifice. They then wash, and clip their hair or shave their heads, to symbolize a new beginning, before returning to Mecca to make the final seven circuits around the Ka'ba.

CLOTHS OF THE KA'BA

The Ka'ba (below) is a stone building, roughly 13 m (43 ft) across, that stands at the centre of the Sacred Mosque at Mecca. It is a sanctuary dedicated to God that dates back to the time of Adam. The Ka'ba is covered with a black cloth embroidered with verses from the Qur'an. Every year, the cloth is renewed and pieces of the old cloth (left) are given away. These fragments are treated with reverence, as is this cloth that once hung inside the Ka'ba.

Piece of cloth from the Ka'ba

GUIDEBOOK

GUIDEBOOK

An ancient guidebook to Mecca illustrates features of the Sacred Mosque. It shows the stepped *minbar*, from which the sermon is preached (p. 257), together with a hanging lamp.

Tile with the Plan of the Sacred Mosque at Mecca, known in Arabic as the Masjid al-Haram

Quotation from the Qur'an saying that the pilgrimage to Mecca is a duty for all who can make their way there

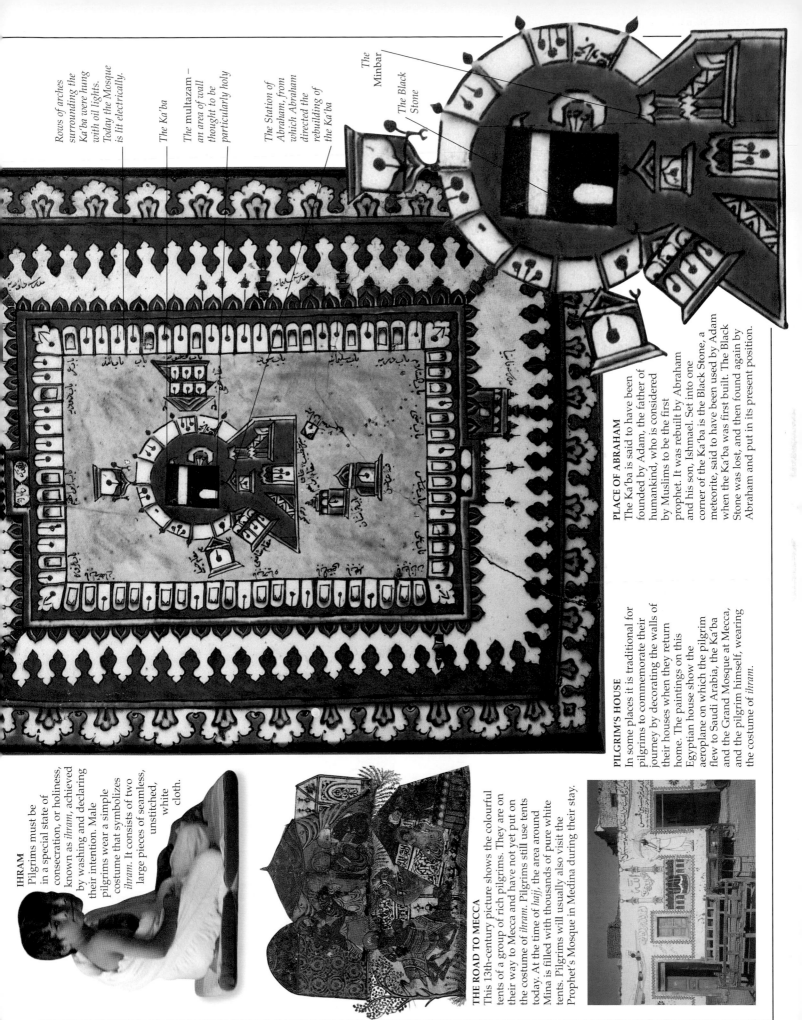

Rows of arches surrounding the Ka'ba were hung with oil lights. Today the Mosque is lit electrically.

The Ka'ba

The multazam – an area of wall thought to be particularly holy

The Station of Abraham, from which Abraham directed the rebuilding of the Ka'ba

The Minbar

The Black Stone

PLACE OF ABRAHAM

The Ka'ba is said to have been founded by Adam, the father of humankind, who is considered by Muslims to be the first prophet. It was rebuilt by Abraham and his son, Ishmael. Set into one corner of the Ka'ba is the Black Stone, a meteorite, said to have been used by Adam when the Ka'ba was first built. The Black Stone was lost, and then found again by Abraham and put in its present position.

PILGRIM'S HOUSE

In some places it is traditional for pilgrims to commemorate their journey by decorating the walls of their houses when they return home. The paintings on this Egyptian house show the pilgrim flew to Saudi Arabia, the Ka'ba and the Grand Mosque at Mecca, and the pilgrim himself, wearing the costume of *ihram*.

IHRAM

Pilgrims must be in a special state of consecration, or holiness, known as *ihram*, achieved by washing and declaring their intention. Male pilgrims wear a simple costume that symbolizes *ihram*. It consists of two large pieces of seamless, unstitched, white cloth.

THE ROAD TO MECCA

This 13th-century picture shows the colourful tents of a group of rich pilgrims. They are on their way to Mecca and have not yet put on the costume of *ihram*. Pilgrims still use tents today. At the time of *hajj*, the area around Mina is filled with thousands of pure white tents. Pilgrims will usually also visit the Prophet's Mosque in Medina during their stay.

The mosque

MOSQUES ARE BUILDINGS that are specifically used for prayer and are open for prayer all the way through the week. In addition, mosques fulfil several other functions in the Muslim community. They provide places where religious discussions can take place, and where education and charitable work can be organized. Most mosques serve their local area and form the spiritual centre of the local community. They are built and run by local people, though they may be funded by donations from the wealthy. In addition, a town has one main mosque, where Friday prayers are held.

CENTRES OF LEARNING
Many big mosques have libraries, which contain books on religious subjects, including Islamic law. In addition, it is common for mosques to have schools where children learn to memorize and recite the Qur'an.

INSIDE A MOSQUE
Mosques vary enormously in design, from simple plain rooms to vast ornate buildings – there is no one standard design. All that is really needed is a space in which the community can pray and some way of indicating the direction of Mecca. But there are standards of behaviour and dress that must be observed inside every mosque. People take off their shoes and cover their heads before going in, and often an area of the mosque is reserved for women.

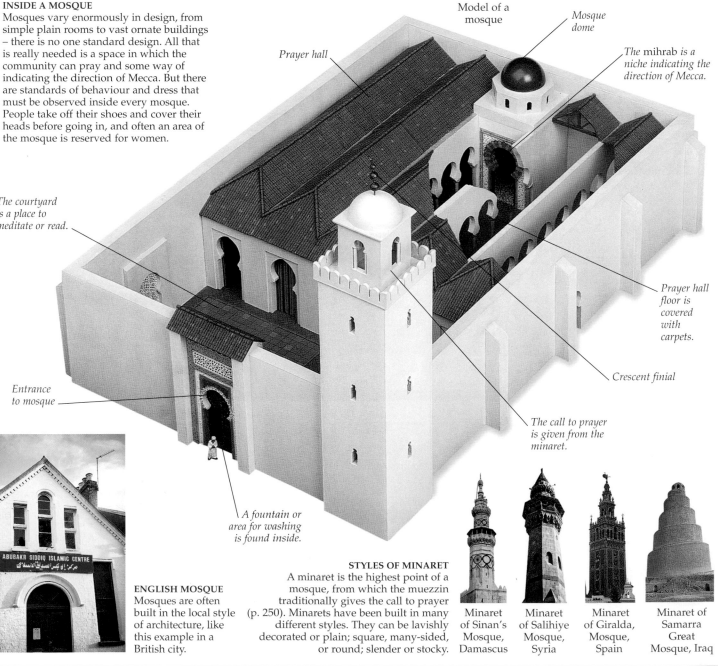

Model of a mosque

Prayer hall

Mosque dome

The mihrab is a niche indicating the direction of Mecca.

The courtyard is a place to meditate or read.

Prayer hall floor is covered with carpets.

Crescent finial

Entrance to mosque

The call to prayer is given from the minaret.

A fountain or area for washing is found inside.

ENGLISH MOSQUE
Mosques are often built in the local style of architecture, like this example in a British city.

STYLES OF MINARET
A minaret is the highest point of a mosque, from which the muezzin traditionally gives the call to prayer (p. 250). Minarets have been built in many different styles. They can be lavishly decorated or plain; square, many-sided, or round; slender or stocky.

Minaret of Sinan's Mosque, Damascus

Minaret of Salihiye Mosque, Syria

Minaret of Giralda, Mosque, Spain

Minaret of Samarra Great Mosque, Iraq

MINBAR

At Friday prayers the congregation listens to the *khutba*, a sermon given by the imam from a raised pulpit called the *minbar*. Some *minbars*, which can be beautifully adorned with inlay and carving, have survived from 1,000 years ago.

OIL LAMP

The traditional way of lighting a mosque was to use oil lamps. These large, hanging lamps could be brightly decorated, like this example of bronze covered with gold and silver, so that they reflected the light and shone more brightly. People who wanted to give alms often made gifts of money for oil for the lamps in their mosque.

15th-century mosque lamp

Mosque finial of Selimiye Mosque in Turkey

Elaborate tile decoration

BLUE MOSQUE IN ISTANBUL

In 1453, the Ottomans took over Constantinople (modern Istanbul). The Christian churches there were lavishly decorated and roofed with domes. Ottoman architects built their mosques in a similar style. One of the greatest is the Sultan Ahmed Mosque, known as the Blue Mosque because of its blue-tiled interior.

SYDNEY MOSQUE

The first Muslims to reach Australia were Afghan and Punjabi camel drivers, arriving between 1867 and 1918 to provide essential outback transport services. Many more Muslims arrived during the late 20th century.

AFRICAN MOSQUE

The earliest mosques had more simple designs, like this 16th-century mosque in Africa. Domes and intricate decoration developed later. The nature of the building, however, is not significant in a mosque. Its function as a meeting place to pray is the most important thing.

MOSQUE DECORATION

As Muslims prospered, they devoted more of their wealth to their faith, and some mosques were adorned with sumptuous decoration, like these tiles atop a minaret in Turkey. Carpets for the prayer hall were another favourite gift.

The caliphate

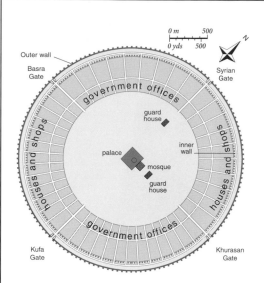

0 m   500
0 yds   500
N

Outer wall
Basra
Gate
Syrian
Gate

government offices

guard house

palace
inner wall

mosque

guard house

government offices

houses and shops

houses and shops

Kufa
Gate
Khurasan
Gate

THE ROUND CITY OF BAGHDAD
The first dynasty of Islam was the Umayyad, who ruled from Damascus, Syria. In 749, they were replaced by the Abbasid caliphs who ruled for over 500 years from their capital in Baghdad, Iraq. The city was founded in 763 and was planned as a great circle. This shape, with gates aligned with the compass points, was like a map of the universe.

THE ROLE OF THE CALIPH
The caliph was the symbolic head of the Muslim community throughout the world. He was expected to rule in accordance with Islamic principles and to lead the army. He also gave authority to Muslim leaders who were often very powerful in their own right. The Mamluk sultanate, for example, ruled in Egypt until the 16th century. This is a Mamluk mosque lamp. Such lamps were often decorated with script from the *Sura al-Nur* of the Qur'an (right).

I_N 632, THE PROHET MUHAMMAD died leaving no obvious successor, so prominent Muslims came together to choose a leader. They elected Abu Bakr and gave him the title *khalifa* (caliph), which means "successor" or "viceroy". Some people thought that the right candidate was 'Ali, the Prophet's cousin, who had married Fatima, the Prophet's daughter. Those who favoured 'Ali as caliph became known as Shi'i Muslims, "supporters" of 'Ali. In 656, 'Ali became caliph, but Muslims were still divided about how the caliph should be chosen. Sunni Muslims supported the system of an elected caliphate. Shi'i Muslims believed that the caliphs should be descended from 'Ali and Fatima.

"Allah is the Light of the heavens and the Earth; the likeness of His Light is as a niche wherein is a lamp."

SURA AL-NUR, LIGHT CHAPTER, THE QUR'AN

THE FIRST FOUR CALIPHS
Abu Bakr, 'Umar, 'Uthman, and 'Ali were the first four caliphs and are greatly revered. As close Companions of the Prophet, they followed his example. Because of this they are known as the Rightly Guided Caliphs.

EARLY CALIPH
Representation of living creatures is discouraged in Islam because it is believed that Allah alone should have the divine right of creation. However this early portrait shows a caliph, in a style imitated from pre-Islamic Persian coins.

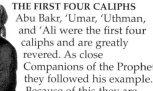

Dhu'l-Faqar, the twin-bladed sword of 'Ali

CALIPH'S GIFT
Rulers like eighth-century caliph Harun al-Rashid were very powerful. Harun exchanged gifts with Charlemagne, the Frankish emperor who ruled a vast area of western Europe. He sent Charlemagne this jewelled jug, with an elephant.

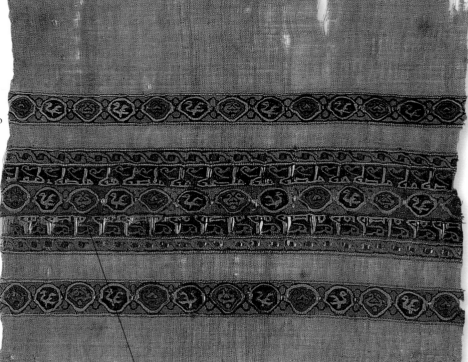

Repeating calligraphic inscription

TIRAZ
Some caliphs gave courtiers, ambassadors, and foreign rulers lengths of specially made cloth – *tiraz* – or robes, woven with calligraphy. In particular, this was a custom of the Shi'i Fatimid caliphs (who claimed to be descendents of 'Ali and Fatima) of Cairo. The cloths were inscribed with the caliphs' names, Islamic prayers, or poems, and were highly prized.

Calligraphy reads, "Allah, Muhammad, Fatima, and 'Ali, Hasan and Husayn."

SHI'I STANDARD
In 680 at Kerbala, the army of the Umayyad caliph killed Hussayn, son of 'Ali and Fatima. The battle standard (above) was used to mark the point at which the Shi'i army collected before the battle began and was then a focal point for the army. What happened at Kerbala divided Shi'i and Sunni Muslims still more deeply. Today, around one tenth of all Muslims are Shi'i.

LADEN WITH GIFTS
One of the duties of the caliph was to protect the holy cities of Mecca and Medina, together with pilgrims journeying there. Pilgrims often travelled with camels heavily loaded with gifts.

Inscription proclaiming the unity of Allah

UMAYYAD COIN
Abd al-Malik, one of the Umayyad caliphs, minted this coin when they ruled from Damascus, Syria. After their defeat by the Abbasids, an offshoot of the Umayyad caliphate ruled Muslim lands in the West from Spain.

ATATURK
The last caliphs were the Ottoman rulers of Turkey. In 1923, Turkey's first president, Kemal Atatürk, came to power. He decided to modernize his country and in 1924 he abolished the caliphate.

First conquests

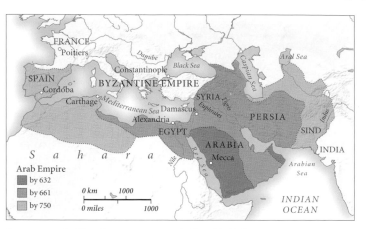

THE FIRST THREE CALIPHS Abu Bakr, 'Umar, and 'Uthman, expanded their territory quickly, creating an empire that eventually stretched from the Arabian Peninsula to Spain. Much land was gained by military conquest, but Islam also spread peacefully into areas where local rulers made alliances with the caliphs. People of other religions living in these areas – Jews, Christians, and Zoroastrians – became known as *dhimmis* (protected people) because they were protected in return for the payment of a tax. Later, other peoples, including Hindus in western India, also became *dhimmis*.

CROWN OF RECCESUINTH
This crown was worn by an early Muslim ruler of Spain, at the request of his wife, who was a princess of the Germanic people, the Visigoths.

EXPANDING EMPIRE
By the end of 'Uthman's reign in 656, the empire included Arabia, Palestine, Syria, Egypt, Libya, Iraq, large parts of Persia (modern-day Iran), and Sind (modern-day Pakistan). The Umayyad dynasty (661–750) expanded into the rest of North Africa and Spain and pushed eastwards.

MAP OF JERUSALEM
This mosaic map shows Jerusalem in the sixth century. It must have looked like this in 638 when, during the reign of caliph 'Umar, the Muslims conquered the city. For many centuries, the city's Islamic rulers governed Jerusalem in a way that was tolerant of the Jews and Christians who lived there and regarded it as a holy place.

ROCK OF GIBRALTAR
Muslim forces landed in Spain in 711, arriving first on the Rock of Gibraltar under their commander, a Berber former slave, Tariq, from whom Gibraltar takes its name (Jebel Tariq). By 715, they had taken over most of Spain, settling mainly in the south, and soon their armies were entering France.

MOSQUE AT DAMASCUS
Under the Umayyad dynasty, the city of Damascus in Syria became the capital of the Islamic empire. The Umayyads built the Great Mosque in the early eighth century.

MOSQUE DECORATION
Mosques were built all around the empire, and many were lavishly decorated. This arch, above a doorway at the Great Mosque in Damascus, shows how Muslim stone masons used different marbles, together with inlays and mosaics made of other brightly coloured stones.

RUINS OF CARTHAGE
The great North African city of Carthage, first the home of the Phoenicians, had been ruled by the Romans before it became an outpost of the Christian Byzantine empire for a short time. The victim of many battles, in 697–8 Carthage fell to Muslim armies. The native Berber population who lived there soon accepted Islam and joined the westward drive of the Muslim forces.

Roman triumphal arch, Carthage

CHARLES MARTEL, KING OF THE FRANKS
In the eighth century, much of western Europe was ruled by a Germanic people called the Franks, under their king, Charles Martel. In 732, Charles defeated the Muslim army between Tours and Poitiers, France, which marked the north-western limit of the Muslim empire. Five years later, he also drove the Muslims out of southern France.

OUT IN FORCE
This image from an early manuscript shows Muslim soldiers gathering near their tents. Soldiers like these, efficient and well disciplined, were greatly feared in western Europe. They advanced as far as France to conquer areas such as Languedoc and Burgundy.

BATTLE STANDARD
In 1212, Spain saw a battle at Navas de Tolosa, between the Almohads, the local Muslim dynasty, and a Christian army. The Almohads, who marched behind this standard, were defeated, and Muslim power in Spain was weakened.

Scholars and teachers

AL-AZHAR UNIVERSITY
Cairo's al-Azhar University was founded in the 10th century and became the world's most famous Islamic university. Renowned for its philosophical and theological scholarship, its name means "the resplendent". Many academic traditions, such as the distinction between graduates and undergraduates, began at al-Azhar.

LEARNING HAS ALWAYS PLAYED a huge part in the Islamic world. A system of education developed in which children learned to memorize and recite the text of the Qur'an at school. When they had mastered this, they could become students at a higher-level school called a *madrasah*. Still more advanced study could be followed at university. From the beginning, Muslim education had a religious basis, and the high standards produced scholars in a range of fields, from mathematics to poetry.

AVICENNA
The scholar Ibn Sina (980–1037), known in the West as Avicenna, wrote many important books on medicine and philosophy. In both fields, he developed the work of the ancient Greeks.

MADRASAH AT CAIRO
A *madrasah* was a school in which subjects such as law, logic, mathematics, and history were taught. *Madrasahs* were usually arranged around a courtyard, with large halls for teaching and smaller rooms for the students.

GLOBE
By the 13th century, Muslim scholars knew a vast amount about astronomy (p. 267). They produced celestial globes like this to show the positions of stars in the sky.

SCHOLAR'S TOMB
Sometimes a famous scholar is commemorated with a large tomb. Bin Ali, a notable scholar of the 14th century from Yemen, was buried in this striking double-domed tomb near Dhofar, Oman.

QUR'AN
Arabic scholarship has always been central to Islam. Muslims traditionally learn to recite the entire Qur'an by heart, and they always recite it in the original Arabic, whatever language they use in everyday life.

LIBRARY BOOKS
Centres of learning grew up in big cities such as Baghdad, Iraq, and Damascus, Syria, and these had libraries that were often much larger than the collections in western cities and universities.

LAW BOOK
Muslim scholars produced some very advanced laws. From the earliest times, for example, Muslim women – unlike women in the West – had the right to own and inherit property. This book contains information about how inheritance was calculated.

A MULLAH
A mullah is a person who is learned in religion. Most mullahs have had a formal religious training, but the title can be given to someone with a reputation for religious scholarship.

POETRY READING
Recited or set to music, poetry was important in Arabia even before the time of Muhammad. It continued to be popular. As well as religious subjects, common poetic themes were love and politics.

Inkpot of agate and gold

AGATE INKPOT
Calligraphy was an important and respected art. While most writing materials were simple, some very fine pieces, like this 19th century inkpot, were also made.

Continued on next page

Writing

For Muslims, writing is one of the most important of all skills. Because Muslims believe that the Qur'an contains the words of Allah, scribes wish to reproduce those words correctly and with as much beauty as possible. Many Muslims therefore practise calligraphy, the art of beautiful writing. Calligraphy does not only appear in books. It is also used to adorn buildings and other objects, providing decoration that carries a meaning.

EARLY SCHOLARS
This illustration from a 16th-century Persian text shows two children at Qur'anic school. Here they would receive the traditional education of young Muslims, learning to read, write, and recite the text of the Qur'an by heart.

Flowing maghribi script is one popular style of Islamic calligraphy.

STUDENTS AT WORK
Some Muslim children, like these in Uzbekistan, still attend traditional Qur'anic schools. In many places, modern schooling has replaced this as the main type of education, although children may attend both kinds of school.

HORSE CALLIGRAPHY
Some Muslim calligraphers can make beautiful pictures using the curving forms of Arabic script. This horse is made up entirely of Arabic script, adorned with different coloured inks.

Inscription written in legible form

STONE BANNERS
Calligraphy is used on many Islamic buildings. At this *madrasah* in Konya, Turkey, bands of carved calligraphy curve around the doorway and cross in a knot-like form above it, like fabric banners.

PEN AND INK
Early calligraphers used pens made out of pieces of reed (left), cut to a point with a sharp knife. Black ink was made from soot, mixed with a little water to make it flow.

Animal-hair calligraphy brushes for larger characters

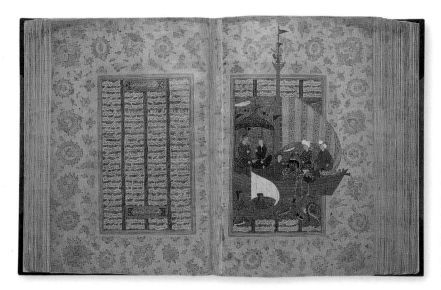

INKWELL
Two bands of calligraphy decorate this inkwell, which was made in Iran in the 16th century. It would have inspired its user to produce writing of beauty and elegance.

BOOK OF KINGS
This book is an epic poem composed in Iran. It is written in a flowing form of Arabic script called *nasta'liq*. The long curves in the script are said to look like birds' wings.

BOOKBINDER
An Indian craftsman holds the pages of a book together to bind them. Bookbinding became an important craft because of the need to protect copies of the Qur'an.

Animal-hair calligraphy brushes for smaller characters

BROAD-BRUSH EFFECTS
Although a lot of calligraphy is done with pen and ink, an animal-hair brush is another useful tool for broad strokes and for filling in colours between black outlines. These brushes are made with goat- and wolf-hair.

ARABIAN NIGHTS
The Thousand and One Nights, or *Arabian Nights*, is a collection of stories said to have been told to a king, Shahryar, by his wife Shahrazad. Full of adventure, these magical stories are still entertaining readers today.

The spread of learning

ISLAMIC SCHOLARSHIP IS NOT just based on the study of the Qur'an. In a famous saying, Muslim scholars are told to "Seek knowledge, even unto China." In the Middle Ages, there were well-known Muslim scholars in many fields, from astronomy and mathematics to medicine and natural science, and in most areas their ideas were among the most advanced in the world. The Islamic scholars gained much of their knowledge from the ancient world. They translated the works of ancient Greek scholars, preserving information that had been lost or forgotten. The Muslim scholars then built on this with their own original work, carefully recording all their discoveries.

BAGHDAD
Under the Abbasids, the walled city of Baghdad became an important centre of learning, with its own university and numerous schools. The city was at its height during the reign of Caliph Harun al-Rashid, who ruled from 786–809. At this time, it was the intellectual centre of the Muslim world.

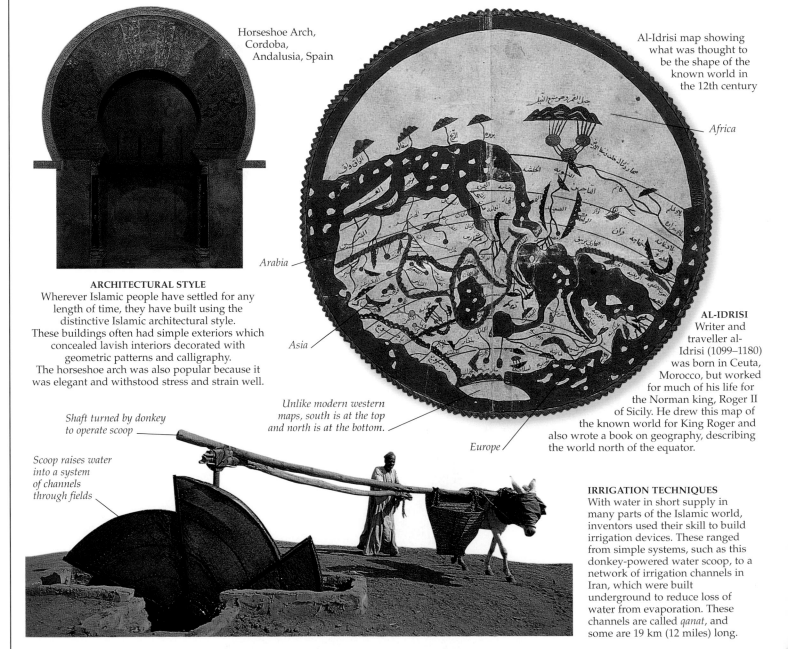

Horseshoe Arch, Cordoba, Andalusia, Spain

Al-Idrisi map showing what was thought to be the shape of the known world in the 12th century

Africa

Arabia

Asia

ARCHITECTURAL STYLE
Wherever Islamic people have settled for any length of time, they have built using the distinctive Islamic architectural style. These buildings often had simple exteriors which concealed lavish interiors decorated with geometric patterns and calligraphy. The horseshoe arch was also popular because it was elegant and withstood stress and strain well.

Unlike modern western maps, south is at the top and north is at the bottom.

Europe

AL-IDRISI
Writer and traveller al-Idrisi (1099–1180) was born in Ceuta, Morocco, but worked for much of his life for the Norman king, Roger II of Sicily. He drew this map of the known world for King Roger and also wrote a book on geography, describing the world north of the equator.

Shaft turned by donkey to operate scoop

Scoop raises water into a system of channels through fields

IRRIGATION TECHNIQUES
With water in short supply in many parts of the Islamic world, inventors used their skill to build irrigation devices. These ranged from simple systems, such as this donkey-powered water scoop, to a network of irrigation channels in Iran, which were built underground to reduce loss of water from evaporation. These channels are called *qanat*, and some are 19 km (12 miles) long.

Astronomy

The science of astronomy was important to Muslims because it could be used to work out the direction of Mecca, so that people knew which way to face during prayers. It also helped them to determine the correct times to pray. As a result, Islamic astronomy became highly advanced. Astronomers developed better instruments, made precise tables showing the movements of the planets, and put together accurate calendars. We are still influenced by these scientists – the names of certain stars derive from Arabic words.

JAIPUR OBSERVATORY
This observatory at Jaipur, India, was built during the 18th century. Many of its instruments are built of stone. These include great curving quadrants, which astronomers used to measure the height of planets as they moved across the sky. The astronomers at Jaipur were successful because they drew on knowledge from both the Arab world and from earlier Indian scientists.

ISTANBUL OBSERVATORY
In 1575, when the Ottoman empire was at its height, the astronomer Taqi ad-Din founded an observatory at Galata (now part of Istanbul, Turkey). This painting of the time shows the astronomers with their equipment, which includes a globe, a sand glass for timing, items for drawing, and all kinds of sighting devices.

Persian astrolabe

ASTROLABE
The astrolabe is an instrument for measuring the height of a star or planet in the sky. It was probably invented by the ancient Greeks, but Muslim scholars and craft workers developed the instrument, making it more accurate and incorporating more data to show the positions of a variety of different stars. It was especially useful to travellers because it could help them to determine their position at sea.

Scales showing the positions of different stars

Central pivot

Rotating arm with pointer

Written instructions for using quadrant

Plumb line

Scale

Arabic quadrant

ASTRONOMY LESSON
This group of scholars is watching as their teacher demonstrates an astrolabe. There were many observatories where lessons like this would have been held. These centres expanded rapidly in the ninth century, during the reign of Caliph 'Abd Allah al-Ma'mun. The caliph founded the House of Wisdom in Baghdad, which included an observatory, and ordered the scientists there to produce more accurate astronomical tables.

QUADRANT
This was the simplest instrument for measuring the height of a star. It consisted of a quarter-circle-shaped framework with a scale on the curving part of the frame and a plumb line hanging down vertically. The user looked at a star through a hole in the frame. The height of the star was shown at the point where the plumb line touched the scale.

Continued on next page

Continued from previous page

Medicine

Early Islamic medicine was very sophisticated for its time. Doctors knew a great deal about the diagnosis and treatment of diseases, anatomy, childcare, public health, and even psychiatry – and much of this knowledge is still relevant today. Medicine was also well taught, with students travelling thousands of miles to study at famous centres such as Baghdad's 'Adudi hospital.

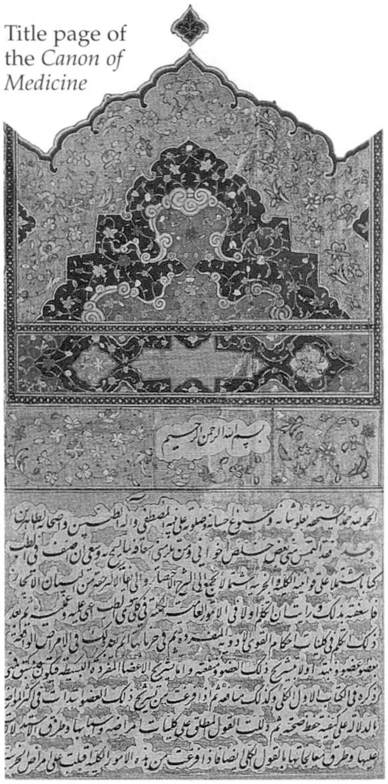

Title page of the *Canon of Medicine*

CANON OF MEDICINE

The most famous book by scholar Ibn Sina (p. 262) is the *Canon of Medicine*. Ibn Sina based much of this book on the writings of ancient Greek physicians. A huge work, it covers such basic subjects as anatomy and hygiene, describes a vast range of diseases and injuries, and lists hundreds of different medicines.

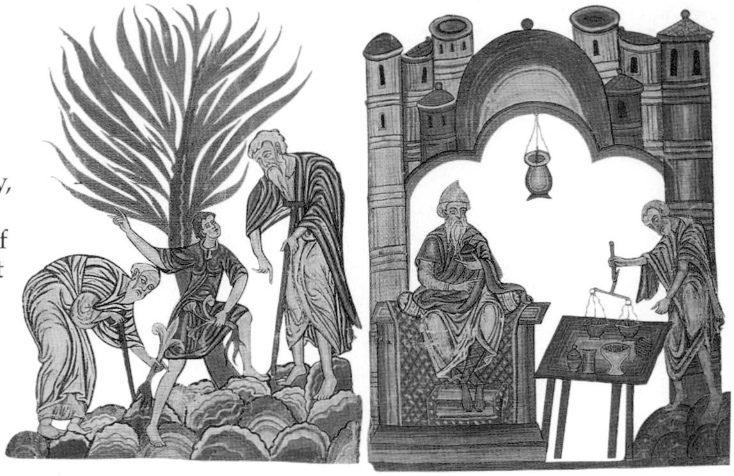

THE ART OF THE PHARMACIST

The Islamic world produced the first skilled, specially trained pharmacists, who made their own medicines and worked closely with physicians. By the early ninth century, privately owned pharmacies were opening in Baghdad, where a flourishing trade with Asia and Africa provided a variety of medicinal herbs and spices. Pharmacies were soon appearing in other cities.

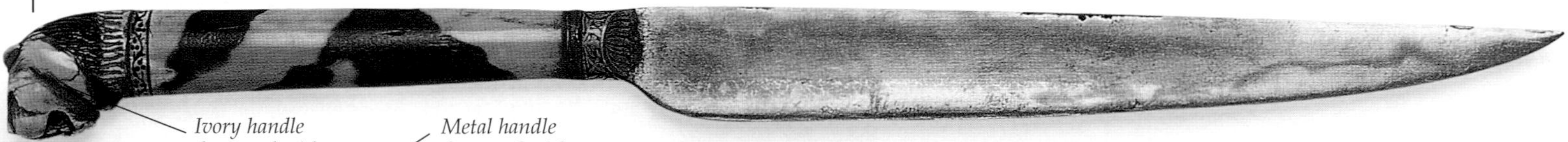

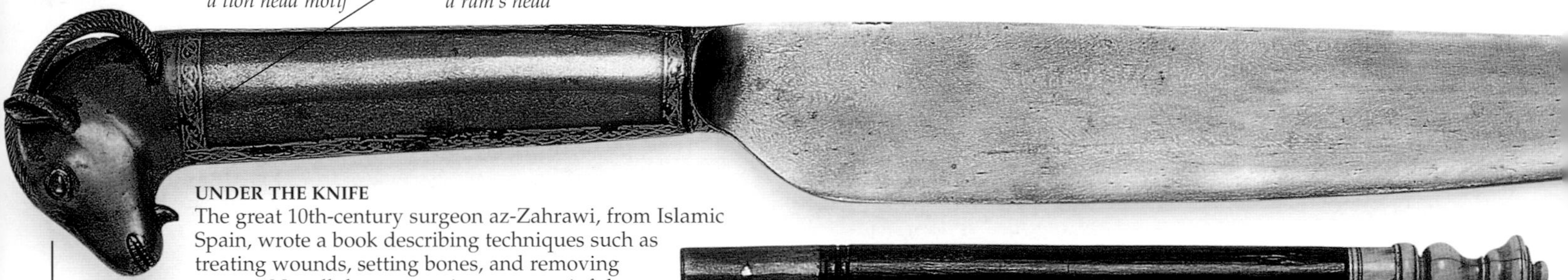

Ivory handle decorated with a lion head motif

Metal handle decorated with a ram's head

Eighteenth-century surgical knives

UNDER THE KNIFE

The great 10th-century surgeon az-Zahrawi, from Islamic Spain, wrote a book describing techniques such as treating wounds, setting bones, and removing arrows. Not all these operations were painful because Muslim surgeons were the first to use painkillers. Az-Zahrawi designed many types of surgical instruments and similar ones were used for hundreds of years.

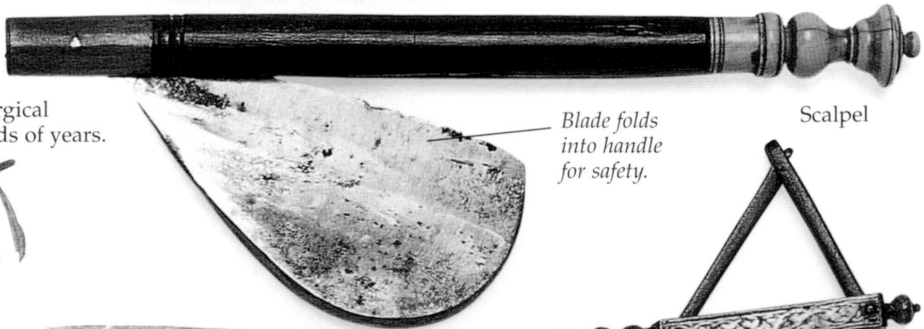

Blade folds into handle for safety.

Scalpel

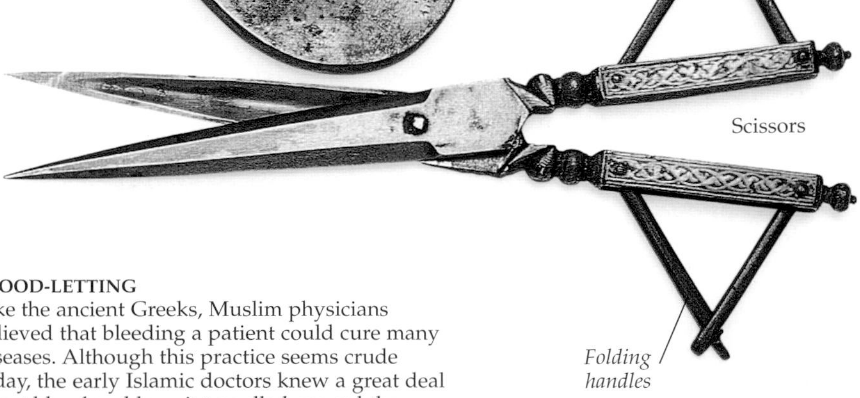

Scissors

Folding handles

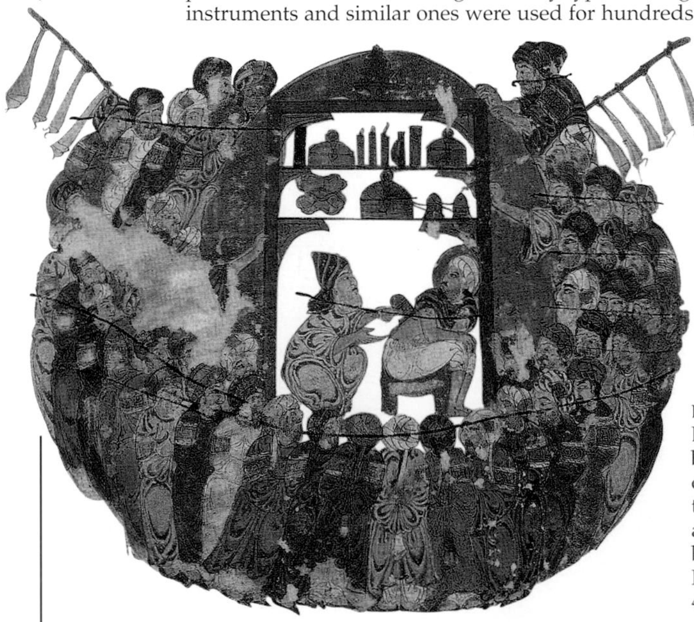

BLOOD-LETTING

Like the ancient Greeks, Muslim physicians believed that bleeding a patient could cure many diseases. Although this practice seems crude today, the early Islamic doctors knew a great deal about blood and how it travelled around the body. One 13th-century Egyptian writer, Ibn an-Nafis, wrote about the circulation of blood, some 400 years before this was "discovered" in Europe.

HERBAL MEDICINE
The ancient Greek surgeon Dioscorides wrote a famous herbal encyclopedia that was translated into Arabic. Its five books describe all kinds of herbs, spices, roots, juices, and seeds that were used to make medicines and other preparations. This page from a 10th-century Arabic version of Dioscorides shows henna, a plant used widely in the Arab world as a dye.

IN STORAGE
Many medicines were made with fresh herbs, but these could not always be found all year round. Herbalists therefore dried leaves, seeds, and other plant parts, so that they were available for use at any time of the year. Herbs were stored in glass or pottery jars, and these were usually sealed with a cork or stopper.

Dark colour to keep out light

Pottery storage jars

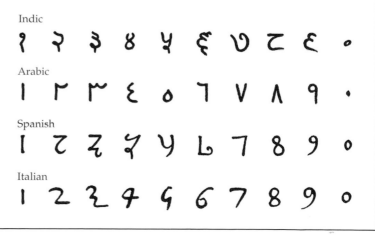

Pointed blade for piercing and then cutting the skin

Vessel has rounded bottom to aid mixing

Pestle and mortar

WELL-PREPARED
Pharmacists and physicians often prepared medicines by grinding the ingredients together using a pestle and mortar. They made their preparations carefully, often following a standard textbook such as the 11th-century al-Aqrabadhin, which describes many different medications.

Mathematics

Modern mathematics was made possible by Islamic scholars. This was because Muslim mathematicians in Baghdad gathered ideas from both ancient Greece and India, as well as adding contributions of their own. In addition to studying subjects such as calculation and geometry, they also founded the science of algebra – a word that comes from the Arabic *al-jabr*, a term describing a method of solving equations.

ARABIC NUMBERS
The numbers we use today began life in India. The Indians used place-value (which gives a value to a number according to its position) and the zero, which was unknown in the West. These ideas, which made calculation much easier than before, were in use in India in the 6th century. They were taken up by Muslims by the 9th century and probably passed to Europe in a 12th-century translation of an Arabic book on mathematics.

Indic

Arabic

Spanish

Italian

1 2 3 4 5 6 7 8 9 0

Nomadic or settled

As ISLAM SPREAD, the faith came to people with many different lifestyles. Some were nomads, living in tents and moving from one place to another in search of new grazing lands for their animals. Others lived in settlements that varied from small oasis villages to some of the world's most sophisticated cities. Even town-dwellers were often on the move, for many were merchants, taking caravans of camels across the desert from one market to the next. In this way, both nomadic and settled people helped to spread Islam across western Asia and North Africa.

OASIS
Water trapped deep under the ground comes to the surface at oases, small patches of green among the desert's rocks and sand. People can settle here and cultivate crops such as date palms. Oases are also vital water sources for nomadic desert peoples.

ON THE THRESHOLD
In Islamic tradition, the door forms the meeting point between the private house interior and the public outside world and may have beautiful carved or painted decorations.

PERCHED ALOFT
For centuries, Yemen has been a prosperous part of Arabia. The area was ideally placed to allow the people to make money from the water-borne trade in the Red Sea and build cities with beautiful tall brick houses like these. The comings and goings in such cities made Yemen a melting pot of ideas where both branches of Islam – Sunni and Shi'i – became well established.

TRADING PLACES
From Tangier in North Africa to Muscat in Arabia, most Muslim cities have always had markets that formed meeting places for traders all over the Islamic world. Everyone came to trade here – nomads, settled farmers and craft workers, and merchants from near and far. This coming together of peoples made markets prime places for the spread of Islam.

Wooden poles, supported by guy ropes, hold up the tent.

RIDER AND CAMEL
Camels provide ideal desert transport because they can go for days without food or water, living off the fat in their humps. This one carries tasselled saddlebags beneath a sheepskin saddle blanket. The rider wears traditional Bedouin costume – a long white tunic covered by a sleeveless cloak with a headcloth secured by two woollen coils. These clothes protect him from both sun and wind.

Flat, wide feet do not sink into the sand.

SUPER SADDLE
Horses have always been important to the Arab people, especially those living a nomadic lifestyle. Arabian horses are still widely prized today. This saddle with matching saddle cloth is fit for the finest Arabian horse.

LIVES OF THE MONGOLS
The Mongols of Central Asia, nomads who traditionally lived in round tents called yurts or gers, conquered Islamic lands in the 13th and 14th centuries, after which many Mongols became Muslims.

BEDOUIN TENT
The Bedouins of Arabia and North Africa are desert-dwellers whose traditional life involves nomadic camel-herding. They were among the first to convert to Islam and to spread the faith. Some Bedouin still live in long, low tents, though few are now nomads.

Merchants and travellers

IBN BATTUTA
Among the early Muslim travellers, Ibn Battuta, from Tangier (in present-day Morocco), was the most remarkable. Setting out on the Pilgrimage in 1325, he carried on travelling, going 120,000 km (75,000 miles) in 29 years. He visited West and East Africa, Arabia, India, and China, and when he returned he told the story of his adventures to the Sultan of Morocco.

TRADE HAS ALWAYS played a key role in the Islamic world. The Prophet himself came from a people who had long ago established the two great caravan journeys from Mecca, the Winter Caravan to the Yemen and the Summer Caravan to the outskirts of the Roman Empire. When Muslim armies took over territory, traders were quick to follow, opening up routes that led east to China, south into Africa, northwest to Europe, and southeast across the Indian Ocean. The faith of Islam was soon spread by merchants as far as Malaysia and Indonesia. Muslims did not only travel for trade, they also went in search of knowledge, on diplomatic missions, and of course to make the Pilgrimage.

MERCHANTS ON THE MOVE
This 13th-century illustration of merchants comes from a book by the writer al-Hariri, who came from Basra, Iraq. Men like these not only carried items for sale. They carried ideas, inventions, and Islam itself, which was often introduced to new areas by merchants who settled far from home.

Silver coins from Baghdad found in a Viking grave in Sweden

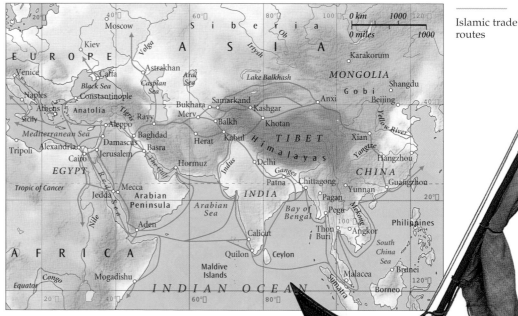

Islamic trade routes

COINS FOR TRADE
Archaeologists have found out where Islamic traders went by unearthing their coins. The Viking lands, Sri Lanka, and the heart of China are three places where Muslim coins have been discovered. Islamic coins were widely respected because of the high proportion of precious metals they contained. These currencies greatly helped the growth of world trade.

TRADE ROUTES
Official reports, travellers' tales, and archaeology have all provided clues about the routes taken by Muslim traders. One route stood out above all – the Silk Road. It was actually a number of roads across Central Asia, linking China and Europe, passing through many parts of the Muslim world on the way.

SALT CARAVAN
This salt caravan is travelling to Timbuktu in Mali (p. 280). Salt was essential for seasoning and preserving food and early Muslims sold it for vast sums. There were rich sources of salt in Africa, at places such as Taghaza, today in Algeria, where the locals even constructed buildings from salt. From here, caravans carried salt south, and the merchants spread Islam as they travelled.

DHOW
The most common trading vessels in the Indian Ocean were dhows, which are still used today. With their triangular sails, these boats are easy to manoeuvre and sail in head-winds. Their captains navigated by looking at the stars and many of them also used the magnetic compass. They also had an excellent knowledge of currents, sea-marks, and winds.

Tasselled saddlebag

BACTRIAN CAMEL
With their great staying power and their ability to produce milk on a diet of bitter vegetation and foul-tasting water, camels enabled the Muslims to survive and travel in inhospitable places. The two-humped Bactrian camel was found on the northern routes, the one-humped dromedary in the south.

Ropes help support mast

Furled lateen (triangular) sail

Main mast

SWEETS ON SALE
In countries such as Saudi Arabia, stores and markets have extremely enticing sweet counters. For centuries, the Arab world has had a reputation for its sweets, and English words such as "sugar" and "candy" come from Arabic.

NOMAD WOMAN SPINNING
This painting shows an Egyptian livestock herder and his wife outside their tent. The woman is spinning wool to make thread. She uses some of this to make clothes for herself and her family. What is left over can be sold at a local market.

Stern rudder

Continued on next page

FRANKINCENSE
A resin from trees growing in southern Arabia, frankincense is burned for its perfume and was also an ingredient in medieval medicines. Frankincense was in great demand in Christian Europe because it was used in religious services. It became a major trading item for Muslim merchants.

NARWHAL TUSKS
Among the marvels on sale in medieval markets were tusks taken from the narwhal, a small species of whale. Stories of the unicorn, the mythical beast with a single horn, fascinated people in the Middle Ages and unscrupulous traders claimed that narwhal tusks were unicorn horns.

HUNTING BIRDS
Nobles in both East and West enjoyed hunting with falcons and the Arab world produced some of the best, and most expensive, birds. When Muslim envoys visited the Chinese emperor during the Ming dynasty, he asked them to bring him falcons.

Exotic goods
The Muslim world had two enormous business advantages. Muslim merchants had a huge range of contacts over land and sea, so they could trade in everything from African gold and Chinese porcelain to European amber and furs. Muslim craft workers were also highly skilled, so merchants could bring back raw materials, which workers then transformed into all kinds of items – leather goods, metalwork, textiles, glass – that always found a ready market.

COTTON
Grown originally in Egypt and Iraq, cotton was a popular material for clothing because it was cool, comfortable, and cheaper than linen.

Cotton plant

OILS
Used in cooking, for soaps and cosmetics, and in lamps like this, oil was traded widely. The fine plant-based oils of the Muslim world were far more pleasant to use than the smelly fish oil that was often found in Europe.

CAMEL CARAVAN
Before modern forms of transport appeared, camel caravans, each beast loaded with bags containing trade goods, were a common sight in Arabia, the Sahara, and on the Silk Road across Asia.

Robe dyed using indigo

COLOURED DYES
Blue was a very popular colour for fabrics and there was a valuable trade in indigo, a blue dye made from plants and used today in clothes such as denim jeans. Other dyes, such as Roman purple made from the murex shellfish, were rarer and more expensive.

SILKS
Muslim merchants brought silk yarns and finished fabrics from China along the Silk Road (p. 274). The yarns were woven into cloth in cities such as Damascus (which gave us the word damask), in Syria, and sold on to Western traders.

Silk fabric

THE IVORY TRADE
Elephant ivory was brought across the Sahara and through Ethiopia to be exported from the ports of North Africa. Much of it went to Muslim Spain, where craft workers produced stunning ivory objects, such as decorated horns and intricately carved caskets.

Oyster shell with pearl

PEARL FISHING
Diving for pearls was dangerous work, but divers risked their lives in the fine pearl beds of the Arabian Gulf and Indian Ocean because of the huge demand. There were thriving pearl markets in Bahrain, Sri Lanka, and around the Strait of Hormuz, between Oman and Iran.

Pearl necklace

Elephant ivory

Food trade

The Muslim world developed a vigorous trade in various types of foods, and this business still continues today. The trade was beneficial in several ways. Not only was there great financial gain for the merchants, but also western Europe was introduced to foodstuffs from all over Asia. Without Muslim merchants, Europeans would have had no rice, sugar, or coffee. In addition, the merchants set up trading colonies in many parts of the world, and this helped Islam to spread eastwards as far as Southeast Asia.

Thai rice pot

Cinnamon sticks

Peppercorns

Ginger

Nutmeg

RICE
The Muslims brought rice from Southeast Asia and it soon became a popular food in parts of Europe. Later, Western farmers learned how to grow rice for themselves.

THE FRUIT TRADE
Muslim travellers introduced new species of fruit, such as the apricot, into Europe. Dried fruit, such as dates, kept for a long time and could be carried for months. Fresh fruit did not travel so well, although highly valued melons were sometimes wrapped in lead to preserve them.

Cherries

Apricots

PRECIOUS SPICES
Grown on the islands of Indonesia, spices fetched high prices in Europe and western Asia, where they were used in both food and medicines. From the time of Muhammad until the 16th century, Muslim merchants ran the spice trade, bringing nutmeg, cloves, cinnamon, and other spices to Arabia by sea and selling them at a huge profit to European traders.

Cloves

Figs

Dates

Bedouin bag for coffee beans and cardamom pods

SUGAR
A great luxury in the Middle Ages, sugar was brought west from Iran and Iraq to Muslim Spain. Access to this expensive ingredient gave Muslim confectioners the chance to create their own specialities – sherbet from Persia, various types of candy, sweets made from the liquorice plant, and Turkish delight – all of which eventually reached Europe through trade.

Sherbet

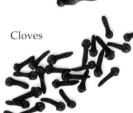

Tea leaves

Green coffee beans

Boiled sweets

TEA AND COFFEE
India and China were sources of tea, while coffee was grown in Yemen and traded from the town of Mocha, which gave its name to a type of high-quality coffee. Both drinks came late to world trade but became very fashionable in the 18th century.

Turkish delight

Liquorice

Sugared almonds

Spain

GREAT MOSQUE AT CORDOBA
Begun in the ninth century and later extended, the Great Mosque, or Mezquita, in Cordoba was a symbol of Muslim power in Spain. It is a dazzling example of Islamic architecture. Over 850 columns of granite, jasper, and marble support a ceiling raised on double arches.

DURING THE EARLY EIGHTH century, Muslims from Morocco invaded Spain – soon they controlled most of the Iberian Peninsula. Muslims ruled in Spain until the 15th century, although they never governed the entire peninsula, as Christian kingdoms survived in the north. After the fall of the caliphate in the 11th century, Moorish Spain began to be conquered by the Christians of the north and the east, but southern cities such as Cordoba and Seville were centres of Islamic art and learning.

MOORISH COIN
The Moors – the name Christians gave to the Muslims from Morocco – brought with them their own coinage and systems of government. After the defeat of the Moors, early Spanish Christian kings continued to use Islamic designs on coins.

MINSTRELS
The musicians of Muslim Spain were among the best in Europe. Some of them were wandering minstrels who introduced European players to the lute, and to the use of the bow to play stringed instruments.

CALIPH'S BOX
A great Moorish craftsman produced this box during the 10th century. It is inscribed with the name of Al-Mughira, son of 'Abd al-Rahman III, who reunited Islamic Spain after a time of disorder and ruled as Caliph of Cordoba.

Scenes showing pleasures of courtly life

THE ALHAMBRA, GRANADA
In the 14th century, Spain was ruled by the Nasrid dynasty who were based in Granada, in southern Spain. Here they built the great fortified palace called the Alhambra, which means "red palace", after the warm colour of its stone. It was designed to represent paradise on Earth and its tall towers and strong outer walls hide luxurious interiors.

ALHAMBRA COURTYARDS
The beauty of the Alhambra lies not only in its exquisite Islamic decoration, but in the clever use of light and water to create a sense of space. Courtyards fill the palace with light, and many have tranquil pools that gently reflect the light. Arched walkways create shaded areas where the Nasrids could walk or relax.

MUDEJAR TOWER
In many parts of Spain, Muslim craftsmen carried on working under Christian rule. They developed a style, now known as *mudéjar*, which used Islamic patterns to decorate brick-built wall surfaces, as in this tower at Teruel.

THE LAST MUSLIM KINGDOM
As the Christians gradually conquered Spain, the Muslim rulers were pushed south. By the 15th century, only the kingdom of Granada, the area in southern Spain around the walled city of the same name, remained in Muslim hands.

THE GARDENS OF THE GENERALIFE
In the Qur'an, paradise is described as a garden – usually an enclosed or shaded garden in which water flows. To escape from the political life of the palace, the Nasrid caliphs created a tranquil garden paradise on their country estate, the Generalife, which looked down over the city of Granada.

MOORISH INFLUENCE
This metalwork decorates a door in the royal palace in Seville. The palace was not built by a caliph but by a Spanish king, Pedro I, and shows the great influence of Islamic art in Spain.

THE LAST CALIPH
Boabdil became caliph in 1482, after a power struggle with his father that weakened Granada. In 1490, the Christian forces of Aragon and Castille laid siege to the city and, after two years, Granada surrendered. On his way to exile in Morocco, Boabdil looked back at the Alhambra and wept at its beauty. This spot is now called "the Moor's last sigh".

Africa

By THE END OF THE UMAYYAD dynasty of caliphs in 750, Islam had spread across North Africa from Egypt to Morocco. From here, the faith spread southwards, as Muslim Berber and Tuareg merchants crossed Africa carrying not just goods, but also ideas. Great cities of Islamic scholarship were established at Timbuktu and Djenne (both in Mali) and Chingetti, in Mauritania. Today Muslims – most of them Sunnis – are in the majority in North and West Africa, and many East African countries. Africa is a vast and varied continent, in which Islam exists side by side with many different local cultures and with political systems that range from socialism to monarchy.

WOMAN WARRIOR
One of the best known accounts of the Muslim conquests in North Africa is an epic called the *Sirat Beni Hilal*. One especially popular character is the heroine Jazia, a warrior who is shown here riding her camel.

BERBER WOMAN
The Berbers are the peoples of the mountains and deserts of North Africa. They are Muslims who have held on to many of their local traditions, such as wearing bright-coloured costumes and silver jewellery.

Wide margin allows the pages to be turned without touching the text.

ILLUMINATED COPY OF THE QUR'AN
Calligraphy and other scholarly skills were as highly valued in Africa as in the rest of the Muslim world, and Africa had some famous centres of learning. One of the largest of these was 15th- and 16th-century Timbuktu. Scholars from all over North Africa came to the city's library to consult precious manuscripts like this copy of the Qur'an.

Earth pinnacle built around wooden post

DJENNE MOSQUE
Earth is the traditional building material in many parts of Africa. As well as being used for houses, large buildings, like this mosque at Djenne in Mali, can be made of earth. Djenne was one of the most important trading centres along the River Niger.

MINARET AT SOUSSE
When the Muslim conquerors took over areas like Tunisia, they founded cities and built mosques in which to pray. The ninth-century mosque at Sousse, with its round stone minaret, is one early example.

WEARING THE QUR'AN
This tunic was worn by a warrior of the Asante people of West Africa. The pouches each contain a text from the Qur'an, which warriors believed would protect them in battle.

Leather pouch containing verse from the Qur'an

TILE PATTERNS
These hexagonal wall tiles from North Africa bear patterns that are based on plant forms. The flowers, leaves, and twining stems have been made into abstract designs in typical Islamic style.

PRECIOUS METAL
The people of West Africa were skilled gold workers before the arrival of Islam. The Muslims put these skills to work to produce gold coinage.

MEMORIZING THE QUR'AN
Islam brought formal education to many parts of Africa for the first time. This Mauritanian student is reading a *sura* (chapter) of the Qur'an, and learning it by heart.

A FAMOUS PILGRIMAGE
Mali was the centre of a large West African empire during the 14th century. Its ruler, Mansa Musa, made the pilgrimage to Mecca in 1324–25 and his long journey is recorded on this map.

Smooth outer coating of mud protects walls.

Wooden beams strengthen the structure.

DOMED TOMB
Most Muslims have simple graves, but there is a tradition of building larger tombs for caliphs and other notable people. The small tomb above, near Khartoum in Sudan, was probably built for a local saint. It is marked by a simple dome so that people can visit to pay their respects.

Mongols and Turks

IN 1219 THE LANDS OF ISLAM were invaded by
Mongol armies from the north. By 1258, the
Mongols – great warriors from the steppes
of Mongolia – had sacked Baghdad and
killed the caliph, devastating Islam's
political centre. But in 1260, the Mongols
were defeated by the Mamluks, and
many converted to Islam. The next
great Muslim power was the Ottoman
empire, founded by the Turks in 1290.
They conquered part of eastern Europe
and, like the Arabs before them, became
the dominant political force in Islam.

GENGHIS KHAN
Genghis Khan was a Mongol warlord
who came to power in 1206 when he
succeeded in uniting warring Mongol
tribes. He then began a campaign of
raiding and conquest. At his death, in
1227, his empire stretched from
China to the borders of Europe.

MONGOL SOLDIER
The Mongol warriors were skilled horsemen and
ruthless fighters. Moving at great speed, they
killed millions and destroyed hundreds of
settlements to bring much of Asia under
the control of Mongol rulers.

WARRIOR BOWL
The Mongols were proud of
their warriors, as this
decorated bowl from the
ninth century shows.
Because they began as a
nomadic people, the
Mongols' detailed
knowledge of the land
meant that they were able to
vanish into the countryside,
reappearing again suddenly to
take their enemies by surprise.

Embroidered cloth

Pillar of skulls

THE NEW MONGOL CAPITAL
After the death of Genghis Khan, his empire
was divided between his three sons and his
grandson, Kublai Khan. The eastern empire
prospered under Kublai Khan, and he founded
the Yüan dynasty in China where he built a
new capital, called Khanbaliq, now Beijing.

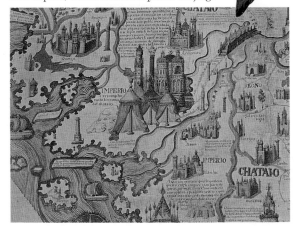

THE RUTHLESS TIMUR
Perhaps the cruellest of all
the Mongol conquerors
was Timur, or Tamerlane.
He was a Turkish-Mongol
leader who claimed to be a
descendant of Genghis
Khan. In the 14th century
he conquered much of the
western part of the Mongol
empire, taking Baghdad in
1390. He liked to display
his victims' skulls after
major battles and this
painting, of his victory at
Baghdad, shows a
gruesome tower of skulls.

FALL OF CONSTANTINOPLE
Constantinople (modern Istanbul) was the capital of the Christian Byzantine empire. During the Middle Ages, the Turks took over more and more of this empire, and in 1453, Constantinople itself fell to the sultan Mehmet II. The city became the new centre of the Ottoman empire.

Fortress of Rumeli Hisari, built by Mehmet II as a base from which to attack Constantinople

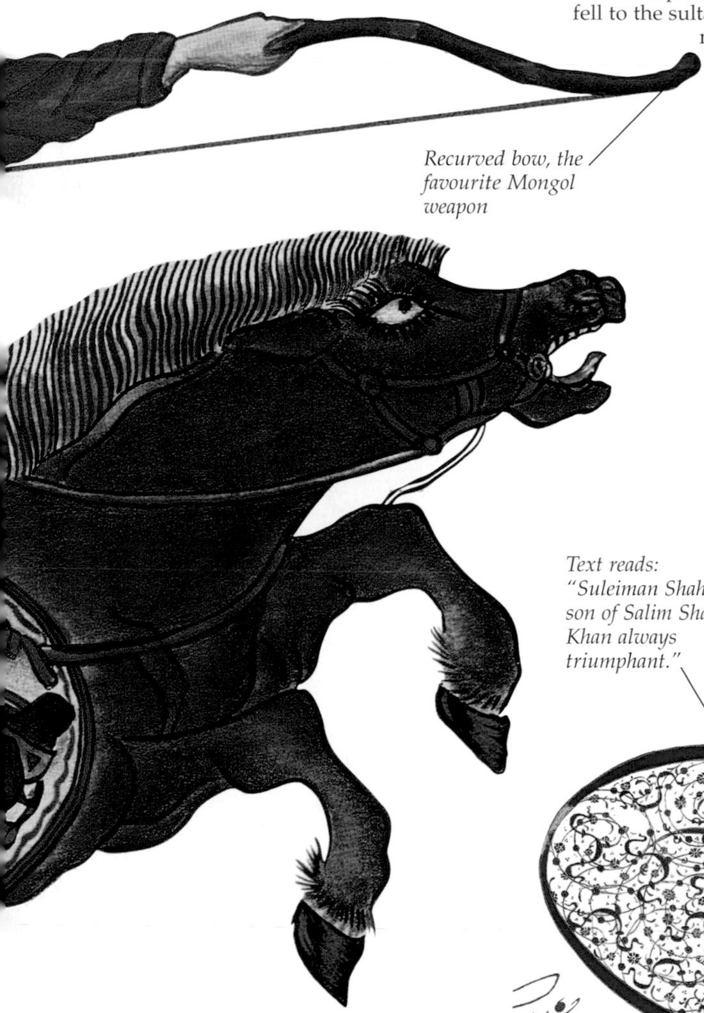

Recurved bow, the favourite Mongol weapon

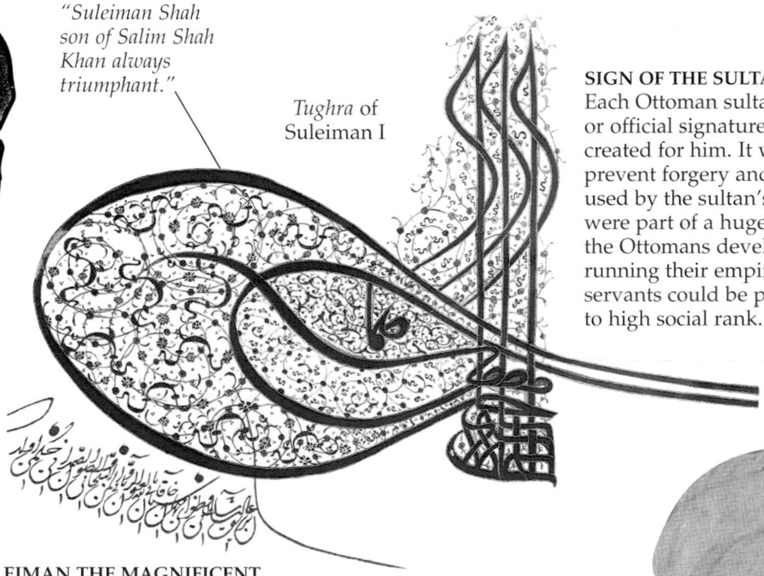

Text reads: "Suleiman Shah son of Salim Shah Khan always triumphant."

Tughra of Suleiman I

SIGN OF THE SULTAN
Each Ottoman sultan had a *tughra*, or official signature, specially created for him. It was designed to prevent forgery and could only be used by the sultan's staff. These staff were part of a huge civil service that the Ottomans developed for running their empire. Able civil servants could be promoted and rise to high social rank.

SULEIMAN THE MAGNIFICENT
Suleiman I, known in the West as "the Magnificent" and in the East as "the Lawgiver", ruled with absolute power from 1520 to 1566, when the Ottoman empire was at its height. Determined to extend the empire, he advanced into Europe and in 1529, he besieged Vienna, in Austria. Despite his powerful army, he failed to capture Vienna.

THE CONQUEROR
Ottoman Sultan Mehmet II, was known as "the Conqueror", after his capture of Constantinople in 1453. He was a broadminded man, interested in all types of culture. His court attracted scholars and craftsmen from all over the Muslim world and he had his portrait painted by the Italian artist Bellini.

Central Asia, Iran, and India

BURNING BRIGHT
The Ghaznavids, whose craftsmen made elaborate metalwork like this lamp, were Seljuk rulers who controlled Afghanistan and much of Iran. They were at the height of their power in the early 11th century. The Ghaznavids were Sunni Muslims who opposed the rival Shi'i dynasty, the Buyids, in Iran.

Pierced decoration

Lamp is made of cast bronze

ISLAM CAME EARLY TO IRAN, an area that was completely conquered by Muslim rulers by the year 641. In the following centuries, a series of ruling dynasties reigned in Iran, including the Seljuks from Turkey, the Mongols from Central Asia, the Timurids (the dynasty of the war leader Timur), and the Safavids. India was also a region of huge variety, with many different religions. Muslims – from the first conquests in Sind in 712 to the Mughal emperors – controlled all or part of India from 1193 to the 19th century, when the subcontinent became part of the vast British Empire. When the country won its independence from Britain in 1947, it was split up and the new Muslim state of Pakistan was created. A growing Muslim minority remains in India.

QUTB MINAR, DELHI
In 1193, Afghan ruler Muhammad al-Ghuri conquered northern India. He built a capital at Delhi from which Muslim sultans ruled, putting up buildings like this tall minaret. For the most part, the rule of the Delhi sultans was ended by the campaigns of Timur in 1398–9, but carried on in some areas until 1526.

TIMUR'S TOMB
The Mongol war leader Timur (p. 282) was a highly successful soldier who had victories in Iran, India, Syria, and Turkey. When he died in 1405, he was trying to add China to his list of military triumphs. The great wealth he amassed from his conquests is reflected by the rich decoration of his tomb at Samarkand in Central Asia.

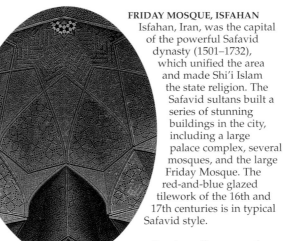

FRIDAY MOSQUE, ISFAHAN
Isfahan, Iran, was the capital of the powerful Safavid dynasty (1501–1732), which unified the area and made Shi'i Islam the state religion. The Safavid sultans built a series of stunning buildings in the city, including a large palace complex, several mosques, and the large Friday Mosque. The red-and-blue glazed tilework of the 16th and 17th centuries is in typical Safavid style.

KHWAJU BRIDGE
One of the achievements of the Safavid dynasty was the construction of the Khwaju Bridge in Isfahan. The bridge is about 133 m (440 ft) long and spans the River Zayandeh with 23 arches. As well as providing a river crossing, this amazing structure acted as a dam to irrigate the nearby gardens.

Openings allow passers-by to enjoy river views in the shade.

The Mughal empire

The Muslim Mughal dynasty ruled in India from 1526 to 1858, with the greatest emperors in power towards the beginning of this period. Under their rule, the diverse Indian subcontinent was united and underwent a unique period of achievement in art, music, literature and architecture. Under the later Mughal rulers, however, the empire began to fall apart.

Babur discusses building progress with his architects

BABUR
The first Mughal emperor was Babur, who came from Iran and was descended from Timur and Genghis Khan. The word Mughal comes from "Mongol", because of Babur's origins. Babur was just 11 when he became a ruler in Transoxiana, and aged 14 when he conquered Samarkand. He established a kingdom in Iran, which he lost, and another in Afghanistan. In 1526, Babur conquered India. A well-educated man, he was a poet and historian who encouraged the arts.

Akbar leads his army into battle

AKBAR
The greatest Mughal emperor was Akbar, who ruled from 1556 to 1605. Skilled in government, Akbar set up an efficient bureaucracy, the structure of which still influences Indian government today. Akbar was also known as one of the most tolerant of rulers. He abolished a tax on the Hindu population, and encouraged artists to combine Hindu and Islamic styles in their work.

AURANGZEB
This book contains the letters of the last important Mughal leader, emperor Aurangzeb (1658–1070), whose rule saw a decline in the health of the Mughal state. He expanded the empire but failed to invest in agriculture and so did not make enough money to support his army or court. He persecuted non-Muslims, taxing Hindus heavily and destroying many of their temples.

China and Southeast Asia

ISLAM HAS BEEN PRACTISED in China since the seventh century when it was introduced to coastal cities by Arab traders. Over the next 200 years, merchants travelling the Silk Road took Islam into the interior. The Muslims of China today are a diverse people descended from many different ethnic groups, including ethnic Chinese, Mongols, and Persians, each with their own customs and cultures. Islam also reached Southeast Asia through trade, and today the largest Muslim population in the world is in Indonesia.

Name of Allah

Outline of bird where wax covered the fabric during dyeing

BY SEA
Some Muslim merchants travelled from the mainland to Southeast Asia in traditional boats with striking curved prows.

Typical Chinese upward-curving roof

BATIK
China and Southeast Asia have always traded in beautiful fabrics, such as silks. This piece has been dyed using the process called batik, which was invented in Java. The dyer applies wax to the parts of the fabric which are to remain uncoloured, then soaks the material in dye. When dry, the material is boiled or scraped to remove the wax.

Carved stone decoration from Xi'an mosque

MOSQUE INTERIOR, BEIJING
By the early 20th century there was a sizeable Muslim minority in China. In the larger cities there are lavish mosques like the Niu Jie mosque (above), which has pillars lacquered in black and gold, and walls decorated with both Arabic and Chinese motifs. Most of China's Muslims live in the rural northwestern province of Xinjiang, where the mosques are usually much plainer.

GRAND MOSQUE IN THE CITY OF XI'AN,
When China became communist in 1949, Muslims were given some religious freedom, but during the Cultural Revolution (1966–1976) all religions were outlawed, and mosques were destroyed or closed. In the 1980s, however, many mosques were reopened or rebuilt. China's oldest mosque, the Grand Mosque in Xi'an, can be visited today.

ROD PUPPET
The shadow puppet theatre called *wayang golek* is performed with carved and painted wooden figures that are manipulated with rods. *Wayang* is a traditional Javanese entertainment, widely enjoyed by Muslims at festivals and celebrations.

Articulated arm

Wooden rod is used to move puppet's arm.

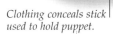

Clothing conceals stick used to hold puppet.

WEARING THE TUDONG
These schoolgirls from Brunei are wearing the *tudong*, a form of head-covering that extends down to conceal the neck and upper body. Wearing the *tudong* is just one way in which women can obey the Qur'an's instruction to dress modestly (p. 288).

BOWL FOR RICE
Rice is the staple food in both China and Southeast Asia. It is eaten from small round bowls made of porcelain – a type of pottery that was widely traded, forging an important link between China, the Muslim world, and the West.

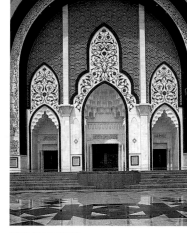

MIX OF STYLES
This modern mosque in Kuala Kangsar, Malaysia, was built after the country became independent in 1957. This was a good time for Muslims in Malaysia because Islam was recognized as the state's official religion.

MALAYSIAN MOSQUE
Because Islam was brought to Southeast Asia by well-travelled merchants, the area has always been influenced by a mix of cultures. This Malaysian mosque is decorated in the style of mosques in Iran and India.

CARAVANSERAI
Merchants travelling by land needed places to stay, so the locals built caravanserais on the routes through Asia to China. In these simple stone buildings, merchants could find a bed and somewhere to stable their camels.

Islamic society

THE QUR'AN TELLS MUSLIMS that man is God's vice-regent on Earth and is responsible for taking good care of everything from the environment to the people around him. Muslims are told to be tolerant of other peoples and to create societies in which justice, personal kindness, and the avoidance of wrongdoing are upheld. Virtues such as these start within the family and the Qur'an describes clearly the roles of men, women, and children. Within these guidelines, which are known as the *sharia*, Muslim society can take a variety of forms.

SULTAN AND HIS SUBJECTS
Muslim countries are governed in different ways. In the past, many had heads of state who ruled with absolute power, like this Moroccan sultan. Since the Second World War and the abolition of the caliphate (p. 258), most Muslims now live in modern nation states.

SELLING SLAVES
Slavery had been an important part of the social system since ancient times, and was still common in the time of Muhammad. It continued to be a part of life in medieval times as this picture of a North African slave market shows. The Qur'an encouraged the freeing of slaves and insisted that they be treated with kindness.

SCALES OF JUSTICE
Islamic law also covers business, encouraging trade, but setting guidelines that ensure fairness. Since Abbasid times (p. 258), markets in Muslim countries had officials who checked weights and measures and the quality of merchandise. The *Muhtasib*, as this public official was called, is still found in some traditional markets.

"Allah created nothing finer on Earth than justice. Justice is Allah's balance on Earth, and any man who upholds this balance will be carried by Him to Paradise."

THE PROPHET MUHAMMAD

TOLERANCE
The Qur'an stresses that there should be tolerance between Muslims and non-Muslims. Jews and Christians, people who, like Muslims, believe in the One God, are given particular respect in the Qur'an. They should be able to coexist peacefully, like the Muslim and Christian chess-players in this Spanish picture.

MARCHING TOGETHER
Many Muslims live side by side with people of very different beliefs. For the most part, they live in harmony, like these Muslims and Buddhists in China.

SPIRES AND MINARETS
In Zanzibar, Tanzania, the mosque and the Christian church are close neighbours. Here, as in many places, Muslims live in a diverse community, side by side with Christians and those who follow other religions.

MEN'S ROLE
Islam makes a clear distinction between the roles of men and women in the home. The man's job is to deal with relations between the family and the outside world, as this man is doing when he entertains his guests.

CHILDREN AND FAMILY
Muslims regard children as gifts of Allah and as one of the great joys of life. Parents are expected to care for their children and to give them a good start in life, making sure they have a proper upbringing and education. Children are expected to respect and obey their parents and to show qualities of kindness, virtue, and conscientiousness towards them.

HENNAED HAND
Henna is used in a traditional ritual that is usually performed on the day before a marriage. The bride's hands and feet are adorned with beautiful patterns using a dye made from henna leaves. This may be done by the bride's female friends and relatives.

MARRIED LIFE
Muslims are usually expected to marry and have children. Marriage not only unites individuals, but it also brings together families, making the Muslim community more unified and reflecting the harmony of Allah's creation.

DOWRY BOX
A Muslim man gives his bride-to-be a dowry, a payment in money or property, which may be presented in a box like this. The amount of the dowry can vary according to the man's wealth.

Pattern is said to symbolize strength and love.

WESTERN WOMEN
In many societies, Muslim women are educated to a high level, are employed in professions such as medicine or law, and may even take prominent part in public life. Baroness Uddin, a Muslim member of the British House of Lords, is a good example.

SUDANESE WOMAN
In traditional Muslim societies such as the Sudan, women usually keep to their roles of home-making and childcare. Even in early Muslim societies, however, there were notable women who worked as scholars and occasionally ruled. Many learned Muslim women, such as the great Egyptian scholar Umm Hani (1376–1466), were famous in the Middle Ages.

Local terracotta pot

MAN AT PRAYER
According to Islam, everything comes from Allah and will eventually return to Allah. Qualities that are loved in family members, friends, and the wider society are all qualities that have come from Allah. So the individual's relationship with Allah is paramount. Each Muslim turns to Allah for guidance, forgiveness, and support.

Festivals and ceremonies

THE MUSLIM CALENDAR contains a number of yearly festivals. Some commemorate key events in the history of the faith, such as the birthday of the Prophet or the Night Journey. Others are connected with the Five Pillars of Islam: *'Id al-Adha* (the feast of the sacrifice) takes place during the time of the pilgrimage, and *'Id al-Fitr* marks the end of Ramadan, the month of fasting. There are also festivals such as *Nauruz* in Iran to celebrate New Year, and celebrations from birth to marriage, that mark key points in a Muslim's life.

LUNAR CALENDAR
The Islamic calendar is based on the phases of the Moon. Each year has 12 lunar months of 29 or 30 days each, and a total of 354 days. Each month begins with the sighting of the new Moon.

RAMADAN
During the month of Ramadan, Muslims fast between sunrise and sunset (p. 253). At sunset each day, people first pray and then eat. Special lights, such as this star-shaped lantern, may be lit during the evening meal.

KERBALA
Kerbala, Iraq, is where Muhammad's grandson Husayn was killed in 680. Husayn's shrine (above) is sacred to the Shi'i Muslims, who are the largest religious group in Iran and Iraq. The death of Husayn is marked by the festival of *Ashura* (see opposite).

MAWLID AN-NABI
These boys from Kenya are taking part in a procession celebrating *Mawlid an-Nabi*, the birthday of the Prophet. This day is a public holiday and is also marked with recitations of a poem called the *Burdah*, in praise of Muhammad.

"EID MUBARAK"
During the festival of *'Id al-Fitr*, people knock on the doors of neighbours, greeting them with the phrase "*Eid Mubarak*" (Blessed *Eid*). Friends or relatives living away are sent *Eid* greetings cards (left).

Eid greetings card

Stained glass panel

'ID BALLOONS
Colourful balloons are a popular feature of the celebrations of *'Id al-Fitr*, which marks the end of Ramadan (p. 253). Celebrations include a festival prayer, a substantial breakfast, and the giving of alms to the poor.

THE ISLAMIC CALENDAR

MUHARRAM	SAFAR	RABI' AL-AWWAL
The sacred month, 30 days	The month which is void	The first spring
1: *Ra's al-'Am* (New Year)	29 days	30 days
10: *Ashura*		12: *Mawlid an-Nabi* (birthday of the Prophet)

SALLAH FESTIVAL
Some Muslim festivals are local celebrations that take part in just one country or region of the Islamic world. For example, the *Sallah* festival is held in northern Nigeria as part of the rituals marking the end of Ramadan. The highlight is a colourful procession featuring chiefs in ceremonial robes, brightly costumed horsemen, and lute players.

ASHURA
The festival of *Ashura* marks the death of Husayn and, in one of the ceremonies, models of Husayn's tomb are carried through the streets. Plays re-enacting the death of Husayn may also be performed.

WHIRLING DERVISH
Members of the Sufi Mevlevi order (p. 273) hold festivals at which they perform their "whirling" dance, known as *sama'*. One such festival marks the death of their founder, the great Sufi poet and mystic, Jalaluddin Rumi (1207–73).

WEDDING CELEBRATIONS
In Islam, a contract of marriage is made by the groom giving the bride-to-be a dowry, and the bride then giving consent to marriage before witnesses. The dowry may be presented in an embroidered purse. Wedding celebrations vary according to the local traditions of the different areas of the Muslim world, but will usually include recitations from the Qur'an and a great feast.

Dowry purse

KHITAN
Muslim boys are usually circumcised in a ceremony called *khitan*. This is often done around age seven, though it may be done any time before a boy reaches 12 years old. These Turkish boys are attending a mosque before their *khitan* ceremony.

LAYLAT AL-ISRA' WA'L-MI'RAJ
On the 27th day of the month of *Rajab*, Muslims celebrate Muhammad's Night Journey, when he rode the beast called the *Buraq*, and his Ascension to Heaven (p. 247). This is called *Laylat al-Isra' wa'l-mi'raj*, the Night of the Journey and Ascension.

The Buraq *is a "miraculous steed", although depictions of the beast vary.*

RABI'ATH-THANI	JUMADA-L-ULA	JUMADA-TH-THANIYYAH
The second spring	The first month of dryness	The second month of dryness
29 days	30 days	29 days

Continued on next page

SWEET TRAY
The availability of sugar meant that many Muslim areas have developed their own traditional types of sweets. These examples come from Malaysia. Known as *kuch*, they are rich cakes flavoured with palm sugar and coconut.

Food

A rich variety of food originated in the Islamic countries, and many of these foods have spread far and wide. This variety is only slightly limited by some simple dietary rules that restrict what a Muslim may eat. Islam forbids the drinking of alcohol, and Muslims are not allowed to eat pork which, as in other traditions, is considered to be unclean. Other animals may be eaten, provided that they are slaughtered in the correct way, with the Name of God pronounced as the creature's life is taken. Meat that is slaughtered in this way is described as halal, or lawful to eat.

MINT TEA
Tea is widely drunk in many Muslim countries. Usually served in a glass, hot, sweet mint tea is very popular and refreshing. Lemon tea is a common alternative.

Cardamom   Cumin

Turmeric

SPICES
The spice trade was always important to Muslim merchants, so many spices from India and Southeast Asia found their way into the cooking of the Middle East. Ingredients such as cumin and cardamom were valued for their fragrance, flavour, and as aids to digestion.

ON SALE
This mother and daughter in Isfahan, Iran, are buying food from a local dealer in dried fruit and spices. In this traditional shop, most of the goods are displayed loose, so that purchasers can see exactly what they are buying.

FAST FOOD
The idea of fast, ready-cooked food is nothing new in the Islamic world, and street sellers cooking and selling their own food are a common sight. In Egypt, street vendors like this man sell passers-by fava bean patties cooked in the open air and flavoured with local herbs.

DATE PALM
Date palms are one of the few crops that are grown all over the dry areas of western Asia and northern Africa. Tasty and rich in carbohydrates, dates are a popular staple food.

RAJAB	SHA'BAN	RAMADAN
The revered month	The month of division	Month of great heat
30 days	29 days	30 days
27: *Laylat al-Mi'raj* (Night Journey)	15: *Laylat al-Bara'ah* (memory of the dead – Iran and India)	27: *Laylat al-Qadr* (Night of the Descent of the Qur'an)

FOR THE SWEET TOOTH
Sweet pastries are one of the delights of western Asia. This shop is in Syria. It is selling local pastries called *hama*, which get their sweetness from a covering of honey. Several different varieties are displayed in the shop window to tempt passers-by.

BREAD-MAKER
Unleavened bread – bread baked without yeast, so that it stays flat and does not rise – is a common staple food throughout the Islamic world. This woman in Kyrgyzstan is making it on an open fire, which is one of the traditional ways to bake bread. Bread like this may also be baked on a hot stone.

ORANGES
Oranges came to Europe along trade routes from the Islamic world, and their juices were quenching thirsts in western Europe by about the 14th century. The very term orange is derived from the Arabic word *naranj*.

LAMB KEBABS
The technique of grilling small pieces of meat on a skewer to make a kebab is used in the eastern Mediterranean and Turkey. Kebabs made with minced lamb, cubes of lamb, or pieces of chicken, are now popular all over Europe and beyond.

COFFEE POT
Another item introduced to the West by the Muslims is coffee. Excellent coffee has been grown for centuries in the south-western corner of the Arabian Peninsula. It is still served there today, usually very strong and sweet, from elegant pots like this.

SHARING A MEAL
Hospitality has always been a virtue in Islam, especially in the desert, where food is hard to come by. This early illustration shows some Persians sharing food with a stranger.

FAMILY FOOD
This family in Senegal is cooking their meal over an open fire. When it is ready, they will all eat out of the one pot. Everyone looks forward to this daily family gathering. It is a chance to catch up on the news, as well as to enjoy a welcome meal.

SHAWWAL	**DHU L-QA'DAH**	**DHU L-HIJJAH**
The month of hunting	The month of rest	Month of the Pilgrimage
29 days	30 days	29 days (sometimes 30)
1: 'Id al-Fitr (Feast of Fast-breaking)		10: 'Id al-Adha (Feast of Sacrifice)

Glossary

GENERAL

ALMSGIVING The act of making charitable gifts to the poor and needy.

BYZANTINE The empire founded in the eastern part of the Roman Empire after the fall of Rome in the 5th century, with its capital at Byzantium, Constantinople (modern Istanbul).

COMPASSION Feeling of sympathy for the suffering of others, linked with the wish to help the sufferer.

CONVERT Person who turns or changes from one faith to another.

COVENANT Formal agreement, usually one made between God and a person or group of people.

CRUSADES Series of wars in the Middle Ages, fought between the Christians of western Europe and the Muslim peoples of the eastern Mediterranean.

DEITY A god or goddess.

DISCIPLE A person who follows or believes in the teachings of a religious leader.

DOWRY Property or money given by one party or the family on marriage.

DYNASTY A series of rulers of the same family.

EMIGRATE To move from one homeland to another country.

ENLIGHTENMENT Heightened state of religious knowledge or fulfilment.

EXILE Enforced absence from one's homeland or country.

FAST To go without food or to follow a severely restricted diet.

GURU A spiritual teacher.

HELLENISTIC Relating to Greek culture, normally during the period around the 4th century BCE, when Alexander the Great was building his Grecian empire in Europe and western Asia.

HUMANIST System of beliefs that puts human concerns first and rejects the supernatural.

IMMIGRATE To enter a new country to set up home.

INITIATION Ritual that signals a person's entry into a group or society, such as a coming of age ceremony where a person gains entry into adult society.

MANDATE Legal authorization for one person or group of people to act on behalf of others.

MANTRA Verse, word, or sound repeated as an aid to meditation, usually in eastern religions.

MARTYR Person who dies for their beliefs.

MEDITATE To quieten and focus the mind on spiritual matters.

MISSIONARY Person who travels in order to spread a religion to other countries.

NOVICE A person who is preparing to be a monk or nun and has entered a monastery, but has not yet taken full vows.

ORDINATION Process of making a person a priest, a minister of religion, or a Buddhist monk or nun.

PAGAN Person following a pre-Christian religion. Alternatively, a dismissive term sometimes used to refer to a person who has no religious faith. Also a modern religion.

PATRIARCH A male religious leader. In Judaism, the head of one of the early Jewish families; in Christianity, the leader of one of the Orthodox churches.

PERSECUTE To harass, attack, or put to death a person or group of people, especially for their religious beliefs.

PILGRIM Person who travels some distance to visit and worship at a sacred place.

PROPAGANDA Spreading of information or doctrine in an organized way, in order to present it in the best possible light.

PROPHECY Prediction of the future or speaking of truths inspired by God.

REPENT To regret or feel sorry for one's sins.

RITUAL Regularly repeated ceremony, service, or other religious observance.

SABBATH Day of the week that is set apart for rest and religious observance.

SCRIPTURES The sacred writings of a religion.

SECULAR Connected to the material world and not concerned with religious or spiritual matters.

SEGREGATE To separate people into groups. For example, according to their race or religion.

SHRINE Place made sacred by its link with a saint or similar holy person or because it houses the relics of such a person.

SPIRITUAL Concerning religion, the spirit, or the supernatural.

TEMPLE Building dedicated to worship, especially in the Hindu and Sikh religions.

VENERATE To hold someone or something in deep respect.

VOW A voluntary and binding promise, such as the promises a monk or nun makes on entering a monastery or those a couple make when they get married.

HINDUISM

AHIMSA Doctrine of the avoidance of doing violence, either through action or thought, to any living beings. This term is used in both Hinduism and Buddhism.

AVATAR One of several forms that a god or goddess may take when he or she appears on earth. The most famous avatars are those of the god Vishnu, which include Rama, Krishna, and the Buddha.

BRAHMAN The supreme, all-powerful being. Gods and goddesses and all of creation, are said to be part of *Brahman*.

BRAHMIN Member of the highest Indian social class, made up of the religious teachers who are priests.

CASTE Social class into which a person is born in Hindu societies.

CONSORT Partner, husband, or wife of a deity. This term is used to describe the goddesses who are seen as the wives of gods in Hinduism.

DARSHAN Act of paying respect to a god or goddess by means of viewing an image of that deity. Through viewing the deity, the worshipper is believed to receive a blessing from the god that is said to dwell within.

DHARMA The practices, truths, and teachings that make life possible, and the moral duty of each person. Every individual has a different *dharma* and may need to study or take advice from a priest or religious teacher in order to discover their own *dharma*.

MAHABHARATA One of the two major epics of ancient Indian literature, composed in the Sanskrit language. The *Mahabharata* tells of the rivalry between two families, culminating in a great battle that is won by the "good" side, the Pandavas.

MOKSHA Release or liberation from the cycle of death and rebirth.

MURTI Image of a deity, understood to be the embodied form of the god or goddess, or the place where the deity is said to dwell.

PUJA Worship of or homage to a god or goddess, which may take many forms including making offerings, chanting, and the action of darshan.

PURANAS Ancient Sanskrit texts containing accounts of Hindu mythology. The *Puranas* are part of the body of *smriti* texts.

RAMAYANA A major epic of ancient Indian literature, composed in the Sanskrit language. The *Ramayana* tells the story of Rama, the seventh avatar of Vishnu.

SADHU Holy person who has left behind the material concerns of the world in order to seek Brahman or God.

SAMSARA The continuous cycle of death and rebirth.

SANSKRIT Ancient sacred language of India, used by those who first wrote down the Hindu scriptures.

SHAKTI The Hindu Great Goddess, normally seen as the consort of Shiva. The Great Goddess is worshipped in many forms and under various names, such as Durga and Kali.

SHRUTI The body of Hindu scriptures that have highest authority because they are believed to be the words of God, heard by ancient holy men in the distant past. They were originally handed down by word of mouth, and later written down in Sanskrit. The Sanskrit word *shruti* literally means "things heard".

SMRITI The second collection of Hindu scriptures. The Sanskrit word *smriti* literally means "things remembered".

TRIMURTI The three-faced image of Hindu gods consisting of Brahma, Vishnu, and Shiva.

UPANISHAD One of a group of Hindu sacred texts containing teachings about the philosophy of Hinduism.

VEDAS Collections of Hindu hymns and chants in praise of the gods. The most sacred part of Hindu scriptures.

YOGA Discipline combining bodily, mental, and spiritual practices designed to bring about release from the round of death and rebirth.

BUDDHISM

ASCETIC Person who achieves holiness by avoiding bodily pleasures and living a life of austerity.

ASURA Power-hungry being, often referred to as a demon,

in Buddhist cosmology.

BODHISATTVA In Theravada Buddhism, the historical Buddha in one of his lives on earth; in Mahayana Buddhism, a person who gives up the chance of achieving nibbana in order to help others towards the same state.

DHAMMA The cosmic law of cause and effect, the teachings of the Buddha, and the living out of a person's life according to those teachings.

KAMMA The consequences of a person's actions, either in this life or a future one.

MANDALA A picture or diagram, showing the universe in symbolic form, used in ceremonies and meditation, especially in Tibetan Buddhism.

MUDRAS Hand gestures adopted by the Buddha and shown in images of him. Each mudra stands for a different quality of activity of the Buddha, such as meditation or gift-giving.

NIBBANA State of spiritual enlightenment in which a person is completely freed from the cycle of death and rebirth.

PALI Sacred language of early Indian Buddhist scriptures which together are known as the Pali canon.

PROSTRATION To lie with the face towards the ground, as a sign of respect to the Buddha, especially as part of the ritual showing that the Buddhist "takes refuge" in the Buddha, his teaching, and the Buddhist monastic community.

SANGHA The community of Buddhist monks and nuns, and laymen and laywomen.

SUTRAS Collections of the

teachings and sayings of the Buddha.

URNA Spot between the Buddha's eyes, a mole with soft hairs that is sometimes referred to as a "beauty spot" but is also called a "wisdom eye".

SIKHISM

AMRIT Sweetened holy water, as used in the ritual of "taking amrit", or receiving initiation into the adult Sikh community.

CHAURI Whisk-like object, representing authority, waved over the *Guru Granth Sahib* as a sign of respect.

GRANTHI Person who looks after the *Guru Granth Sahib*, is skilled in reading it, and also cares for a *gurdwara* in which it is housed.

GURDWARA Sikh place of collective worship, in which a copy of the *Guru Granth Sahib* has been correctly installed.

GURMUKHI Script, usually said to have been invented by Guru Angad, used to write the Sikh scriptures.

GURU GRANTH SAHIB The Sikh sacred book. Also known as the *Adi Granth*.

KACCHA Long shorts worn as underwear by Sikhs. One of the "Five Ks" or distinguishing items worn by Sikhs.

KANGHA Small comb, usually made of wood or ivory, worn to keep the hair tidy. One of the "Five Ks" or distinguishing items worn by Sikhs.

KARA Steel bangle worn by Sikhs on the right wrist. One of the "Five Ks" or distinguishing items worn by Sikhs.

KESH Hair left uncut by Sikhs, because to cut the hair is to

Glossary

KHALSA The community of Sikhs who have been initiated into the adult community.

KHANDA Two-edged sword, symbolic of Sikhism. Such a sword was used by Guru Gobind Singh in the ceremony that marked the founding of the *Khalsa*.

KIRPAN Sword worn by Sikhs. One of the "Five Ks" or distinguishing items.

KIRTAN Communal hymn-singing, often with accompaniment on instruments, forming part of Sikh worship.

SEVA The Sikh ideal of service to others, including the giving of alms to the poor and service in the *gurdwara*.

JUDAISM

ASHKENAZI Jews from eastern and central Europe and their descendants in other parts of the world.

BAR/BAT MITZVAH The ceremony of reaching religious adulthood in Judaism, and the state of having reached this position. The phrase *Bar mitzvah*, meaning "Son of the Commandment", is used for boys and men, *Bat mitzvah* for girls and women.

CIRCUMCISION The removal of all or part of the foreskin, an operation performed on male Jewish babies to show that they are members of the Jewish community.

CONSERVATIVE Branch of Judaism taking the middle ground between Orthodox and Reform Jews.

DIASPORA The dispersion and migration of Jews outside Israel.

GHETTO Part of a city where Jews lived, often in poor conditions and with restricted movement beyond.

HANUKKAH Jewish festival of lights commemorating the rededication of the Temple after the revolt led by Judah the Maccabee in 164 BCE.

HEBREW BIBLE Term used to describe the principal collection of Jewish sacred writings, made up of the *Torah* (law), *Nevi'im* (prophets), and *Ketuvim* (writings).

HOLOCAUST The mass murder of Jewish people by the Nazis during World War II.

KIBBUTZ Farming communities in Israel where land and produce are shared between the inhabitants and decisions are made democratically at meetings.

KOSHER Term used to describe food that is fit for human consumption according to Jewish dietary laws.

MENORAH Seven-branched candlestick. The menorah is one of the most important symbols of Judaism and the Jewish people.

ORTHODOX Term describing Jews who follow most closely the traditional practises of the faith.

PASSOVER Festival celebrating the time when the people of Israel were led out of captivity in Egypt by Moses.

POGROM A violent attack on a group of people, especially those on Jews in Poland and Russia between 1880 and 1920.

RABBI Jewish person learned in the *Torah* and the spiritual leader of a specific Jewish community.

REFORM Term describing Jews who adapt their faith to life in the modern world. Reform Jews believe that, rather than containing God's actual words, the *Torah* contains the words of people who were inspired by God.

SEMITIC Term used to refer to Jewish people.

SEPHARDIC Jews from Spain, Portugal, or North Africa, and their descendants in other parts of the world, including many whose ancestors settled in Holland.

SYNAGOGUE Jewish place of worship, or, a gathering of Jews for worship or study of the *Torah*.

TORAH The Five Books of Moses, the scriptures that make up the most important of the Jewish sacred writings.

YIDDISH A language spoken by many Ashkenazi Jews, containing words derived from both German and Hebrew.

YOM KIPPUR The Day of Atonement, the holiest day in the Jewish calendar, when Jews fast and pray in atonement for their sins.

ZIONISM Political movement that came to prominence in the 19th century to support the establishment of a Jewish state in Israel. Modern Zionists support today's Israeli state.

CHRISTIANITY

ADVENT Period, including four Sundays, which forms the lead-up to the celebration of Jesus' birth at Christmas.

ANNUNCIATION Announcement to the Virgin Mary by the angel Gabriel that she was to give birth to God's son, whom she should name Jesus.

ASCENSION Event that took place after the Resurrection, when Jesus joined his father in heaven.

ASSUMPTION The belief that both the body and the soul of the Virgin Mary were taken up to heaven at the end of her life.

BAPTISM Ceremony performed to admit a person to the Christian church. The ritual involves either immersion in water or the sprinkling of water on the head.

BAPTIZE To perform the ritual of baptism.

BIBLE Collection of writings making up the scriptures of the Christian faith. The Bible is divided into two sections or testaments. The Old consists of the Hebrew Bible, and the New is made up of writings mainly dealing with the life and ministry of Jesus and his early followers.

CATHEDRAL Christian church which is also the seat of a bishop or archbishop and contains his throne, or cathedra.

CHRISTMAS Christian festival held on 25 December to celebrate the birth of Jesus.

CHURCH Christian place of worship.

COMMUNION The taking of the consecrated bread and wine during the rite of eucharist or mass.

CONFIRMATION Ritual in which those who have already been baptized renew or confirm their Christian faith. People who have been baptized as babies often confirm their faith at adolescence or early adulthood.

CRUCIFY To put to death on a cross.

DIOCESE The area under the care and control of a bishop.

EASTER Christian festival marking the resurrection of Christ.

EUCHARIST Christian rite in which consecrated bread and wine, representing the body and blood of Christ, are distributed and eaten. Eucharist is also known as Mass, Holy Communion, and the Lord's Supper.

EVANGELICAL Relating to the Christian Gospel or to those people who are convinced that it is their duty as followers of the faith to spread the word of the Gospel.

EXCOMMUNICATE To ban a person from taking Holy Communion.

EXORCISE To perform a ceremony to drive away an evil spirit.

HOST The consecrated bread representing Jesus' body, consumed at Mass or Eucharist.

ICON Image used in Orthodox Christianity to decorate churches and to act as a focus for private devotion.

INCARNATION The belief that God was made human flesh in the person of Jesus.

LENT Period, between Ash Wednesday and Easter (or slightly longer in the eastern churches), which Christians mark with solemnity and fasting, in remembrance of Jesus' time of fasting in the wilderness.

MASS Name for the Eucharist, used generally in the Roman Catholic Church.

MIRACLE Event that occurs, against the normal laws of nature, as a result of God's divine intervention.

MONASTERY Community of monks or nuns living together apart from society and following vows of poverty, chastity, and obedience.

MONSTRANCE Vessel used for carrying and displaying the host (consecrated bread), especially in processions.

PARABLE Story used to make a specific moral or religious point, especially such a story told by Jesus.

PENANCE Act of punishment or humiliation undertaken as a way of expressing a person's sorrow for their sins.

REFORMATION Movement that took place in the early 16th century in Europe, during which time people campaigned for the reform of the Christian Church and established new, Protestant churches.

RELIQUARY Container for holy relics.

RESURRECTION Coming back to life after death.

ROSARY Ritual in which a person recites a set number of prayers and devotional phrases, using a string of beads (often also called a rosary) to count them.

SACRAMENTS The solemn religious rites of Christianity.

SALVATION The state of being safe or rescued from the normal sinful human condition through belief in Jesus Christ.

SERMON Spoken discourse on a religious theme, usually as part of a religious service.

SYNOD Formal meeting of bishops or other church leaders

VESTMENTS Special garments worn by those officiating at a religious service.

ISLAM

HADITH Traditional accounts of the words and deeds of the prophet Muhammad, as related by his companions.

HAJJ Pilgrimage to Mecca, especially the pilgrimage undertaken during the month of *Dhu'l-Hijja*. Hajj is one of the Five Pillars of Islam.

IMAM Leader of a Muslim congregation, usually a man who is learned in the *Qu'ran* and the *Hadith*.

KHALIFA A term used for a political leader of the Muslim community. Also, more widely used to describe human beings as representations of God in the world.

KHITAN Male circumcision, usually practised on boys aged seven or older.

MADRASAH Islamic school, linked to a mosque and teaching both children and adults.

MIHRAB Niche in the prayer hall of a mosque which indicates the direction of the city of Mecca.

MINARET Tower attached to a mosque from which the call to prayer is given.

MINBAR Raised pulpit in a mosque, from which the sermon is given at Friday prayers.

MOORS Muslims from North Africa or the Muslim rulers of Spain during the medieval period.

MOSQUE Building where Muslims gather for worship.

MUEZZIN Official who gives the call to prayer to the Muslim community five times each day.

MULLAH Muslim religious scholar, sometimes a teacher and preacher who leads communal prayers.

QUR'AN The sacred book of Islam, believed to consist of the words of God as revealed to the prophet Muhammad.

RAK'A Cycle of movements performed during regular prayers.

RAMADAN Ninth month of the Islamic year, during which Muslims fast.

SALAH Regular worship through prayer, performed by Muslims five times a day.

SHARIA Islamic law, based principally on the Qur'an, hadith, and the practices of the prophet Muhammad.

SHI'I One of the two major groups of Muslims, made up of those who believe that the Prophet's cousin 'Ali was Muhammad's legitimate successor as caliph.

SUFIS Groups of Muslims who follow a mystical faith, hoping for a personal and direct contact with God.

SUNNI The majority group of Muslims, made up of those who supported the system of an elected caliphate.

SURA Division or chapter of the Qur'an; the Qur'an is divided into 114 suras, each with its own name.

ZAKAT A tax, calculated as a percentage of a person's wealth, which is collected and given to the poor in Islamic communities. Paying zakat is one of the Five Pillars of Islam.

Index

Acknowledgements

Dorling Kindersley would like to thank: Virpal Kaur at The Sikh Museum, Leicester; Sawag Singh, model on pp. 124–125; Ritesh and Darshana Patel, models on pp. 48–49; Darshana Patel for her knowledge and patient guidance on the details of a Hindu wedding ceremony; Nancy Arnott for kind loan of props; Joshi fabric shop, Wembley, London; Julie Ferris for proof reading; Sue Lightfoot for the index; Father Francis Baird; Father Stephen Horton; Julian Brand; Valerie Brand; Sister Susanna Mills; Sister M Anthony; Sister Irene Joseph; Rev. Malcom Allen; Rev. Stephen Tyrell; Rev. Felicity Walters; Amber Mullins; the monks of Prinknash Abbey, Cranham, UK; the nuns of the Convent of Poor Clares, Woodchester, UK; Birminham Buddhist Vihara, UK, especially Venerable Dr. Rewata Dhamma and Yann Lovelock; Karma Ling Temple, Birmingham, UK; Lama Rabsang; Venerable Nagesena Bhikkhu; Stiematzky and Jerusalem the Golden; Sheila Collins; Fran Jones; Sadie Smith; Clare Lister; Zahavit Shalev; Philip Letsu; Wilfrid Wood; and Batul Salazar

The publishers would like to thank the following for their kind permission to reproduce their photographs:

a=above; b=below; c=centre; l=left; r=right; t=top

A-Z Botanical Collection: Matt Johnston 294bl.

AKG London: 129tl, 135c, 138c, 146b, 147tr, 149tc, 161cbr, 184br, 185, 195tr, 197cb, 198bl, 199tl, 204tr, 211tl, 213tc, 214bc, 216tl, 216tc, 221t, 221t, 253cr, 259br, 280c, 282tl; British Library 241t; British Museum, London 247tr; Stefan Diller 139l; Erich Lessing 178tr, 184tl, 185bc, 185cbr, 185r, 189bl, 193C, 196tr, 198tr; Victoria and Albert Museum 285tr, 285cl.

Ahuzan Gallery, Ahuzan Islamic Art, London: 272c.

Alamy Images: 206bc; Bryan & Cherry Alexander Photography 15br; Jon Arnold Images 14bc; Paul Doyle 119tr; Brian Harris 232b; Christine Osborne 124b; Robert Harding Picture Library 37tr; Robert Preston 16c.

Photograph by Alexander Stone Lunde: 252cr, 256bl.

All Saints Church: 204br, 205tr, 205cl.

Ancient Art & Architecture Collection: 33bc, 134cr, 136b, 160bl, 188clb, 192r, 195tl, 239br, 248tl; R. Sheridan 204tl, 205cr.

Andes Press Agency: 81cr, 81br; C & D Hill 85tl; Carlos Reyes-Manzo 101br, 104bl, 107tl.

Arcaid: Alex Bartel 210tl; Alan Weintraub 152cl.

Archivo Fotografico: 261br, 279br.

The Art Archive: Archaeological Museum, Madrid 260tl; Biblioteca Nacional Lisbon/Dagli Orti 173br; Bibliotheque des Arts Decoratifs Paris/Dagli Orti 129cb; Dagli Orti 130cl; Museuo Capitolino Rome/Dagli Orti 137br; Nationalmuseet Copenhagen Denmark/Dagli Orti (A) 139br; Topkapi Musuem, Istanbul 283br.

Art Directors & TRIP: 29tl, 35tl, 35br, 40tl, 42bl, 44bl, 118c, 118br, 118l, 119b, 120tr, 121tr, 122cr, 122-123, 123cr, 124tl; Ask Images 168tr; T. Bognar 70cl, 106tr; R. Daniell 41tl; Dinodia 46-47; I. Genut 160c; F. Good 105cr; J. Highet 66bc; T. Morse 100tl; Christopher Rennie 87br; Resource Foto 43tl, 47cr; H. Rogers 7br, 13cr, 159tl, 167br, 54cr, 106t; S Shaprio 174tr; J. Sweeney 12tr, 25car, 77tr; B. Turner 51tr.

Art Resource: The Jewish Museum, New York 176c.

Ashmolean Museum, Oxford: 74bl, 74bc, 78b, 88c; Bibliotheque Nationale, Paris 110tl.

Barnabas Kindersley: 71c, 71c, 91cr, 95bl, 97tr, 97c, 99tl, 101tl.

Baroness Udin/Universal Pictorial Press: 291clb.

Beth Hatefutsoth, Photo Archive, Tel Aviv: 138bl, 145tr, 152cr, 164tl; Central Zionist Archives, Jerusalem 142cl, 144tr, 145br, 145c; Courtesy of E. M Stern 165cb; Ghetto Fighter's House- Photo Archive 150c; Jewish National and University Library, Jerusalem 159tr; Municipal Archives of Rome 140tr; Tel Aviv, The Gross Family Collection 144br.

Bodleian Library, University of Oxford: 266c, 273cl.

Bridgeman Art Library, London/New York: 38bl, 190cr, 199b, 203br, 213bc, 213br, 216c, 219clb, 219bcl, 239bl, 257tc, 262bl, 263bl, 270tr, 272tr, 282cl, 282br, 283tr, 283b; Alte Pinakothek, Munich, Germany 219cla; American Museum, Bath, Avon 216cl; Basilica di San Marco, Venice, Italy 128tr; Bible Society, London 5tl; Govt. Museum and National Art Gallery, Madras, India 35tr; Bible Society, London, UK 201tr, 201br; Biblioteca Publica Episcopal, Barcelona 227bc; Bibilioteque Mazarine, Paris 199cr; Bibliotheque Nationale, Paris, France 132bl, 138br, 268tl, 290c; Bradford Art Galleries and Museums 212bl; British Library, London 132c, 202br, 264tr, 266tr, 295bl; British Museum 82tr, 282bl; Egyptian National Library, Cairo, Egypt 273cr; Eton College, Windsor 268tr; The Fine Art Society 216bl; Giraudon 158tl; Insititute of Oriental Studies, St Petersburg, Russia 255bc, 268bl, 274tr; Instituto da Biblioteca Nacional, Lisbon 199cl; Koninklijk Museum voor Schone Kunsten, Antwerp 227tr; Kunsthistorisches Meseum, Vienna, Austria 258br; Lauros/Giraudon 177br; Louvre, Paris 262cr, 278cr; Monasterio de El Escorial, Spain 261bl, 278c, 290cr; Musee Conde, Chantilly, France 204cl, 248-249; Musee de la Revolution Francaise, Vizille, France 141tl; Musee Guimet, Paris 56c, 58tl, 59b, 65br, 75tr; Museo Real Academia de Medicina, Madrid 262tr; Museo di San Marco dell' Angelico, Florence, Italy 196bl; Museum of the City of New York, USA 215tl; National Museum of Ancient Art, Lisbon, Portugal 219c; National Museum of India, New Delhi 67br, 92; Oriental Museum, Durham University 64c, 64tl, 65tr, 66bl, 75tl, 77br; Private Collection 20tl, 72b, 89tl, 93tr, 140cr, 159br, 205br; Rafael Valls Gallery, London, UK 214cal; Richardson and Kailas Icons, London 210cal; Royal Asiastic Society, London 265bc; Sarnath, Uttar Pradesh, India 68l; Sixt Parish Church, Haute-Savoie, France 208c; Stapleton collection 250tl, 250bc, 258bl, 259bl; Surya Temple, Somnath, Bombay, India 40bl; Topkapi Palace Museum, Istanbul, Turkey 263br, 267br; Le Tresor de L@Abbaye de Saint-Maurice, France 259tl; University Library, Istanbul, Turkey 267tl; Volubilis, Morocco 261tl; Victoria and Albert Museum, London 84b, 204bc; Wesley's Chapel, London, UK 215tr.

British Library: 23, 20tr, 20cl, 20cr, 20br, 20l, 21l, 32cr, 32bl, 36tr, 39br, 40tr, 40bc, 41b, 69tr, 72tl, 72c, 73cr, 73bl, 167tr, 202tr, 202bl, 232c.

British Museum: 57b, 83c, 90tl, 128cl, 128c, 194r, 200ca, 207tr, 207tr, 220c, 221br, 226tl, 237cr.

Buddha Padipa Temple, Wimbledon: 96r.

Camera Press: 149cb, 149br.

Christine Osborne: 59tl, 66tl, 92c, 98tl, 99tc, 102cl, 107c, 176tc, 220tcl, 236bl, 256br, 257cr, 262br, 263cr, 266bl, 267tr, 270cr, 274bl, 276tr, 280tl, 286tl, 287bl, 292tr, 292cb; Nick Dawson 78tr, 88tl; Paul Gapper 95cb; Liam White 225tr.

Coca Cola Company: 167bl.

Collection Ali Bellagha: 293br.

Corbis: 24cl, 239tl, 279cl; Paul Almasy 244bl, 284b; James L. Amos 182-183; Archivo Iconografico, S.A. 10c, 245br, 261tr; Nathan Benn 137tl; Bettmann 142bl, 148c, 148bl, 151cl; D.Boone 89; British Museum 264bl, 264-265; Kathleen Brown 12bl; Burstein Collection 180–181tc © ADAGP, Paris and DACS, London 2003; Michael Busselle 279br; Sheldan Collins 69br, 284cr; Dean Conger 128–129b, 131tr; Cordaiy Photo Library Ltd/Eve Miessler 12-13b; Gianni Dagli Orti 12cr, 130b, 134tl; Gerard Degeorge 281tr; Edifice 279bc; Ric Ergenbright 279tl; Eye Ubiquitous: David Cumming 21br, 28bl, Bennett Dean 18-19, 43tr; Michael Freeman 99bl; Keerle Geo/Sygma 79tr; Shai Ginott 166br; Philip Gould 237br; Dallas and John Heaton 207br; Lindsey Hebberd 22-23, 28cr, 33br, 47tc, 50c, 52-53, 123bc; John Hesletine 278-279; Angelo Hornak 34tr, 35bl, 61bl; Dave G. Houser 50-51; Hanan Isachar 22bl, 174b; Historical Picture Archive 36c, 36cr, 36cb; Rabbi Naamah Kelman 164c; Christine Kolisch 21tr; Earl & Nazima Kowall 290bl; Charles & Josette Lenars 14-15, 270-271; Barry Lewis 135tr; Chris Lisle 120bl, 124tc; Araldo de Luca 244br; Lawrence Manning 16-17, 24c; Roy Morsch 126-127; Richard T. Nowitz 134b, 152tr, 178br; Tim Page 61bl, 105tr; Philadelphia Museum of Art 39ca; Roger Ressmeyer 11tr, 37br; Albrecht G. Schaefer 46cl; Moshe Shai 178tl; Ariel Skelley 18tl; Janez Skok 46bl; Joseph Sohm/Chromo Sohm Inc. 25br; Paul. A. Souders 154br; Stapleton Collection 156tr; Sygma: Baldev 45cl, 45br; Richard Ellis 25cb; Desai Noshir 116-117; Leonard de Selva 144cl; Ted Spiegel 151bc; Unger Kevin/Sygma 165cra; Luca I. Tettoni 64cl; Graham Tim 51c; Travel Ink/Abbie Enock 270cl; David Turnley 17cb; endpapers; Peter Turnley 166bl, 241cr; Penny Tweedie 17pr; Brian A.Vikander 10bl; West Semitic Research/Dead Sea Scrolls Foundation 157tc; Peter M. Wilson 158bl; Janet Wishnetsky 287br; Roger Wood 260br; Adam Woolfit 264cr, 278tr; Alison Wright 96tl, 262; Michael S. Yamashita 105b, 107bl, 108-109.

Danish National Museum: 192t.

www.dinodia.com: M.Amirtham 36bl; Anil A.Dave 45tr; Pramod Mistry 44tl; Satish T. Parashar 50tl.

DK Picture Library: American Museum of Natural History 17cr; Ashmolean Museum 42tr, 249tl, 258c,

303